Mere Mormonism

A Defense of Mormon Theology

Mere Mormonism

A Defense of Mormon Theology

Ronald R. Zollinger

CFI
Springville, Utah

ISBN 13: 978-1-59955-264-4
Published by CFI, an imprint of Cedar Fort, Inc., 2373 W. 700 S., Springville, UT 84663
Distributed by Cedar Fort, Inc., www.cedarfort.com

LIBRARY OF CONGRESS CATALOGING-IN-PUBLICATION DATA

Zollinger, Ronald R.
Mere Mormonism : defense of Mormon theology / Ronald R. Zollinger.
p. cm.
Includes bibliographical references and index.
ISBN 978-1-59955-264-4 (acid-free paper)
1. Church of Jesus Christ of Latter-day Saints--Apologetic works. 2. Mormon Church--Apologetic works. I. Title.

BX8635.5.Z66 2009
230'.9332--dc22

2009008932

Cover design by Angela D. Olsen
Cover design © 2010 by Lyle Mortimer
Edited and typeset by Megan E. Welton

Printed in the United States of America

10 9 8 7 6 5 4 3 2 1

Printed on acid-free paper

To my mother and father,
My wife and children.

Contents

Acknowledgments

A work such as this surely could not come to pass through my instrumentation alone. Many have directly as well as indirectly contributed to this work. I express appreciation to Sharon Berger and Dan Hogan for their expertise in providing a critical read through; to my daughter, Vicki Zollinger, for sharing her unique perspective during the initial drafts; to Alisha Weston and her friends who helped redesign my Plan of Salvation graphic; and to Robin Johnson for her help with early design graphics.

In a college literature class, I was told that Hemingway rewrote some sections of *Old Man and the Sea* a hundred times before he felt it was right. Likewise I've expended a great effort in an attempt to produce an excellent work. However, a fool is his own critique. I express appreciation to those friends and family who read early drafts and provided wonderful insights in its evolution.

Initially, I defaulted to experience the path of self-publishing. I came to recognize how difficult it was for a first time author to have a manuscript accepted for publishing. One publisher in the East catered to first-time authors but required the author to provide a significant subsidy to cover production costs. I am appreciative to Cedar Fort and their professional staff who accepted this manuscript. Their acceptance not only confirmed in my own mind the value of this work but made available to this project many professional and skilled people who helped create the finished product. To all those at Cedar Fort I express appreciation.

Preface

You have not done enough, you've never done enough, so long as you have something more to contribute.—Dag Hammerskjold

The final two assignments of my career within the Church Educational System (CES) allowed me to teach at the Ogden and Berkeley institutes of religion. Teaching on the collegiate level these nine years enabled me to crystalize and mature my intellectual grasp of the principles and doctrines of the gospel of Jesus Christ and the plan of salvation. During these assignments, I developed two courses that were unique within the standard CES institute curriculum. The first was entitled "The Gospel and Comparable Christian Religion." The second, developed during my last three years, was "The Historical Development of the Standard Works." For each of these courses I developed an extensive printed supplement that documented much of the information I presented during classroom sessions. However, the supplements were essentially an accumulation of my research put together in an informal handout format. Even in this form, it was very gratifying to receive feedback from my students as they came to prize this information. Several students encouraged me to bring all of this information together into a book format. In addition to these courses, I taught other classes based on the principles and doctrines found within each of the standard works of the Church of Jesus Christ of Latter-day Saints. Again, many students encouraged me to "write a book" because of the unique perspectives I presented that helped them see the principles and doctrines within a unified whole. The synergy created from this holistic*[1] approach enabled students to better view the gospel within one grand design. The idea of writing a book continued to resonate* within me but the actual format and content hadn't become apparent.

After the funeral service of my dear mother, I was visiting with one of my nephews who asked me how I had reconciled all aspects of the principles and doctrines of the Church within a logical and reasonable framework, which he admitted he had failed to do. It was then that I gained the impetus* for this project. The format and content soon followed during a trip to the Canadian border with my brother Clair. The hours of travel allowed us to pursue a discussion of many of these ideas. Once again came a request to "write a book."

I acknowledge full responsibility for these ideas. I am not writing as an official voice of the Church, but to say I am fully responsible is actually a misnomer.* Throughout my life I have recognized a certain proclivity* toward a serious study of the scriptures and have worked to gain an intellectual grasp of spiritual principles. My educational degrees empowered me with skills of logic, design, and synthesis.* My professional career in religious education and my teaching service within the Church provided not only study hours but also an opportunity to consider these principles within a classroom or teaching dynamic. Lastly, the tender guidance of the Spirit has enlightened my mind and directed my course, which I gratefully acknowledge.

A Mormon Apologist

I assume the position of an apologist.* Historically, many of the early fathers of the Catholic Church (claimed by both Roman and Greek traditions) were labeled as apologists, meaning defenders of the Christian faith. These third- and fourth-century converts to Christianity felt a need to present a treatise* of logical defense that positioned Christianity as a legitimate religion in the Roman empire (Latin: *religio licitus*). The Roman government conveyed a tolerance for existing religions in lands they had conquered. The leaders of Judaism were allowed to govern their own religious affairs unless the acts of disobedience were against the state. This is why the Jewish Sanhedrin needed to charge Jesus with sedition and treason in order to bring a death penalty. The charge of blasphemy, which carried a death penalty in Jewish law, was not allowed to be executed by the Jews. Later in the first century when Christianity, viewed initially as a Jewish sect, separated itself from its Jewish connection, it became a new and novel religion in the empire. As viewed by the Romans, it surrounded itself with customs that seemed strange, curious, and dangerous. Hence, it became *religio prava.* or an illegal religion to be viewed with great suspicion.

Some of the early charges that came against the Christians were a result of misinformation and skewed reporting by Jewish leaders and government officials. These included charges of:

1. Cannibalism (partaking of the flesh and blood of Christ).
2. Disruption of business (refraining from idolatrous practices and commerce).
3. Gross immorality and incest (meeting in secret; greeting each other with a holy kiss).
4. Anti-family (identifying themselves within a community of believers).
5. Poverty (accepting converts from lower classes and slaves).
6. Atheism (rejecting the polytheism contained within the Roman religious tradition).
7. Novelty (rejecting Greco-Roman philosophy and tradition; however, Rome did allow Jews to worship according to their ancient traditions).
8. Lack of patriotism (rejecting Caesar worship and religious ceremonies and festivals of the state; promoting pacifism; loving enemies).
9. Anti-social behavior (appearing to be self-righteous; meeting in secret; partaking of a communal meal with members only).
10. Cause of disaster (offending the gods who had built up Rome, thus causing impending conquest and destruction).

Many of the Christian apologists came out of the neo-Platonic* school of philosophy and used their skills of logic to present a defense. Unfortunately, their developing understanding of Christian doctrine became tainted with their prior Greek philosophic orientation. Christianity has from that time on been forever altered away from original truth and clarity. As Isaiah prophesied, "the earth also is defiled under the inhabitants thereof; because they have transgressed the laws, changed the ordinance, broken the everlasting covenant. Therefore hath the curse devoured the earth, and they that dwell therein are desolate" (Isaiah 24:5–6).

Isaiah also foresaw the solution to this state of apostasy. He anticipated the coming forth of the Book of Mormon from plates as they had lain buried in the earth since the fifth century after Christ. Isaiah spoke of a people who "shalt be brought down, and shalt speak out of the ground, and thy speech shall be low out of the dust, and thy voice shall be, as of one that hath a familiar spirit, out of the ground, and thy speech shall whisper out of the dust" (Isaiah 29:4).

Isaiah further clarifies that these words would come from a sealed book and be delivered to one who was unlearned. Through this person the Lord would perform "a marvellous work among this people, even a marvellous work and a wonder: for the wisdom of their wise men shall perish, and the understanding of their prudent men shall be hid" (Isaiah 29:13–14).

When the gold plates were received by Joseph Smith, part of the compilation was sealed and Joseph was instructed to not translate the contents. Truly, the story of the coming forth of the Book of Mormon is an amazing drama and reasonably qualifies as a marvelous labor, the product of which has frustrated Christian scholars ever since.

Christianity is probably the most fractionalized religion in the world. There are over 33,800 different Christian denominations.[2] There is not a common theology or organization and there is no "unity of the faith," such as the Apostle Paul encouraged (see Ephesians 4:11–13). But once again, the Lord has restored the "familiar voice" back to the earth to become a spokesman for truth and doctrine. That "familiar voice" is positioned within the Church of Jesus Christ of Latter-day Saints in the role of prophet, seer, and revelator. I have been blessed to drink from not only the well of sacred canon,* including all of the LDS standard works, but also from the revelatory declarations that come through these inspired men. Throughout my personal and professional study experiences, I have labored not only to come to a more perfect understanding of restored gospel principles and doctrines, but also to place them holistically into a beautiful architecture of logical design, synthesis, and reason.

Purpose and Scope

As a Mormon apologist, I intend to defend the position of The Church of Jesus Christ of Latter-day Saints and debunk misinformation. The title of this work reflects that used by C. S. Lewis, who wrote one of the great apologies for the Christian religion, *Mere Christianity*. I am in awe of Lewis's writing style and skill and claim no pretext to the same. I use the colloquial* term Mormonism only because it is more common and shorter than the official name of the Church.

Within a scriptural context, the LDS position is stated in Doctrine and Covenants 1:30: "And also those to whom these commandments were given, might have power to lay the foundation of this church, and to bring it forth out of obscurity and out of darkness, *the only true and living church upon the face of the whole earth, with which I, the Lord, am well pleased*, speaking unto the church collectively and not individually" (emphasis added).

From instructions received by the boy Joseph Smith from the Father and the Son during the First Vision, Joseph records the divine answer to his question about which church he should join: "I was answered that I must join none of them, for *they were all wrong*" (Joseph Smith—History 1:19; emphasis added). The term wrong seems to imply a dichotomy* or an initial connotation of black or white, good or bad, right or wrong. Though our critics ignorantly suggest this to be our position, the restored gospel of Jesus Christ actually teaches a wonderful plan of inclusion and near universal salvation. I intend to present a defense of this position.

In addition to these scriptural declarations, it is my personal position that the plan of happiness (as taught within Mormonism) provides not only a unique perspective to the "salvation" issue of religion, but also a paradigm that is unequaled in logic, potential, and self-actualization.* I intend to extend my scope beyond mainstream and fringe Christianity to align Mormonism in an unequaled position among the religions of the world and philosophic schools of thought.

Poetic Sense of Mission

I have put to memory three literary pieces that provide a poetic sense of mission. The first comes from a French author, René Daumal (1908–1944):

> You cannot stay on the summit forever; you have to come down again. So why bother in the first place? Just this: what is above knows what is below, but what is below does not know what is above. One climbs, one sees, one descends, one sees no longer, but one has seen. There is an art of conducting oneself in the lower regions by the memory of what one saw higher up. When one can no longer see, one, at least, still knows.

One of the most gifted literary figures in France in the early part of the twentieth century, René Daumal was a genuine seeker of truth. Sadly, only a few of his writings saw the light of day during his lifetime; Daumal did not truly come into his own until the publication of *Mount Analogue* nearly a decade after his death. In this allegorical novel the author sets sail on the yacht *Impossible* to search for Mount Analogue, the hidden peak that reaches inexorably toward heaven. Daumal's symbolic mountain represents a way to truth that "cannot not exist."

The second piece comes from the observations of an eleventh century scholar from Liege, Belgium, which I entitle "Love of Learning":

> Olbert was not able to satiate his thirst for study. When he would hear of someone distinguished in the arts he flew there at once, and the more he thirsted the more he absorbed something delightful from each master. Afterwards just like the bees among flowers, gorged with the nectar of learning, he returned to the hive and lived there studiously in a religious way, and religiously in a studious manner.[3]

Finally, the third work is a poem entitled "The Crossroads." It was originally written to leaders of boys and is cited at times by President Thomas S. Monson:

> He stood by the crossroads—
> All alone with sunlight in his face.
> He had no thought for the world unknown
> But he was set for a manly race.
> The road stretched East and the road stretched West
> But the lad knew not which road was best.
> So he chose a road which lead him down—
> He lost the race and the victor's crown.
> He was caught at last in an angry snare
> Because no one stood at the crossroads there
> To show him a better way.
> Another day at this selfsame place
> A lad with high hopes stood.
> He too was set for the manly race.
> He too was seeking the things that are good.
> But one was there who the roads did know
> And that one did show him which way to go.
> Today he walks the highways fair

Because one stood at the crossroads there
To show him the better way.[4]

As I reflect back on my own climb to the summit of Mount Analogue, the trail I followed wound its way through scripture study hours, bounced around illuminating classroom discussions, and elevated itself in personal moments of pondering and reflection. The geography included religious, educational, and scholastic terrain. The views I received at the top provided me understanding, clarity, vision, perspective, and, greatest of all, conviction. I have been blessed to gorge myself in the broad-base nectar of religious, philosophic, and academic study. It is my hope that this attempt to harmonize the restored gospel and plan of salvation into a logical, reasonable, and incomparably holistic paradigm* may provide strength to the spiritual and religious heritage held by my posterity, extended family, and associates. It is also my desire that the words of this defense, coupled with the spirit of the Holy Ghost, may be part of a process of reconciliation for individuals who have misunderstood the plan and possibly removed themselves from their alliance with the Restoration. I am humbled even to anticipate such an attempt. I am, however, driven by spiritual impressions that provide the incentive for such a task. I am aware that there is risk inherent in such a project, for it exposes the author's mind to public scrutiny. If I didn't have the conviction I possess for the claims of truth presented herein, I could be otherwise thwarted. Truth, however, is supernal* and faith overcomes fear. Onward and upward. I proceed.

1. A glossary of words is provided after the Appendices. An asterisk (*) will note the words selected.
2. Barrett, *World Christian Encyclopedia*, 2nd edition, 1:3–19.
3. Shelley, *Church History In Plain Language*, 195.
4. Lyon, *Best-Loved Poems of the LDS People*, 313.

CHAPTER ONE:

In Search of Truth

And ye shall know the truth, and the truth shall make you free. – John 8:32

If any man seeks for greatness, let him forget greatness and ask for truth, and he will find both. – Horace Mann

Methodology

Reasoning is the cognitive* process involved in determining the logic for beliefs, conclusions, actions, or feelings. In terms of convincing someone of religious constructs and design, there is no methodology available with the power to alter a differing mind, especially a closed mind. Even truths conveyed by angelic messengers were of little significance to the minds of individuals bent on a different course and an unreceptive disposition (see 1 Nephi 3:29; 15:16; 16:22; 18:20; 2 Nephi 5:3). Early in my missionary service, I came to recognize that logic and reason, though useful and helpful to illuminate, were insufficient in and of themselves to convince. For example, there is no convincing argument using biblical sources to prove beyond doubt whether the Christian God is a triune* spiritual essence or three divine and separate beings, each possessing physical or spirit bodies. But my objective is not to use a word picture that will convince but one that will defend.

In philosophy, the study of reasoning typically focuses on what makes reasoning efficient or inefficient, appropriate or inappropriate, good or bad. Philosophers do this by either examining the form or structure of the reasoning within arguments, or by considering the broader methods used to reach particular goals of reasoning. The most fundamental concept in logic is that of an argument. An "argument" must be distinguished from "arguing," which is a debate or disagreement between different people. The logical concept of an argument includes a set of statements, a conclusion, and premises, which support the conclusion. In other words, it is a statement along with the evidence that supports it. My defense will utilize the following tools:

1. Propositions, premises and inferences within the structure of arguments;
2. Thesis statements supported by rules of
    a. Logic and reason
    b. Analogy
    c. Internal consistency
3. Experimentation
4. Contrast and comparison

Avenues of Truth

In the Savior's final interview before an earthly magistrate, Pilate asked Christ what turned out to be a rhetorical question which received no reply: "What is truth?" (John 18:38). This question has been the quest of historic humanity. Truth, from a dictionary definition, is that "body of things or events . . . being in accord with fact or reality."[1] The Doctrine and Covenants further clarifies that "truth is knowledge of things as they are, and as they were, and as they are to come" (D&C 93:24).

Down through recorded history, mankind has sought truth. Various sources have provided insight helpful to understanding the purpose of life, mankind's relationship to the natural world, and laws existing within the natural world. With uncertainty, natural man has ventured into theories of prior existence and anticipated realms of reality beyond the barrier of death. The realms of religion, voodoo, the paranormal, and the occult are venues claiming "more sure knowledge" to the realities of life prior to and beyond the grave. Many early cultures of man relied upon superstition to understand the supernatural dynamics of life. The development of myth produced caricatures* and personalities that personified natural phenomena.

Classic philosophy rose up out of the seedbed of early Greek thought. Though not the first philosophers, Democritus, Socrates, Plato, and Aristotle gave philosophy the foundation for its developmental canon. Aristotle's extensive project of assimilating and cataloging the whole body of existing knowledge on all subjects within the natural world gave impetus to the modern scientific method, which relies on controlled experimentation to produce objective, empirical results. Moving from the philosophic to the empirical and finally applying scientific methodology has helped to refine truth concerning the natural world. Some truths so discovered are labeled as "laws." The accumulation of a knowledge of these laws of the natural world has been impressive and essential in understanding the mortal experience within the atomic, cellular, organic, and stellar domains. Unfortunately, because of bias, some theories popularly supported yet inconclusively proven have moved into the realm of scientific canonical law. The theory of complete organic evolution originating from the observations and writings of Charles Darwin is classic evidence of such a phenomenon. Just watch any nature program to see the depth of conviction with which this theory has ingrained itself into "law."

There is an avenue of truth that lies beyond the realm of philosophy, science, and situational relevancy. The truths from this domain are eternal, everlasting, and come from a source beyond the shifting sands of human reason and empiricism. The source of such absolute truths must come from a domain where absolutes exist. In this realm of reality, the existence of beings of absolute omnipotence, omniscience, and perfect character development qualifies this source to communicate absolute truths to mankind. If man's existence is integrally related to such beings, and if these beings have a vested* interest in the final outcome of the mortal experience, then it is incumbent upon seekers of truth to come to know, with certainty, the realm of this "heavenly" environment and the makeup and origin of such beings.

Mormonism's Love Affair with Truth

Ironically, access to absolute truth through divine channels antedates all other avenues. Adam and Eve's first tutorial in the Garden of Eden set the divine pattern of heavenly beings conveying counsel and instruction. Post-Edenic angelic messengers communicated laws and ordinances. These communications began a covenant relationship between God and Adam and Eve and their posterity. This pattern has characterized the story of mankind as recorded in Judeo-Christian canon. This pattern is also repeated within the pages of scripture added through the Restoration. Mormons are interested in all truth from every legitimate source. Two of our Articles of Faith state the following: "We believe all that God has revealed, all that He does now reveal, and we believe that He will yet reveal many great and important things pertaining to the Kingdom of God." Also: "If there is anything virtuous, lovely, or of good report or praiseworthy, we seek after these things" (Articles of Faith 1:9, 13).

Truth is one of the paramount jewels that Mormons prize above all. This love affair with truth is captured in the lyrics of a beautiful Mormon hymn written by John Jaques. Being introduced to the message of the Restoration as a young man, John sought the support of his father in his decision to embrace this new religion—which support was not given. Desiring the truths of the Restoration at the expense of fatherly approval, John embraced Mormonism and later penned these poetic words as he immersed himself in this new nectar of learning.

> Oh say, what is truth?
> 'Tis the fairest gem that the riches of worlds can produce,
> And priceless the value of truth will be when
> The proud monarch's costliest diadem*
> Is counted but dross and refuse.
>
> Yes, say, what is truth?
> 'Tis the brightest prize to which mortal or Gods can aspire.
> Go search in the depths where it glittering lies,
> Or ascend in pursuit to the loftiest skies:
> 'Tis an aim for the noblest desire.
>
> The sceptre may fall from the despot's grasp
> When with winds of stern justice he copes.
> But the pillar of truth will endure to the last,
> And its firm-rooted bulwarks outstand the rude blast
> And the wreck of the fell tyrant's hopes.
>
> Then say, what is truth?
> 'Tis the last and the first, for the limits of time it steps o'er.
> Tho the heavens depart and the earth's fountains burst,
> Truth, the sum of existence, will weather the worst,
> Eternal, unchanged, evermore.[2]

The Mormon tradition of fast and testimony meetings is essentially unique in religious practice. Many Christian bodies also provide opportunity for standing utterance of spiritual experience; however, in Mormon testimony meetings not only do members of the congregation share spiritual experiences and appreciation of common values, they also express their absolute conviction of the truthfulness of Mormonism and the essential doctrines and principles revealed through the Restoration. This practice is not unique to a certain locale or ethnic group; it can be found in any LDS congregation, anywhere in the world. These congregations are composed of people from all classes of society, all levels of education, all career fields, and from every ethnic group. How can such a premise of Mormonism be received and held onto with confidence by such a fast-growing mass of humanity? The answer is found within the concept of "testimony" and how this witness is obtained.

1. *Webster's New World Dictionary of the American Language*, 2nd edition, s.v. "truth."
2. *Hymns,* no. 272.

CHAPTER TWO:

The Three Pillars of Truth

Truth is the most valuable thing we have. – Mark Twain

Surrender your pride to truth. – Rabindranath Tagore

As Nephi of old, I also was born of goodly parents. During the early years of their marriage, my parents purchased a weed-infested farm located in Thatcher, Utah. This "morning glory farm" was to become a laboratory of experiential learning as well as the primary source of income for our family of six sons and a daughter. Each child contributed to the family's financial success through deposits of blood, sweat, and tears.

One of my personal duties required my presence alongside our family cow every night and morning. Our family developed a large-capacity feed yard where we fed over a thousand head of beef cattle, but we maintained one milk cow to provide that butter-rich white liquid that Mother always needed to strain through a cheesecloth so as to remove the foreign elements that dropped in during the hand milking process.

Receiving very little on-the-job training, I inherited a one-legged stool from an older brother. I set about to determine for myself the easiest posture to perform this twice-daily task of milking the cow. It soon became apparent that it was better to sit on something than to squat or kneel in barn conditions that were less than ideal. The one-legged stool was versatile and supported my small frame, but it proved less than stable when Mrs. Cow decided to kick me out of the way. After a little thought and experimentation, I added two more legs and invented my very own milking stool. It was stable, versatile, and enabled me to resist the kick from the hind legs often coming from an irritated cow. In my childhood imagination, I was sure I was the first to invent the three-legged milking stool. This childhood invention became a memory icon, symbolizing, for me, the three pillars of Mormon testimony.

First Pillar—The Empirical Method

During a festival celebration, Jesus entered into the courtyard of the temple and began to be questioned by his Jewish critics. They were amazed at the doctrine Jesus taught but discounted his lack of formal Jewish credentials that equipped rabbis of the Pharisaic and Sadducean traditions. Jesus countered their assault on his professionalism by qualifying that the doctrines he taught were not his but came from a divine source, his Heavenly Father. He then gave them this challenge couched in the format of an if-then thesis statement: "*If* any man will do his will, [*then*] he will know of the doctrine, whether it be of God, or whether I speak of myself" (John 7:17; emphasis added).

A principle of the gospel is simply a divine truth to live. I know of no principle of the gospel as taught within Mormonism that fails to bless, sanctify, inspire, and encourage those that apply these divine principles into their lives. Once these principles are acted upon, they then produce the blessings associated with that principle. This is taught in the following scripture: "There is a law, irrevocably decreed in heaven before the foundation of this world, upon which all blessings are predicated—And when we obtain any blessing from God, it is by obedience to that law upon which it is predicated" (D&C 130:20–21).

Our Father in Heaven understands the human domain perfectly. Because He is integrally vested in our welfare, He has revealed anew through his living prophets a restoration of every principle that can bless us in the mental, spiritual, physical, and social domains of life. Part of our testimony emanates from a confirmation that comes as we live the principles of the Restoration and receive an experiential witness to the veracity* of their truth.

Each principle of the gospel can be tested in order to receive personal confirmation as to its goodness, its enabling power, and its importance to be incorporated into our lives. Values or principles that are not based upon divine truth will not pass the divine test. This is because they lack the germ of truth. Alma spoke of this testing process as he taught the poor but humble Zoramites in the land of Antionum, which was just east of the land of Zarahemla. He compared the word to a seed. In our discussion, any principle of the gospel or a personal value can be equated with the seed and assessed through this testing process. Alma taught:

Now, we will compare the word unto a seed. Now, if ye give place, that a seed may be planted in your heart, behold, if it be a true seed, or a good seed, if ye do not cast it out by your unbelief, that ye will resist the Spirit of the Lord, behold, it will begin to swell within your breasts; and when you feel these swelling motions, ye will begin to say within yourselves—It must needs be that this is a good seed, or that the word is good, for it beginneth to enlarge my soul; yea, it beginneth to enlighten my understanding, yea, it beginneth to be delicious to me.

Now behold, would not this increase your faith? I say unto you, Yea; nevertheless it hath not grown up to a perfect knowledge.

But behold, as the seed swelleth, and sprouteth, and beginneth to grow, then you must needs say that the seed is good; for behold it swelleth, and sprouteth, and beginneth to grow. And now, behold, will not this strengthen your faith? Yea, it will strengthen your faith: for ye will say I know that this is a good seed; for behold it sprouteth and beginneth to grow.

And now, behold, are ye sure that this is a good seed? I say unto you, Yea; for every seed bringeth forth unto its own likeness.

Therefore, if a seed groweth it is good, but if it groweth not, behold it is not good, therefore it is cast away.

And now, behold, because ye have tried the experiment, and planted the seed, and it swelleth and sprouteth, and beginneth to grow, ye must needs know that the seed is good.

And now, behold, is your knowledge perfect? Yea, your knowledge is perfect in that thing, and your faith is dormant; and this because you know, for ye know that the word hath swelled your souls, and ye also know that it hath sprouted up, that your understanding doth begin to be enlightened, and your mind doth begin to expand.

O then, is not this real? I say unto you, Yea, because it is light; and whatsoever is light, is good, because it is discernible, therefore ye must know that it is good; and now behold, after ye have tasted this light is your knowledge perfect?

Behold I say unto you, Nay; neither must ye lay aside your faith, for ye have only exercised your faith to plant the seed that ye might try the experiment to know if the seed was good.

And behold, as the tree beginneth to grow, ye will say: Let us nourish it with great care, that it may get root, that it may grow up, and bring forth fruit unto us. And now behold, if ye nourish it with much care it will get root, and grow up, and bring forth fruit.

But if ye neglect the tree, and take no thought for its nourishment, behold it will not get any root; and when the heat of the sun cometh

> and scorcheth it, because it hath no root it withers away, and ye pluck it up and cast it out.
>
> Now, this is not because the seed was not good, neither is it because the fruit thereof would not be desirable; but it is because your ground is barren, and ye will not nourish the tree, therefore ye cannot have the fruit thereof.
>
> And thus, if ye will not nourish the word, looking forward with an eye of faith to the fruit thereof, ye can never pluck of the fruit of the tree of life.
>
> But if ye will nourish the word, yea, nourish the tree as it beginneth to grow, by your faith with great diligence, and with patience, looking forward to the fruit thereof, it shall take root; and behold it shall be a tree springing up unto everlasting life.
>
> And because of your diligence and your faith and your patience with the word in nourishing it, that it may take root in you, behold, by and by ye shall pluck the fruit thereof, which is most precious, which is sweet above all that is sweet, and which is white above all that is white, yea, and pure above all that is pure; and ye shall feast upon this fruit even until ye are filled, that ye hunger not, neither shall ye thirst.
>
> Then, my brethren, ye shall reap the rewards of your faith, and your diligence, and patience, and long-suffering, waiting for the tree to bring forth fruit unto you (Alma 32:28–43).

In addition to our irrigated farm in Thatcher, Utah, we also had two dry farms that supplemented our family income. One summer I received an assignment from my father to clean out the grain bin on our dry farm in Blue Creek, Utah. Dad had other labors to perform as the two of us spent the day at this location. I climbed up the bin to enter from its roof opening. It was a large bin. The descent down was about forty to fifty feet. There below me on the cement floor was a pile of old grain. Instead of climbing down the attached wood ladder, I thrust myself out and landed in the pile of grain. Young boys seek for this kind of thrill to break up the monotony inherent in some farm labor. My task was to shovel this pile of old grain down the exit chute so it could be discarded. As I worked, I began to wonder why this grain, which appeared to be good grain, was to be discarded. Later I asked my father this question. His answer not only resolved my farm query but also had great theologic implications to which I have returned many times in my life. He said simply, "Ron, the rain ruined the wheat." From an opening in the top of the bin, rain had fallen through an opening in the top of the bin. I learned that moisture created an environment which caused the grain to ferment and heat up to such a degree that it killed the germ inside the seed. It is from the germ that sprouts emerge, beginning the life cycle process, bringing it through its flowering stage, and culminating in its seed-producing potential.

The germ is that element in every seed from which life springs. When the conditions are right, the germ activates to produce the emerging cotyledon or its first leaf stem. The cotyledon, fueled by the endosperm (the substance usually ground to make flour), produces primary roots, which assist to further energize the plant to rise toward light. After breaking through the soil, secondary roots begin to grow. With these roots—and through photosynthesis—the plant is fueled to develop toward maturity.

There are many human metaphoric applications that could be developed from the plant cycle. For our current discussion, gospel seeds like life principles, values, and so on, are determined to be good if they possess the germ of truth. If not, they are just imitations not based on divine truth (in other words, these lack the essential germ of life). As such, they have not the power to swell, sprout, and grow to produce the desired blessing. There certainly exist in life many imitations that feign likeness but possess little power to produce happiness and joy. When we place our faith in these counterfeit values and principles in our lives, the outcome falls short of a fulness of happiness and joy and results in sadness and despair. The following represents some good versus counterfeit values or principles:

GOOD SEEDS	COUNTERFEITS
• Spirituality	• Spiritualism
• Restored Church of Jesus Christ	• Splintered offshoots
• Seeking peace through the word of God.	• Seeking peace through war
• United Order	• Communism
• Love and commitment	• Lust and situational morality
• Prophets	• False prophets
• Priesthood	• Priestcraft
• Sabbath as the Lord's Day	• Sunday as a fun day

GOOD SEEDS	COUNTERFEITS
• Family	• Gangs
• Self-discipline and self-control	• Gratification from self-indulgence
• Plan of Salvation (agency honored)	• Plan of tyrants (freedom repressed)
• Selfless service	• Self-centeredness
• Temples	• Cathedrals
• Confession to a bishop	• Confession of sins to a therapist
• Temple ceremony	• Secret combinations
• Honoring priesthood authority	• Loyalty within criminal societies

One of the common observations reported by outside observers (including media reports) is the high quality of life that is characteristic of Mormon homes and society. When true principles are lived, lives are blessed. On the flip side, we also find Mormon homes and individuals that are plagued with the problems associated with the violation of these principles. These problems can be corrected. Through scriptural study, humility, and obedience to heavenly principles, spiritual hearts are born anew, new insights are embraced, and appreciation for divine truths returns. Correct attitudes, behaviors, and commitments bring or restore the repentant person to the blessings of righteousness.

Jesus said, "Wherefore by their fruits ye shall know them" (Matthew 7:20). To the Nephites he reiterated this principle as taught by Moroni, the custodian of the gold plates. "For I remember the word of God which saith by their works ye shall know them: for if their works be good, then they are good also. . . . For behold, a bitter fountain cannot bring forth good water; neither can a good fountain bring forth bitter water. . . . Wherefore, all things which are good cometh of God (Moroni 7:5, 11–12).

Second Pillar—The Test of Logic and Reason

The historic trail of Christianity is paved with the firm resolve of some individuals who dared to challenge the religious institution that currently held power over the minds and freedoms of its members.

Hundreds of scenarios describe individuals who, through their own study and contemplation (especially those having access to biblical canon), deduced a differing interpretation to the practices or foundational beliefs of the governing Christian church.

These were honorable individuals being guided by their own sense of what was right or wrong about current Church practices. Sparked by the Spirit through their own study and analysis, many initiated challenges to mainstream belief and practice. However, few, if any, individuals or groups claimed their ideas resulted from prophetic guidance or were given by angelic messengers. There is one prime question that rises from splintered Christianity: who has the correct interpretation if, in fact, Christianity represents God's endowment of true religious belief and practice? A common proclamation in most every testimony borne by members of the Church of Jesus Christ of Latter-day Saints is to their witness that "the Church is true!" Let's examine both what is meant by this proclamation and the logic supporting this claim.

The Role of Prophets

If Christ, in the meridian of time, established his true church with its unique organization, doctrines, and principles, where does that church exist today? What has happened to it? Modern Christianity accepts the idea that Christ's church was established in the meridian of time. Most Christian theologians use Acts 1 and 2 to document the genesis of the Christian church. The premise of Mormonism lies in a careful reading of the Bible. One of the first tenets* of Mormonism is the primary role of prophets, who shoulder a unique responsibility as spokesmen for God to his children. It is difficult to read the Old Testament and not discover this repetitive design. Amos, one of those Old Testament prophets, documented his unique role when he declared, "Surely the Lord God will do nothing, until he revealeth his secret unto his servants the prophets" (JST, Amos 3:7). Paul declared that the very groundwork of Christ's church in New Testament times was "built upon the foundation of the apostles and prophets" with Christ as the cornerstone (Ephesians 2:19–20). As spokesmen for God, prophets' inspired teachings and instructions were written down and later collected and canonized. These men were responsible to reconcile their new dispensation of the gospel message with those messages from the eras of the Old Testament. To do this was not the prerogative of lay members or those with outside interests. The apostles, led by Peter, continually met this challenge. Peter taught this principle when he said, "No prophecy of the scripture is of any private interpretation. For the prophecy came not in old time by the will of man: but holy men of God spake as they were moved by the Holy Ghost" (2 Peter 1:20–21).

This pattern was continued when Peter, the leading apostle, was taught through inspired events that "God was no respecter of persons." The consequence of this doctrine prompted Peter to open the waters of baptism to include Gentiles who desired to embrace the gospel and enter into a covenant relationship with Christ. As a confirmation of Peter's apostolic direction, the Holy Ghost fell upon these gentile proselytes (see Acts 10). This same apostolic, prophetic direction was needed to resolve the issue of circumcision, which was debated in early church counsels (see Acts 15).

Inherent in the roles of apostle and prophet is the authority to interpret former sacred scripture and also to become living oracles for current revelatory needs. The apostles differed from the many Christian disciples in that they received separate instruction, responsibility, and authority from Christ directly. The four Gospels reveal numerous occasions when the Twelve were privy to personalized instruction and examples of the Lord preparing them to assume leadership responsibility of the Church after his ascension (see Matthew 10:1; 16:13, 20–21; 17:1ff;* 19:28; 23:1ff; 26:20ff; 28:18–20). Matthew tells of keys of authority conveyed to Peter and to all of the apostles (Matthew 16:19; 18:18). The Apostle John records that the Twelve were specially chosen and ordained (John 15:16). The book of Acts provides a more historic account of how the Church was specially directed by the Twelve with Peter, James, and John leading as a presidency. As long as the office of apostle and prophet existed in the church in New Testament times, true principles, doctrines, and practices were vouchsafed.* Within the New Testament, other offices of authority are named. Some of these include the seventy, bishops, deacons, teachers, evangelists, priests, high priests, and elders (see Ephesians 4:11–14; Acts 14:23; Philippians 1:1; 1 Timothy 3:1,8; Hebrews 5:1). Unfortunately, the New Testament was not written as an operations and procedures manual. A complete understanding of the responsibilities and limits attached to these secondary and tertiary* offices is not found. What is clear is that they were subordinate to and received direction from the Twelve, who held the keys of leadership of the kingdom.

Maintaining a complete quorum seemed to be a high priority. One of the first leadership acts arising from the Twelve was the calling of Matthias to fill the vacancy left by Judas Iscariot. Whoever was selected needed to possess two important credentials: (1) "[he] must . . . be ordained to be a witness with us of his resurrection" (Acts 1:22), and (2) he must be "called of God, as was Aaron" (Hebrews 5:4). An apostle, then, is a special witness of Christ and his resurrection to all the world. Saul, who received a vision of the resurrected Lord, became Paul and was known as an apostle of the Lord Jesus Christ. Paul applied the title to James, the Lord's brother (Galatians 1:19), and also to Barnabas (1 Corinthians 9:5–6; Acts 14:4, 14). When this foundational position and quorum failed to endure after the turn of the first century, the void of leadership was filled by men possessing various motives and credentials, none of whom were "called of God as was Aaron—through prophecy" (see Numbers 27:15–20) to witness of His resurrection.

The Apostasy Foretold

Paul, possessing prophetic vision, warned the saints at the meridian of time that there were dark days ahead—even that of apostasy (see 2 Thessalonians 2:1–4). There were forces without and within plaguing the lifeblood of Christ's infant Church. During the first century and into the second, the Church struggled against

1. Individual wickedness.
2. Rejection of authorized priesthood leaders.
3. A lack of faithful devotion due to the pursuit of wealth, luxury, and personal ambition.
4. The rise of false teachers introducing heretical doctrines, philosophies, unauthorized ceremonies, and organizational changes.
5. Ecclesiastical positioning and aspiring to high positions in the Church.
6. Imprudent enthusiasm for martyr worship and aspiration for the same reward.
7. Returning to pagan practices in response to the fear of Roman reprisals.
8. Persecution coming from jealous adherents of Judaism who viewed Christianity as a rival religion to their own monotheistic and special religious position.

9. Persecution coming from Roman (pagan) rulers.

Finally, as John the Revelator saw in apocalyptic vision, the true Church, which was endowed with correct doctrine, principles, and practices, was taken into heaven (the child) and the external remnant (the women) fled into the wilderness (see Revelations 12:1, 5–6; D&C 86:1–4). The Apostle Paul continually warned the early Church of this impending demise (see Acts 20:29–30; Galatians 1:6; 2 Thessalonians 2:1–3; 1 Timothy 4:1–3; 2 Timothy 3:1–4). Christ himself foresaw these events, and he warned those with listening ears (see Matthew 13:25; 24:5, 24). John dates the length of this wilderness epoch as 1,260 years (see JST Rev. 12:5). John's mortal apostolic ministry came to a close in Ephesus, his abode after he was released from his island prison at Patmos. The historic life of John, the last of New Testament apostles, ended around A.D. 100. If we add 1,260 years to this date, we should observe some historic activity that would represent the process of bringing the women back out of the wilderness. This brings us to events during the fourteenth century that must have some prophetic significance.

Reformers and the Reformation

The Lord, who sees in grand vision the beginning from the end, allowed his Holy Spirit to distill truth upon selective receptive minds even though the gift of the Holy Ghost had been lost to the Christian church. Down through the centuries of Christian history, there were many individuals and groups seeking to reclaim original Christianity, which they also believed had been lost or replaced. Peter Waldo's conversion to Christianity (AD 1175) prompted his desire to return to the practices of New Testament Christianity. The Waldensians were very active in France during the twelfth and thirteen centuries. Their movement spread throughout Europe, but had its greatest influence in the central and eastern regions. Waldensians joined other reformation movements and eventually lost their unique identity. The Anabaptists represented a widespread movement originating in the sixteenth century. Though disjointed, they also sought a return to original Christianity. The Anabaptists centered on doctrine (rejected infant baptism, pacifists, and so on) instead of following charismatic leaders. Their influence began in Switzerland and then spread throughout the continent. It was met with much resistance by the established church as well as by some of the emerging reformers. Many Anabaptists ended their life as martyrs. During the twelfth and thirteenth centuries, the Cathars and the Manicheans promulgated their dualistic Christianity or the belief in two gods: one who created the spiritual realm of goodness and the other who was responsible for the material realm, which was evil. Many of these individuals and movements were isolated to specific regions and periods of time.

My candidate for the morning star of the Reformation developed his ideas and writings, which acted like ashes of change diffused into the waterworks of Europe. John Wycliffe was not a sixteenth century contemporary of great Reformers like Luther, Melanchthon, Calvin, Zwingli, and Knox. During the 1360s, Wycliffe was actively challenging the doctrines and practices of the Catholic Church in England. Wycliffe, a professor at Oxford, concluded from his intense study of the Bible that the Catholic Church had strayed significantly from the Church that practiced in New Testament times. The Archbishop of Canterbury attempted to silence this menacing voice by taking away his teaching duties and thereby limiting his access to the great library at Oxford. Using this time of reprieve, Wycliffe felt inspired to direct his labors and those of his colleagues to translating the Latin Vulgate Bible into the English language. Wycliffe felt that each individual could be empowered by the Spirit to drink directly from the pages of the Bible if available in his own native tongue. Wycliffe had no confidence in the tainted interpretation and lack of scholarship existing within the clergy. Through great personal sacrifice, he and his followers, referred to as Lollards, translated, made copies, and distributed these new scriptures throughout Europe. His teachings and his desire to provide easy access of the scriptures to each believer had profound impact on Christian history. In 1428, years after his death, the English Catholic Church disinterred his body and performed a public burning. His ashes were cast into the river Swift, carried by the current, and disseminated into the waterways of Europe. Unknowingly, the Church's action provided symbolic representation of the influence that John Wycliffe had upon Europe and upon all of Christianity.

John Huss of Czechoslovakia carried Wycliffe's Reformation spirit into the fifteenth century, to be followed by the explosion of Reformers traditionally associated with the sixteenth century. The philosopher Ernst Block said this about the Protestant Reformers: "Despite their suffering, their fear and trembling in all these souls, there glows the spark from beyond and it ignites the tarrying kingdom."[1]

Latter-day Saints pay homage to these valiant reformers. Elder M.

Russell Ballard said of the reformers: "I believe these reformers were inspired to create a religious climate in which God could restore lost truths and priesthood authority."[2] President Thomas S. Monson eulogized these reformers:

> Honest men with yearning hearts, at the peril of their very lives, attempted to establish points of reference, that they might find the true way. The day of the reformation was dawning, but the path ahead was difficult. Persecutions would be severe, personal sacrifice overwhelming, and the cost beyond calculation. The reformers were like pioneers blazing wilderness trails in a desperate search for those lost points of reference which, they felt, when found would lead mankind back to the truth Jesus taught.[3]

The Reformation and America

The Book of Mormon suggests that the Spirit "wrought upon" Columbus and others among the "gentiles" to forge into the unknown to establish themselves in the new world of America. The work of the Protestant Reformation had impact not only on religious life but it also fueled the fire for the ideals of democracy and personal freedoms, especially freedom of religion, religious toleration, and separation between church and state. It is not an exaggeration to state that America's study for independence came from the political theory fueled by the Reformation. Thomas Jefferson was acquainted with Martin Luther's treatise, "The Freedom of a Christian Man," written in A.D. 1520. The writings of John Locke, though not considered a religious reformer, advanced ideas such as liberty, the proper role of government, individual rights, religious toleration, and separation between civil and religious authority. We can see Locke's ideological fingerprints in the establishment of our nation based on life, liberty, and the pursuit of happiness—a nation in which the Restoration could take place. The historian Frank Bristol states in his book, *Providential Epochs*:

> It was the Reformation that raised up and sent forth colonizers and settlers of deep religious life, of advanced and liberal ideas—men of high and heroic character, men of prayer and faith and independent conscience, men of convictions and bibles and Sabbaths. Without that Reformation no such race of moral giants could have been thrust out into this New World, and without such a race of men the problem

> of self-government could not have been solved, this continent-wide Republic could not have been established.[4]

After America had gained its independence and documented its code of laws into a written constitution, it set its sail toward becoming a "land of the free and home of the brave." William E. Gladstone, four-time prime minister of Great Britain, wrote: "the American Constitution is the most powerful work ever struck off at a given time by brain and purpose of man."[5] Elder Dallin Oaks positioned America's constitution with this statement: "The United States' Constitution was the first written constitution in the world. It has served Americans well, enhancing freedom and prosperity during the changed conditions of more than two hundred years. Frequently copied, it has become the United States' most important export."[6]

People with eyes of faith recognize the hand of God in the establishment of this great democratic republic. As revealed to the Prophet Joseph Smith, the Lord "established the Constitution of this land, by the hand of wise men whom I raised up unto this very purpose." Part of that purpose ensured that "every man may act in doctrine and principle pertaining to futurity, according to the moral agency which I have given unto him" (D&C 101:77–80). President Gordon B. Hinckley has said: "All of this is part of a miracle . . . . But beyond it all is the wonder of a nation that for more than two centuries has remained free and independent and strong, the envy of the world, the hope of the world, the protection of free men everywhere, the manifestation of the power of the Almighty."[7]

America's Manifest Destiny—The Restoration

However, the true manifest destiny of America was not necessarily to inhabit land from sea to sea or even to disseminate the principles of freedom through democratic government, though both of these ends were of tremendous significance. During the end of the eighteenth century and the start of the nineteenth century, America experienced a spirit of religious revivalism, which was especially heated in the New England area. The time was right, the conditions were in place, and true Christianity was about to be restored. The Restoration became the crown jewel in the divine destiny of America.

As a young lad, the prophet Samuel sensed a divine communication being directed his way. As he responded to this prophetic call, he became one of the great prophets of Israel. Joseph, son of Jacob, remained true in his youth to the religious convictions he learned as a son of the Abrahamic covenant. Because of his integrity, he became a savior to his extended family and the father of a chosen posterity. Scriptural history reflects back with eyes of awe at the courageous valor of the young shepherd boy, David. Though less than exemplary during his tragic episode with Bathsheba, his poetic pleas of forgiveness and his songs of love for God form a literary masterpiece in Judeo-Christian tradition. The Book of Mormon provides additional examples of valiant and righteous youth called to spiritual duty (Nephi, Mormon, the sons of Helaman, Alma, and so forth).

Clearly, God's call for individuals to serve while yet in youth has historic precedence. In the spring of 1820 in upper New York state, such a call came to a boy of fourteen tender years. Being of a serious mind about his relationship to God and desiring to discover the correct church to join, he went to a secluded grove of trees near his parents' home to begin his private supplication. Thus began the events surrounding what Latter-day Saints refer to as "the Restoration."

Just as the idea of apostasy was a subject included in the epistles of the apostles, we also find that they had understanding about a future period of restoration. In his epistle to the Ephesians, Paul wrote "that in the dispensation of the fulness of times he [Christ] might gather together in one all things in Christ, both which are in heaven, and which are on the earth; even in him" (Ephesians 1:10).

At the ascension of Christ into heaven, those who witnessed this spectacular occurrence were taught by angelic witnesses of a future period called "the times of restitution of all things, which God hath spoken by the mouth of all his holy prophets since the world began" (Acts 3:21).

In summary, Christ established a Church in the meridian of times with organization, doctrines, principles, and ordinances. Christ endowed his apostles with keys of jurisdiction and authority. These men and their replacements took seriously the charge to take the gospel to every nation, kindred, and tongue. Because of conditions outside and inside the Church, these men continually combated a spirit of apostasy, which "entered into the flock." When the keys of the last living apostle were removed from the Church, the leadership void was filled by both noble and ignoble representation. The Church entered into a period of apostasy. There were many attempts to return to New Testament Christianity as men recognized true Christianity's drift. The end of the Middle Ages produced a plethora* of Reformers driven by an inspired conviction to rediscover true Christianity. However, the once-unified Church of Jesus Christ became splintered into several thousand various denominations. These denominations can be classified into the following groups with European origins: Catholic (the Roman, Orthodox, and Anglican families), Lutheran, Reformed (Presbyterians), and Radicals (Anabaptists, Mennonites, Quakers).

The Only True and Living Church

The foregoing traced the importance of apostolic authority and the meridian organization, early apostasy, a period of reformation, and conditions which preceded the eventual restoration of the gospel and of Christ's church. This review was necessary in order to understand the logic behind the claim that the Church of Jesus Christ of Latter-day Saints is the only true church and the literal restored Church of Jesus Christ. This claim is central to each testimony born by every member. Peter encouraged every member of the meridian Church to "be ready always to give an answer to every man that asketh you a reason of the hope that is in you with meekness and fear" (1 Peter 3:15). Our claim is not a boast which we cram into the Christian milieu.* Rather, with loving concern we proselytize the message of the Restoration to every human being without regard to religious persuasion, ethnicity, or economic status.

The Test of the Book of Mormon

The key to conversion to Mormonism rests upon the validity of the Book of Mormon. If the Book of Mormon is not what Mormonism claims it is, then we have perpetrated one of the greatest hoaxes the world has ever witnessed. However, if the Book of Mormon is truly an inspired translated record taken from gold plates which were deposited within the Hill Cumorah and delivered to Joseph Smith by the angel Moroni, then the events that followed as Joseph continued to respond to divine command throughout his life were truly of God. The confirmation of the Book of Mormon as the work of God comes primarily from a spiritual witness. However, it is the logic of this claim I wish to pursue at present. If this work is of God, then, once again, God has established his ancient divine pattern of prophetic direction. From that prophetic direction came the following events:

1. The restoration of ancient scripture created an open canon concept, which is of primary contrast to the closed canon of traditional Christianity.
2. True apostolic priesthood and keys were restored through divine means.
3. The creation of Christ's true church followed the form and likeness of its meridian counterpart.
4. The restoration of correct ordinances, principles, and doctrines is linked historically to their very genesis when God began the great human drama and established a covenant relationship with Adam and Eve.
5. A continuous line of living prophetic oracles has become responsible for the tender direction of God's church through contemporary times.

There have been many critics and criticisms of the Book of Mormon. Some have attempted to explain away its existence by claiming that Joseph copied or plagiarized other historic writings. Alexander Campbell, influential in the early Disciple of Christ movement, initially dismissed the Book of Mormon as a crude product of a single author. Later, as the complexity and erudition* of the book became apparent, Campbell rescinded his first argument and resorted to the idea that the more intelligent Sidney Rigdon must have authored it. Scholarly investigation has debunked both of these positions. Others credit the Book of Mormon as a result of Joseph's extremely fanciful and imaginary genius (see Appendix J). This position seems to validate the "marvelous work" that the Book of Mormon represents, but falls short of acknowledging its divine origin. One extreme explanation credits the Book of Mormon to Joseph's secret use of psychedelic drugs. These same imaginative critics use this same reasoning to describe how the highly symbolic and metaphoric texts of Ezekiel, Daniel, John the Revelator, and other biblical apocalyptic prophets came about.

Textual analysis of the Book of Mormon identifies many different writing styles, and vocabulary uncommon to the 1800s, including unique kinds of expressions that appear to be uncharacteristic of English in any time and place; some of these expressions are Hebraistic in nature, including examples of chiasmus parallelisms.* The Book of Mormon contains hundreds of new proper names, a complex geography, and several interwoven story lines. It was written in the style of the King James English Bible, which was not the common communicative nomenclature* used in any area where Joseph and his family lived. The Book of Mormon continues to amaze its critics as it continues to be scrutinized. Documented history testifies of the extremely short duration in which the Book of Mormon was translated. In contrast, it took Gregory Martin of Rheims, France, fours years to translate the Latin Vulgate New Testament into English. He averaged a little over one page of translated text per day. It took nearly fifty scholars seven years to complete the King James Bible project. They also averaged one page per day. Joseph Smith completed his 520-page translation of the reformed Egyptian text from the gold plates in approximately sixty-five days. This amounted to about eight pages of translated text per working day. Those who assisted Joseph as scribes testified that after interruptions during translation, Joseph would continue in context, even from a word stop, without rehearsal or asking for a restatement of the previous text. Those Bible scholars had the best resources available to them. Joseph, though enjoying minimal public education, possessed only two transparent stones, a portable fixture called a breastplate in which the Urim and Thummim were placed, and a scribe. We might add that he also received the divine gift of translation from the Holy Ghost.

We have not seen the end of attempts by skeptics to find textual errors sufficient to discredit its stated origin. It is a real, tangible book. Truly the Book of Mormon is an either/or scenario. If a reader allows himself to accept the story of the coming forth of the Book of Mormon, then he must also accept the full parameters tangent to that acceptance. To not accept the Book of Mormon, whether out of fear of defeat, pride sealing an open mind and heart, lack of interest to investigate truth, complacency in life, or fear of change and commitment, the Book of Mormon poses a veritable and legitimate conundrum.*

Humanity has benefitted from the great treasure houses of wonderful literature. Unfortunately, not every civilization has treasured the written word outside its own culture. Some of the greatest devastation from military conquests, beside the loss of human lives, has come with the destruction of libraries and special writings. Such was the case when the library of Alexandria, with at least five hundred thousand volumes, was destroyed. Tragedy struck again when Catholic priests burned and destroyed thousands of Mayan bark books, which contained special history and literature. Only three of these books were saved to remind us of what the world could have known about this intriguing culture. When the barbaric tribes east of the Rhine invaded Western Europe, their intrusion helped usher in the "dark ages" of ignorance. The modern world owes gratitude to the Irish monks who helped salvage and disseminate throughout Europe the great literary treasures of the Occident. Conversely, the Roman Catholic Church in England suppressed the translation of biblical writings into the evolving, vulgar* tongue of English. The translations of Wycliffe and Tyndale were both suppressed and when found, fueled the arrogant fires of religious prejudice.

Joseph Smith was taught by the Lord that there is truth mixed within writings outside the Biblical canon that can be discerned with the companionship of the Spirit, just as each individual must sift the wheat from the chaff and tares (see D&C 91). In principle, the same is true of canonized writings. One of the great contributions arising from the Prophet's gift of translating was to produce a corrected Bible commonly called the Joseph Smith Translation (JST). This work came as divine instruction from the Lord (D&C 45:60). One of the verses Joseph corrected is found in 2 Timothy 3:16. Instead of reading "All scripture is given by inspiration of God, and is profitable. . . ," Joseph's spiritual insight taught the following: "All scripture given by inspiration of God is profitable. . . ." There exists within the Bible some content that doesn't meet the high standards of inspired writing, either because of inappropriate inclusion by ignorant translators, careless transcribers, or designing and corrupt priests. The Bible is viewed within Mormonism to be the word of God "as far as it is translated correctly" (Articles of Faith 1:8).

There is a literary spirit unique to prophetic writings not found within the great writings of classical literature. This literary spirit is a power in the word of God written by prophets and is manifested within various affective domains. Jacob, son of Lehi, suggested that the "word" of God "healeth the wounded soul" (Jacob 2:8). Alma testified that the preaching of the "word" had "a great tendency to lead the people to do that which was just—yea, it had had a more powerful effect upon the minds of the people than the sword, or anything else, which had happened unto them—therefore Alma thought it was expedient that they should try the virtue of the word of God" (Alma 31:5).

Nephi chose to read to his rebellious brothers from the writings of Isaiah found on the plates of brass that he might "more fully persuade them to believe in the Lord their Redeemer" (1 Nephi 19:23). Jesus appeared incognito* to two disciples who were traveling to Emmaus and rehearsed with them from the scriptures all things pertaining to himself. Afterwards, they reflected how their "hearts [did] burn within [them], while he talked with [them] by the way, and while he opened to [them] the scriptures" (Luke 24:32). The Jews who had returned to Jerusalem from their Babylonian exile received leadership from Ezra, the priestly scribe. In order to cleanse the people from the elements of the world they had acquired over time, he read to them from "the book of the law of Moses, which the Lord had commanded to Israel. And Ezra the priest brought the law before the congregation both of men and women, and all that could hear with understanding" (Nehemiah 8:1–2). The reading of these scriptures had such a powerful effect upon the people who had long been withheld from the written word that "all the people wept, when they heard the words of the law" (Nehemiah 8:9). Aaron, one of the sons of Mosiah, used the scriptures to teach the king of the Lamanites about the true God and the plan of redemption. The Spirit confirmed the teachings of these scriptures with such great power that the king was willing to "give away all [his] sins to know [God]" (Alma 22:18).

The spirit of scripture enlightens our minds with truths of eternal significance. It was Joseph's scripture study—especially his reading of James 1:5—that prompted him to seek in personal prayer for the answers he fervently desired. Joseph reflected:

> Never did any passage of scripture come with more power to the heart of man than this did at this time to mine. It seemed to enter with great force into every feeling of my heart. I reflected on it again and again, knowing that if any person needed wisdom from God, I did; for how to act I did not know, and unless I could get more wisdom than I then had, I would never know; for the teachers of religion of the different sects understood the same passages of scripture so differently as to destroy all confidence in settling the question by an appeal to the Bible (Joseph Smith—History 1:12).

The process of scripture study seems to yield unending metaphoric, symbolic, and interpretive insights and provides answers to our personal and daily dilemmas. Truly, as Nephi proclaimed, "I did liken all scriptures unto us, that it might be for our profit and learning" (1 Nephi 19:23).

Such is the power of inspired prophetic writings found in the Book of Mormon, as well as the other canonized writings from the hand of the Prophet Joseph Smith, including the Doctrine and Covenants and the Pearl of Great Price. Also included in this set of sacred canon are other inspired declarations of latter-day prophets. There is a vindicating consistency found throughout the LDS standard works. They pass the test of being the "word of God." They are the products of prophets, seers, and revelators. They are not a hoax. A test of writing scripture was given to the early members of the Church who challenged Joseph's ability to write revelation. The Lord, knowing of these men's thoughts, challenged any person to chose what he felt was the least significant revelation that had been compiled within the soon-to-be-published Book of Commandments, the forerunner of the Doctrine and Covenants. One William E. McLellin took up the challenge.

> McLellin, perhaps under the urging of others, accepted the challenge. He retired from the conference and, in the solitude of his room, attempted to write that which might sound like a revelation from the Lord. On November 2nd he appeared again in the conference and with tears in his eyes begged the forgiveness of the Prophet, of his brethren, and of the Lord. He could not write a revelation. Try as he might, he could not write that which would sound as if it were a revelation from the Lord. Everyone who puts the matter to the test must come to the same conclusion. The uninspired man can only write those thoughts presently in his mind; and when he has put them in writing, he finds that they are but a rehash of ideas long known to mankind. The writings may have literary or educational value—but if nothing new is revealed, they are not revelation. On the other hand, if writings enrich the world with ideas and information not previously known, then by the same test, they are revelation and, the newly found truth should be accepted and followed[8].

Finally, the Book of Mormon, the Doctrine and Covenants, and the Pearl of Great Price fulfill the primary purpose of scripture as stated by John the Revelator: "But these [scriptures] are written, that ye might believe that Jesus is the Christ, the Son of God; and that believing ye might have life through his name" (John 20:31).

Nephi, in his desire to understand his father's dream of the Tree of Life, received his own angelic interpretation. The angel showed Nephi in vision the records of the Jews as well as other records which would come forward representing the record of Joseph (cf.* Ezekiel 37:15–17). This angel told Nephi of "other books" which "came forth by the power of the

Lamb" (1 Nephi 13:39). Then the angel spake, saying:

> These last records, which thou hast seen among the Gentiles, shall establish the truth of the first, which are of the twelve apostles of the Lamb, and shall make known the plain and precious things which have been taken away from them; and shall make known to all kindreds, tongues, and people, that the Lamb of God is the Son of the Eternal Father, and the Savior of the world; and that all men must come unto him, or they cannot be saved.
>
> And they must come according to the words which shall be established by the mouth of the Lamb; and the words of the Lamb shall be made known in the records of thy seed, as well as in the records of the twelve apostles of the Lamb; wherefore they both shall be established in one; for there is one God and one Shepherd over all the earth (1 Nephi 13:40–41).

The official name of the book translated from the plates of gold is "The Book of Mormon: Another Testament of Jesus Christ." As such, it takes its place as the "keystone of our religion."

A Test of Comparison

During the early 1800s, a group of American Christians began labeling themselves as Restorationists or Seekers. They sought for a church which possessed the true elements of New Testament Christianity. Thomas Campbell and his son, Alexander, were among this group. They were convinced that the elements of true Christianity included the following:

> One must have faith in God. One who thus believed would repent of their sins. They would seek forgiveness through an immersion baptism. After baptism would come a laying on of hands for the gift of the Holy Ghost. The priesthood of God must be acquired to authorize the establishment of Christ's true church on earth. However, there is no one on earth capable of laying hands on people to bestow the Holy Ghost because no one on earth possesses the priesthood of God to do it or to organize Christ's church.[9]

These Seekers sought out any legitimate voice who suggested such a return. In an earlier century, one of the forerunners of these Seekers, Roger Williams, was actually responsible for bringing to America the Baptist brand of Christianity but left it in Providence, Rhode Island, to further his search of seeking out true Christianity. He stated: "There is no regularly constituted church on earth, nor any person qualified to administer any church ordinance; nor can there be until new apostles are sent by the Great Head of the Church for whose coming I am seeking."[10]

Together, these statements represent those who sought for the New Testament Church but could not find it throughout Christendom. Thus, a major tenet of Mormonism is stated in its sixth article of faith: "We believe in the same organization that existed in the Primitive Church, namely, apostles, prophets, pastors, teachers, evangelists, and so forth." This article of faith rests upon the premise that a true church of modern times will reflect organizational patterns found in the Church that was set up by Christ back in the meridian of time. Since Christ always sought to do the will of his Father (see 3 Nephi 27:13; John 6:39–40; 10:25), the organization that came through Christ's administration and direction had divine approval. The true Church of modern times should also have this same divine stamp of approval and reflect the will of the Father through the administration of the Son.

As shown earlier, the New Testament identifies organizational positions that functioned in the Primitive Church. An analysis of ancient biblical scripture yields other characteristics, unique to the organization and functions found in the Church whenever it functioned within a gospel dispensation. Unfortunately, the New Testament was not produced to be a manual of instruction for organizing the meridian Church. We can only reflect upon these writings to deduce a pattern or mode of correct organization and principles of operation. However, a parallel organization does not necessarily prove a true organization; it can only suggest invalidity to the ancient pattern. This fallacy of reasoning is usually called "affirming the consequent." For example, if a church is the true church, it will have New Testament characteristics. The logical consequence could yield several churches who all claim to be the true church having common New Testament characteristics. The premise, however, can only be used to recognize a FALSE church:

- If a church is the true church, it will possess unique characteristics;
- Church X does not have these [or all of these] characteristics;
- Therefore, Church X is not the true church.

There have been several "lists" in modern circulation that identify the "points of the true church." The validity of the story behind how some of these lists came about may be questionable, but the use of the lists stands on its own merit. Many individuals in the early 1800s were like Wilford Woodruff, who had his own list, which he used to determine whether he would seriously investigate a particular church. Wilford was continually disappointed with ministers of local churches until he was invited to a meeting conducted by two Mormon missionaries who introduced him and his brother to the restored gospel. Some of the early converts to the restored gospel who became significant leaders in the Restoration were also among this group of Seekers. Some of these included Sidney Rigdon, Frederick G. Williams, Parley P. Pratt, Orson Hyde, Edward Partridge, and Newel K. Whitney.

A comprehensive list of forty-two points was printed in *The Greatest Quest* by Brent and Blaine Yorgenson. A copy of their list is found in Appendix A. The claim of these authors suggests that all forty-two points on the list reflect characteristics of biblical origin and that all points are reflective within the operations of the Church of Jesus Christ of Latter-day Saints. Therefore, this test of comparison provides reasonable validity to support, but not necessarily to prove, the premise of Mormonism. The proof beyond doubt is a function of the spiritual witness that comes to all who humbly seek it and that complies with the prerequisites as stated in Moroni 10:4–5.

Reconciling Salvation Between Old and New Testament Models

Though the forty-two points are comprehensive, there is an additional feature the true Church must reconcile. There are seemingly two different models of salvation as described in the Old Testament and the New Testament. One of the dilemmas of mainstream Christianity is in harmonizing the message of salvation through Christ as taught in the New Testament with the mode of salvation as taught in the Old Testament, which emphasizes obedience to the Law of Moses. One of the tenets of those subscribing to the doctrine of Christian Trinity is that it is an unchanging essence: the same yesterday, today, and forever. How, then, can modern Christianity proclaim salvation through Christ, either by the Catholic adherence to church sacraments or the Protestant message of being saved by grace, and then reconcile either mode against the emphasis in the Old Testament of obedience to the Law of Moses? The two seem to be products of different modalities of salvation—a conflict of internal consistency in modern Christianity and certainly an item of discussion between the three world religions that hold sacred reverence to biblical scripture. The message of traditional Christianity is very adamant* about the importance of being "saved." Carried to the extreme, unless a person is saved, he is eternally damned. If this is the case, then the mode of salvation should be consistent down through the history of man.

Salvation is a tenet shared by all three biblical religions. Many religionists ascribe the early origins of this covenant relationship between God and man to the point in history when Abram discovered Yahweh (Y-H-W-H; see Appendix F) in Ur of Chaldea. F. E. Peters, professor of Middle Eastern studies, history, and religion at New York University, discussed this covenant shared among the three religions of Judaism, Christianity, and Islam. Peters explained:

> Each monotheistic community has validated the revealed covenant of its predecessors, even as it departed from it in the name of a new revelation that represented both the continuation and the transcendence of what had gone before. The Israelites who gathered with Moses at the foot of Sinai affirmed the truth of what had been announced to Abraham and the tribal patriarchs, and read it into the record of Scripture; indeed, in its finished version the sacred history of the Jews began with Creation itself. The early followers of Jesus, some Jews, some not, re-affirmed, like Jesus himself, the experience of the Covenant. There was, the Christian agreed, a New Covenant, but the New was inexplicable without the Old and so the sacred history of the Jews, the history of both law and the community, became the holy past of the Christian movement.[11]

Peters described Christianity's movement away from the old law into a new covenant:

> Christianity was a revolution in Judaism in that it announced not simply a reform of the Mosaic law but its effective abrogation. It instructed the new Christians, more and more of them from among the Gentiles, that the Torah—its observance and its study, both linchpins of what rabbinic Judaism defined as a Jew—was neither obligatory nor indeed praiseworthy. Christians of strict or even regular observance were not distinguished by their voluntary embrace of the rabbinic ideal but by the pursuit of an asceticism that was radically alien to the world of the Talmud.[12]

Traditional Christianity effectively dismisses both the Law of Moses and the New Testament covenant as single modalities of salvation within an eternal time and space continuum. According to Traditional Christianity, the covenant within the Law of Moses was abrogated* to a New Testament covenant. Furthermore, the Christian Church is the institution which vouchsafed* its perpetuation. Within this perspective comes the justification of the Roman Church to utilize pain of awful death in order "that one man should die for the people, and that the whole nation perish not" (John 11:50). Fox's *Book of Martyrs* documents the extreme forms of execution the Church utilized in order to dictate compliance. Thousands of sincere but differing minds placed their convictions upon the embers of the martyr's stake or dozens of other forms of execution. People were hard pressed to find the "gospel of peace on earth and good will toward all mankind" once Christianity became the religion of state. Jesus might have been the new "way, the truth, and the life" (John 14:6), but it was hard to find the gospel forest for the trees of "Christian might makes right."

Revealed insight found within the pages of Mormon canon sheds a whole new light on the historic origins of the gospel of Jesus Christ and the significance of the Mosaic dispensation. There is, in actuality, only one mode of salvation. From Adam and Eve and through every dispensation of man, the gospel of Jesus Christ was taught, including its most basic principles of faith in Jesus Christ, repentance through the Atonement of Christ, the initial ordinances of baptism by immersion for the forgiveness of sins followed by the bestowal of the gift of the Holy Ghost. Adam and Eve were Christians (see Moses 5:9–12; 6:51–62, 64–66), as were their descendants (see Moses 7:10–11; 8:23–24). Many elements of Christ's life and of his person were documented in pre-Christian scripture. A knowledge of the resurrection, final judgment, and the abode of the dead were also known by pre-Christian societies led by prophets. Contrary to every denomination of Christianity today, a knowledge of a spirit birth and of a premortal existent realm was known even by antediluvian* prophets (see Abraham 1:3, 23). This knowledge, however, was exorcized* from the Christian Church during the fourth and fifth centuries (see Chapter Six: The Plan of Salvation—Spirit Birth and Pre-existence). A knowledge of these ancient principles and ordinances is documented within LDS scripture, which originates translated writings of ancient prophets and continues through modern-day revelation.

If the message of salvation has been continuous in each gospel dispensation, what is the role of the Mosaic Law with its emphasis upon animal and plant offerings, sacrifices, and festivals? What was its purpose in the Mosaic dispensation? The apostle Paul taught that "the law was our schoolmaster until Christ, that we might be justified by faith" (JST, Galatians 3:24). The family of Lehi (circa 600 B.C.) "did observe to keep the judgments, and the statutes, and the commandments of the Lord in all things, according to the law of Moses" (2 Nephi 5:10). It was Nephi who best explained how the Law of Moses connected itself to the gospel of Jesus Christ. He taught: "Behold, my soul delighteth in proving unto my people the truth of the coming of Christ; for, for this end hath the law of Moses been given; and all things which have been given of God from the beginning of the world, unto man, are the typifying of him" (2 Nephi 11:4).

The Nephites understood that the Law of Moses was a preparatory law that helped them look to Christ for salvation. Nephi further warned his people against relying upon the works of the law for salvation, but to look unto Christ for their saved condition.

> For, for this end was the law given; wherefore the law hath become dead unto us, and we are made alive in Christ because of our faith; yet we keep the law because of the commandments.
>
> And we talk of Christ, we rejoice in Christ, we preach of Christ, we prophesy of Christ, and we write according to our prophecies, that our children may know to what source they may look for a remission of their sins.
>
> Wherefore, we speak concerning the law that our children may know the deadness of the law; and they, by knowing the deadness of the law, may look forward unto that life which is in Christ, and know for what end the law was given. And after the law is fulfilled in Christ, that they need not harden their hearts against him when the law ought to be done away (2 Nephi 25:24–27).

King Mosiah reminded his people, who began to harden their hearts, that "the law of Moses availeth nothing except it were through the atonement of his [Christ's] blood" (Mosiah 3:15).

A careful analysis of the Mosaic Law, the Levitical Priesthood, and its ceremonies throughout the books of Exodus and Leviticus, reveals wonderful insights of the veiled but symbolic doctrines of Christ and his gospel. Had the Jews of Jesus' day been as well instructed and prepared as the Nephites, one can only guess how history would have been dramatically altered.

In addition to apostolic priesthood and keys being restored by Peter, James, and John (see D&C 27:12; 128:20), the Levitical or Aaronic Priesthood was also restored in these latter days of restoration by John the Baptist, who held keys to this appendage of authority (see D&C 13; 27:8). Joseph was taught by revelation about these two priesthoods.

> There are, in the church, two priesthoods, namely, the Melchizedek and Aaronic, including the Levitical Priesthood.
>
> The second priesthood is called the Priesthood of Aaron, because it was conferred upon Aaron and his seed, throughout all their generations.
>
> Why it is called the lesser priesthood is because it is an appendage to the greater, or the Melchizedek Priesthood, and has power in administering outward ordinances (D&C 107:2, 13–14).

Mormonism declares only one method of salvation, which is in and through the Atonement of Jesus Christ by being obedient to the ordinances and principles of the eternal gospel of Jesus Christ. This has been taught in every age and dispensation of man and in every society which has been blessed with the voice of prophets. The work of God in other societies where the prophetic voice has had no representation will be a topic of Chapter Six.

Third Pillar—A Spiritual Witness

The apocalyptic vision experienced by John represents one of the grandest visions recorded in scripture. John's awe of the angelic messenger who guided him through these visionary epochs brought him to his knees in reverential worship. The angel resisted John's attempt at worship and acknowledged that he also was a fellow servant who had a testimony of Jesus. Then the angel declared, "The testimony of Jesus is the spirit of prophecy" (Revelations 19:10). Without this third pillar of conviction, a Mormon testimony would be incomplete and without enduring strength. A testimony born of the Spirit permeates every sinew and fiber of one's being. That's the power of spiritual confirmation. It cannot be acquired by money, by request of another, or by deceit. It is the sole product of a very simple but demanding formula. Once received, it is as difficult to verbalize as it is to accurately convey the taste of salt to a person who has never tasted salt. Testimony borne of the Spirit is the oil in the lamp which could not be given to another (see Matthew 25). Some members acknowledge that their testimony of the Church came only from a spiritual witness. Others acquired this spiritual confirmation as they studied, prayed, and began to live the principles contained within the gospel parameters. Realistically, some members bearing testimony possess a "social or familial"* witness only. They have grown up within Mormon society and recognize that their lives have been thus blessed. However, the strength of each member's conviction will surely be tested, and without this spiritual foundation, some fall away into the vain and foolish traditions of men.

The very foundation that is a sure anchor within Mormonism is this personal rock of revelation. A careful reading of Christ's conversation with his neophyte* apostles in Caesarea Philippi establishes this tenet. During one of their group conversations, Jesus asked what people were saying about him. Their reply is almost comical as they reported that Jesus was one of the old prophets who had come back to life. But Jesus turned personal when he asked how *they* personally felt about him. Peter, seizing the occasion, answered, "Thou art the Christ, the Son of the living God." Jesus blessed Peter for his acknowledgment and reminded him, "Flesh and blood [human resources] hath not revealed it [Peter's testimony] unto thee, but my Father which is in heaven" (Matthew 16:17).

Peter's testimony continued to grow and develop and was eventually tested further. The day of Pentecost brought to all of the apostles a confirmation of the spirit. This sealing of the Spirit empowered Peter's conviction and helped him to endure lifelong faithfulness, even experiencing a martyr's death by crucifixion upside-down, as he requested. Back at Caesarea Philippi, Christ, addressing Peter (see Matthew 16:18a for a subtle wordplay upon "Peter" and "rock") again, then said: "and upon this rock I will build my church; and the gates of hell shall not prevail against it." The antecedents of *this* and *it* refer back to the process of receiving personal revelation, or of how divine knowledge is received (see Matthew 16:13–19). Christ's church was not nor now is built upon a human foundation but upon the rock of revelation.

Moroni, in the closing chapter of the Book of Mormon, wrote to future readers of his record. He knew there would be skeptics, doubters, and those who would attempt to explain away the veracity of the sacred text. However, he knew truth would prevail, and he described the formula through which the truth of the Book of Mormon can be acquired, even today:

> Behold, I would exhort you that when ye shall read these things, if

> it be wisdom in God that ye should read them, that ye would remember how merciful the Lord hath been unto the children of men, from the creation of Adam even down until the time that ye shall receive these things, and ponder it in your hearts.
>
> And when ye shall receive these things, I would exhort you that ye would ask God, the Eternal Father, in the name of Christ, if these thing are not true; and if ye shall ask with a sincere heart, with real intent, having faith in Christ, he will manifest the truth of it unto you, by the power of the Holy Ghost.
>
> And by the power of the Holy Ghost ye may know the truth of all things (Moroni 10: 3–5).

The way is sure. The primary question is in the two-letter conjunction: *if.* The results are that he *will* manifest the truth. This is the strength of Mormonism—personal testimony.

Handling Difficult Issues within Mormonism

Within Mormonism, some people struggle with what they perceive as difficult issues, whether it be doctrine, practice, or history. Some of these may involve the practice of plural marriage, gender roles, women and the priesthood, blacks and the priesthood, the Church's stand on sexual orientation, hierarchical authority structure (patriarchy), confession to a priesthood leader, interpersonal social relationships, Church involvement in political issues involving morality, the Mountain Meadows conflict, the Council of Fifty, organic evolution, and the list goes on. Any one of these issues, if given only a cursory investigation, could lead a member to question his or her allegiance to the Church if that member's testimony has not been anchored to a spiritual witness of the Restoration. It is important then to develop deep moorings to these basic tenets of testimony:

1. God lives. He is our loving Father in Heaven, and we are His Children.
2. Jesus Christ is the Son of the living God and the Savior of the world.
3. Joseph Smith is the prophet of God through whom the gospel and the Church of Jesus Christ was restored in the latter days.
4. The Book of Mormon is the word of God.

5. President Thomas S. Monson (or our current prophet), his counselors, and the members of the Quorum of the Twelve Apostles are the prophets, seers, and revelators in our day.[13]

Hold on to these pillars as you proceed to investigate, study, analyze, ponder, and at times, put issues back on the shelf and wait for the spirit to massage your mind and heart until a reconciliation comes—because it will.

Sometimes errors in judgment are assessed against the Church as being true, when the real issue has been a relationship issue. The principles of the gospel are intended to help people in the perfection process. In reality, each of us is striving to overcome our many weaknesses and imperfections. This is true at every level of Church leadership. It is wrong to assume that every leader functions perfectly in each and every calling he receives. One of the hallmark characteristics of the Church is the concept of a "lay ministry." Ordinary members, both male and female, are called to function extraordinarily in positions of leadership and service.

When people are placed in supervisory positions, there is always a possibility of misconstrued behavior or mishandled actions. In addition, there are many opportunities, even within normal social interactions within a religious community, for offense to be taken. Sometimes people, both young and old, just behave badly.

The goal is to follow the example of the Savior. He taught that we should forgive all (D&C 64:10) and that we should love even our enemies (Matthew 5:44). He further instructed us that if we have an offense against our neighbor, it is our duty to go to our neighbor and reconcile those feelings in forgiveness (Matthew 5:22–25; D&C 42:92). In actuality, to be offended is a choice we make. Elder David A. Bednar taught this truth: "However, it ultimately is impossible for another person to offend you or to offend me. Indeed, believing that another person offended us is fundamentally false. To be offended is a choice we make; it is not a condition inflicted or imposed upon us by someone or something else."[14]

The ideal, of course, is to be full of meekness, possessing a forgiving heart. Like the Savior, we are to "give no heed" (1 Nephi 8:33; D&C 20:22) to those situations which might be offensive. Gratitude is given to every member who attempts to serve faithfully in each and every calling received. We are also grateful for fellow members who are quick to forgive and support each other even in our imperfections and shortcomings. Isn't that, in essence, one of the virtues of true charity? Hyrum Smith, the prophet's supportive older brother, said:

> Never undertake to destroy men because they do some evil things. . . . Put down iniquity by good works. Many men speak without any contemplation; if they had given the matter a little contemplation it would not have been spoken. We ought to be careful of what we say and take the example of Jesus; cast over men the mantle of charity, and try to cover their faults. We are made to enlighten and not to darken one another; save men, not destroy them.[15]

1. George, *History of Christianity* video series, 2003.
2. M. Russell Ballard, "Restored Truth," *Ensign*, Nov. 1994, 66.
3. Thomas S. Monson, "They Way Home," Ensign, May 1975, 15.
4. Bristoll, *Providential Epochs*, 227.
5. William Gladstone, cited in the BYU devotional address by President Ezra Taft Benson "The Constitution—A Heavenly Banner," September 16, 1986.
6. Dallin H. Oaks, "The Divinely Inspired Constitution," *Ensign*, Feb. 1992, 68.
7. "News of the Church," *Ensign*, Aug. 1999, 75.
8. Berrett, *Teachings of the Doctrine and Covenants,* 6.
9. Alexander Campbell, cited by T. Edgar Lyon in *BYU Speeches*, (Provo, Utah: Brigham Young University Press, 1960) 7.
10. Richards, *A Marvelous Work and a Wonder*, 29.
11. F. E. Peters, "Abraham's Miraculous Journey," *U.S. News and World Report* Mar. 2007, 18.
12. ibid., 19.
13. Dieter F. Uchtdorf, "The Power of Personal Testimony," *Ensign*, Nov. 2006, 38.
14. David A. Bednar, "And Nothing Shall Offend Them," *Ensign*, Nov. 2006, 90.
15. Corbett, *Hyrum Smith, Patriarch,* 350.

CHAPTER THREE

The Gift of the Holy Ghost

Howbeit when he, the Spirit of truth, is come, he will guide you into all truth.—John 16:13

For they that are wise . . . have received the truth, and have taken the Holy Spirit for their guide. —D&C 45:7

And by the power of the Holy Ghost ye may know the truth of all things. —Moroni 10:5

The Prophet Joseph Smith journeyed to Washington to seek help in recovering compensation for injuries and losses the Saints had suffered during the era of Missouri persecutions. In a conversation between Joseph Smith and President Martin Van Buren, Joseph was asked how this Church differed from other religions of the day. The Prophet replied that "we differed in mode of baptism and the gift of the Holy Ghost by the laying on of hands."[1] He later explained that this answer was given because "all other considerations were contained in the gift of the Holy Ghost."[2] President Wilford Woodruff called the gift of the Holy Ghost the greatest gift we can receive in mortality.[3] One of the most important principles of the gospel, as well as being a primary subject of discourses in LDS worship services, is the encouragement to be guided by the influence of the Holy Ghost. After a person is baptized by immersion for the remission of sins, the candidate receives a second ordinance referred to as "confirmation," which means he is confirmed a member of the Church of Jesus Christ of Latter-day Saints. The words used when this ordinance is performed admonish the new member to "receive the Holy Ghost."

During this ordinance, the newly baptized member is given the "gift of the Holy Ghost." When Brigham Young was the prophet and president of the Church, he had a dream wherein Joseph Smith appeared to him. In the course of their visit together, Brigham Young requested counsel from Joseph Smith on a specific question. He reported that Joseph came toward him and, speaking in earnest, said:

> Tell the people to be humble and faithful, and be sure to keep the spirit of the Lord and it will lead them right. Be careful and not turn away the small still voice; it will teach you what to do and where to go; it will yield the fruits of the kingdom. Tell the brethren to keep their hearts open to conviction, so that when the Holy Ghost comes to them, their hearts will be ready to receive it. They can tell the Spirit of the Lord from all other spirits; it will whisper peace and joy to their souls; it will take malice, hatred, strife and all evil from their hearts; and their whole desire will be to do good, bring forth righteousness, and build up the kingdom of God. Tell the brethren if they will follow the spirit of the Lord they will go right. Be sure to tell the people to keep the Spirit of the Lord.[4]

This encouragement to be led by the Spirit is central to our sacramental covenant and an important doctrine to clarify. Our sacramental ordinance acts as a memorial service, which allows each member to renew the covenants he made at the time of baptism. The prayers offered on the emblems of the sacrament (an ordinance performed in our Church each Sunday), position the elements of bread and water as symbolic reminders of our prior baptismal covenant to "take upon them the name of thy Son, and always remember him and keep his commandments which he has given them." The promise is made at the conclusion of the sacramental prayer that if this course is obediently followed, "they may always have his Spirit to be with them" (D&C 20:77; Moroni 4:3; 5:2). The more sure witness of the Holy Ghost produces nomenclature within testimonies such as "I know beyond a shadow of doubt," or "I know with every fiber of my being."

Mormons are not unique in their desire to be led by the Spirit. We are unique, however, in our doctrine of the personage of the Holy Ghost and our position that only through priesthood ordinance can the gift of the Holy Ghost be received. Truths related to these topics have been woven into latter-day scripture and have been clarified by latter-day prophets and apostles.

Holy Ghost—Third Member of the Godhead

The idea of a "holy ghost" may conjure up wild imaginations (if not fear) in the minds of innocent children who are steeped in the traditions of Halloween. Be that as it may, one of the primary doctrines clarified in the First Vision was the doctrine of the Godhead (Mormons use this term rather than "Trinity" because of the doctrinal differences). The Father and the Son appeared as separate and distinct personages possessing resurrected bodies. The Holy Ghost was present as it had been when Moses was brought into the presence of the Lord on Mount Sinai or when Jesus was transfigured on a mountain top. Joseph Smith was taught by revelation that "the Holy Ghost has not a body of flesh and bones, but is a personage of Spirit. Were it not so, the Holy Ghost could not dwell in us. A man may receive the Holy Ghost, and it may descend upon him and not tarry with him" (D&C 130:22, 23).

Joseph continued to teach and develop the doctrine of the Godhead throughout his prophetic ministry. (A discussion of the doctrine of God the Father will be included in Chapter Six, "Nature and Character of God—LDS"). As the Holy Ghost relates to the others in the Godhead, Joseph taught this eternal truth: "An everlasting covenant was made between three personages before the organization of this earth, and related to their dispensation of things to men on the earth; these personages, according to Abraham's record, are called God the first, the Creator; God the second, the Redeemer; and God the third, the Witness or Testator."[5]

Elder Bruce R. McConkie taught that the Holy Ghost is a "personage of spirit, a spirit person, a spirit man, a spirit entity. He can be in only one place at one time, and he does not and cannot transform himself into any other form or image than that of the man whom he is, though his power and influence can be manifest at one and the same time through all immensity."[6]

President Joseph Fielding Smith clarified that "the Holy Ghost should not be confused with the Spirit which fills the immensity of space and which is everywhere present. This other Spirit is impersonal and has no size, nor dimension; it proceeds forth from the presence of the Father and the Son and is in all things. We should speak of the Holy Ghost as a personage as 'he' and this other Spirit as 'it,' although when we speak of the power or gift of the Holy Ghost we may properly say 'it.' "[7]

There has been some discussion within LDS circles concerning the origin and destiny of the Holy Ghost. In regard to these matters, President

Joseph Fielding Smith counseled: "We cannot compare ourselves and our destiny with the Holy Ghost and the position he occupies. Speculation on such things is not edifying."[8] Supporting this conclusion, Elder Bruce R. McConkie stated: "In this dispensation at least, nothing has been revealed as to his origin or destiny; expressions on these matters are both speculative and fruitless."[9]

That we can receive inspired guidance, enlightened impressions, and confirmed feelings from the Holy Ghost is viewed by Latter-day Saints as one of our most sacred gifts. We acknowledge, as the Prophet Joseph Smith did, that "without this companionship we are nothing; our minds could not be enlightened; and our comprehension of the everlasting gospel would be impaired."[10]

The Light of Christ and the Spirit of the Lord

Vince Rause, a writer for the *Los Angeles Times* magazine, came across a passage written by Bede Griffiths, a contemporary Benedictine monk. Griffiths described his boyhood experience of walking one night when he was suddenly dazzled by the beautiful song of a flock of birds. Their singing awakened senses he had never used before. Instantly the world seemed transformed as if he'd stepped into the presence of an almost unfathomable mystery that seemed to draw him to itself. Rause said of this experience: "That was it: no burning bushes, no flaming chariots. Just a gentle subtle awakening, a soft epiphany that many might simply shrug off. But it changed Griffith's life forever."[11]

Soon Rause found accounts of similar revelations: people surprised by a thrill of wonder as they read poetry, pondered the cosmos, or prayed. Rause further explained: "Mystical experience, I was beginning to understand, was not a magical ascension into some distant literal paradise. It was a quiet, personal epiphany that the miraculous and the mundane are one and the same, and that both are right before our eyes. For the first time since I was a kid, I felt the presence of something mysterious and fine. What that something was, I couldn't fathom."[12]

After this experience, Rause decided to approach life somewhat differently. He said his new master plan for his life was to "shut up and listen for a while." Humble people who try to be in tune to their "inner selves" admit to hearing a special voice within that helps them appreciate the good in life and to recognize right from wrong. However, many may be like Vince Rause, who hadn't any idea what that special inner voice could be or from whence it came. As Latter-day Saints with Restoration scriptures, we know what it is and the source from whence it comes. "For the word of the Lord is truth, and whatsoever is truth is light, and whatsoever is light is Spirit, even the Spirit of Jesus Christ. And the Spirit giveth light to every man that cometh into the world; and the Spirit enlighteneth every man through the world, that hearkeneth to the voice of the Spirit. And everyone that hearkeneth to the voice of the Spirit cometh unto God, even the Father (D&C 84: 45–46).

Moroni tells us the same thing: "For behold, the Spirit of Christ is given to every man, that he may know good from evil; wherefore, I show unto you the way to judge; for everything which inviteth to do good, and to persuade to believe in Christ, is sent forth by the power and gift of Christ; wherefore ye may know with a perfect knowledge it is of God" (Moroni. 7:16).

Our understanding of the Light of Christ is limited. Finite powers and capacities cannot comprehend that which is infinite. But we do know certain basic principles, among which are these[13]:

1. It is the light which proceeds forth from the presence and person of Deity to fill the immensity of space and is therefore everywhere present (D&C 88:12).
2. It is the agency of God's power, and the law by which all things are governed (v. 13).
3. It is the divine power which gives life to all things, and if it were completely withdrawn, life would cease (v. 13).
4. It enlightens the mind and quickens the understanding of every person born into the world (all have a conscience!) (v. 11).
5. It strives with all men (the Holy Ghost testifies but does not strive) unless and until they rebel against light and truth, at which time the striving ceases, and in that sense, the Spirit is withdrawn (D&C 84:46).
6. Those who hearken to its voice come unto Christ, receive his gospel, are baptized, and gain the gift of the Holy Ghost (Moroni 7:12–18; D&C 84:43–53; 88:7–13).

Sometimes it is difficult to distinguish between the influences of the Spirit of the Lord and the promptings which come from the Holy Ghost.

Elder George Q. Cannon clarifies this difference.

> This is a gift of itself, to be able to distinguish that which suggests itself to our own hearts and that which comes from God. And we are misled sometimes by our own feeling because of our inability to distinguish between the voice of the [Holy Ghost] and the suggestions of our own spirit. There is a still, small voice in the heart of every human being. There is an influence [that] comes with every son and daughter of Adam that is born into the world. What! Outside of the Latter-day Saints? Certainly, we are all the children of God. There is an influence born with every person that to a certain extent is a spirit of revelation.[14]

The benefit of receiving the Spirit of the Lord as well as promptings from the Holy Ghost throughout our lives may produce a situation where the overall effect of these influences may not be wholly understood and fully appreciated. Empirically,* the total loss of these influences would produce the knowledge that unfortunately would come at a great cost. Sometimes a person doesn't appreciate a possession until after the possession is lost or made unavailable. We may come to a greater understanding of the influence of the Holy Ghost in our lives when we, through transgression, lose it. But at what cost? Those who have received church discipline that results in a loss of Church membership and its attendant blessings soon recognize some of the effect of losing the gift of the Holy Ghost. Those who have turned their hearts from allegiance to the Restored gospel and their ecclesiastical leaders oftentimes become hard-hearted and vindictive. In these situations, pride becomes an enemy to humility. A spirit of rebellion and retaliation replaces spiritual promptings. If a forgiving and humble heart cannot be restored, the course that follows is certainly dolorous,* becoming a path of sorrow and spiritual anguish.

It is a historic observation that some of the greatest enemies of our Church have been those who had once received fellowship but were removed because of transgression. The Amalekites and the Amulonites were Nephite dissenters. The Book of Mormon characterized them as having more hardened hearts than even the Lamanites among whom they were living. Alma said of these dissenters: "And thus we can plainly discern, that after a people have been once enlightened by the Spirit of God, and have had great knowledge of things pertaining to righteousness, and then have fallen away into sin and transgression, they become more hardened, and thus their state becomes worse than though they had never known these things" (Alma 24:30).

Recognizing the Witness of the Spirit

As experienced within the Restored Church, the influence of the Holy Ghost is one of the most precious gifts God bestows upon his mortal children. The Lord, in a revelation to Joseph Smith, reminded Oliver Cowdery, who was then acting as Joseph's scribe, of the divine witness he had received during an evening when Oliver was pouring out his heart to the Lord: "Did I not speak peace to your mind concerning the matter? What greater witness can you have than from God?" (D&C 6:23). Joseph Fielding Smith explained the power of this third member of the Godhead:

> A person who will walk in the light as that light is revealed by the third member of the Godhead, will know with a positive and unerring understanding that Jesus is the Christ and the Redeemer of the world, and the plan of salvation will be plainly comprehended. . . . The Spirit of God speaking to the spirit of man has power to impart truth with greater effect and understanding than the truth can be imparted by personal contact even with heavenly beings. Through the Holy Ghost the truth is woven into the very fibre and sinews of the body so that it cannot be forgotten.[15]

The manifestations of the Holy Ghost are primarily centered upon our minds and upon our hearts—in our thoughts and our feelings. The Lord, again in speaking through Joseph, told Oliver: "I will tell you in your mind and in your heart, by the Holy Ghost, which shall come upon you and which shall dwell in you heart" (D&C 8:2).

President Spencer W. Kimball taught the Saints during an area conference:

> The burning bushes, the smoking mountains, the sheets of four-footed beasts, the Cumorahs, and the Kirtlands were realities; but they were the exceptions. The great volume of revelation came to Moses and to Joseph and comes to today's prophets in the less spectacular way—that of deep impressions, without spectacle or glamour or dramatic events. Always expecting the spectacular, many may miss entirely the constant flow of revealed communication.[16]

For each member of the Church, the blessing of "always having his

Spirit" to be with you is translated as receiving personal revelation and inspiration. Elder Dallin H. Oaks taught, "In its more familiar forms, revelation and inspiration comes by means of words or thoughts communicated to the mind (see D&C 8:2,3; Enos 1:10), by sudden enlightenment (see D&C 6:14,15), by positive or negative feelings about proposed courses of action, or even by inspiring performances, as in the performing arts. As Elder Boyd K. Packer has stated, 'Inspiration comes more as a feeling than as a sound.' "[17]

A favorite scripture reference quoted by members on this topic is found in Doctrine and Covenants 9. The background of this revelation concerns the relationship of Oliver Cowdery as a scribe to Joseph Smith during the translation of the plates of gold. Oliver also desired to participate in the translation process. The Lord allowed Oliver an attempt to translate—and he failed. The Lord taught Oliver, "Behold, you have not understood; you have supposed that I would give it unto you, when you took no thought save it was to ask me" (D&C 9:7). The two verses following continue the Lord's counsel and are often cited in counsel on receiving answers to prayer:

> But, behold, I say unto you, that you must study it out in your mind; then you must ask me if it be right, and if it is right I will cause that your bosom shall burn within you; therefore, you shall feel that it is right.
>
> But if it be not right you shall have no such feelings, but you shall have a stupor of thought that shall cause you to forget the thing which is wrong. (D&C 9:8–9)

Interestingly, the rest of the verse is not usually cited: "therefore, you cannot write that which is sacred save it be given you from me." It is important to understand the historical setting behind scripture references and avoid applications taken out of context. The Lord's specific counsel was given to Oliver regarding how to translate. In principle, as we take our concerns and questions to the Lord, we also must "study it out in our minds." There are examples in the scriptures when the Lord provided solutions upon request or assistance in dire circumstances (compare Ether 2:19–21; Exodus 3:10–15; and 1 Nephi 16:10; 17:8). There are other occasions when the Lord declined an answer and instead asked the person for a proposed solution—which he then vindicated or turned down (Ether 2:23; see historical background of D&C 3). However, we should not always expect the "burning in the bosom" or "the stupor of thought." More often than not, the answer comes in gentle whisperings or in the warm feelings of sweet peace.

As members of the Church strive for the companionship of the Spirit in their lives, it is sometimes difficult to recognize all of the subtle ways in which the Holy Ghost manifests himself. This may have been the condition of the converted Lamanites who had been "baptized with fire and with the Holy Ghost, *and they knew it not*" (emphasis added; 3 Nephi 9:20). The apostle Paul desired members of the Church in Ephesus and Colosse to understand the workings of the Spirit in their lives. He taught that the fruits of the Spirit are love, joy, peace, long-suffering, gentleness, goodness, faith, meekness, temperance, and walking in the spirit. He also included mercy, kindness, humbleness of mind, forbearance of one another, forgiveness, charity, peace, and thankfulness (compare Galatians 5:22–25; and Colossians 3:10–15).

President Benson taught the Saints:

> We hear the words of the Lord most often by a feeling. If we are humble and sensitive, the Lord will prompt us through our feelings. That is why spiritual promptings move us on occasion to great joy, sometimes to tears. Many times my emotions have been made tender and my feelings very sensitive when touched by the Spirit. The Holy Ghost causes our feelings to be more tender. We feel more charitable and compassionate with each other. We are more calm in our relationships. We have a greater capacity to love each other. People want to be around us because our very countenances radiate the influence of the Spirit. We are more godly in our character. As a result, we become increasingly more sensitive to the promptings of the Holy Ghost and thus able to comprehend spiritual things more clearly.[18]

Counterfeits to the Spirit

As with all principles of the gospel, counterfeits exist here as well. Elder Gerald N. Lund spoke of these counterfeits: "If something is counterfeit, it means it resembles the original so closely that it is difficult to distinguish which is the true and which is the false. We must ever be on guard against being deceived by our emotions or by revelation from an unworthy source."[19]

Brother Lund suggested five guidelines or principles to help determine whether information or feelings are from the Lord or from a counterfeit source.[20]

1. It is God who determines all aspects of revelation. "We must remember that when all is done, it is still up to the Lord to determine when the revelation comes, how it is given, what is revealed, and to whom."

2. The content given in a revelation is more important than the form in which it comes. God reveals his mind and will to man across a broad spectrum of experiences. Quiet premonitions, gentle thoughts, a feeling of peace . . . are by far the most common. Don't expect the dramatic.

3. Revelation from God does not contradict gospel principles or go contrary to established Church policy and procedure. New doctrine and procedure comes in one of three ways:

    a. A formal press conference will be called by the leaders of the Church, at which an official announcement will be made.

    b. It will be announced through the *Church News*, the *Ensign*, or other official Church communications.

    c. It will be announced in general conference by those in authority.

2. The Lord wants us to use our agency and develop spiritual self-reliance. The Lord counsels us that "it is not meet [it is not proper or good] that I should command in all things. There are some things that don't matter to the Lord; he leaves the choice up to us (see D&C 58:26; 27:2; 60:5; 61:22; 62:5; 63:40; 80:3) Similarly, the Spirit of the Lord is not likely to give us revelations on matters that are trivial. Elder Dallin H. Oaks gives further clarification on the matter: "If a matter appears of little or no consequence, we should proceed on the basis of our own judgment. If the choice is important for reasons unknown to us, the Lord will intervene and give us guidance. Where we are living in tune with the Spirit and seeking its guidance, we can be sure that we will receive the guidance we need to attain our goal. The Lord will not leave us unassisted when a choice is important to our eternal welfare."[21]

5. A person is not given revelation to direct another person unless they have priesthood or family responsibility for that person. Elder Oaks calls it the principle of "stewardship in revelation."

> Only the President of the Church receives revelation to guide the entire Church; the stake president receives revelation for the stake; and the bishop for his ward. "When one person purports* to receive revelation for another person outside his or her own area of responsibility . . . you can be sure that such revelations are not from the Lord."[22]

Elder Lund's final point is driven home in an anecdotal story of a beautiful BYU student who came home from class reporting that she had five boys throughout the day each declare that he had a personal witness that she should be his wife. Obviously, only one could be right, if any.

The Apostle Paul concluded his epistle to the Philippians with this counsel: "Finally, brethren, whatsoever things are true, whatsoever things are honest, whatsoever things are just, whatsoever things are pure, whatsoever things are lovely, whatsoever things are of good report; if there be any virtue, and if there be any praise, think on these things" (Philippians 4:8).

Latter-day Saints seek guidance from genuine sources bearing divine approval. Historically, some societies and cultures have placed much credence upon omens, astrological observations, and superstitious inclinations. Members of the Church who desire to be lead by the Spirit of the Lord and the Holy Ghost will not place any value upon these false imitations. Putting credence upon an omen is not the same as the Spirit providing a sense of concern. We believe in the freedom of the will and not fatalism or determinism. Good luck is as much earned as it is happenstance. We are not concerned about Friday the 13th, walking under ladders, carrying rabbit's feet (they weren't much good to the rabbit!), black cats crossing our path, or worrying about our future if a mirror breaks. Elder Bruce R. McConkie stated:

> Religious beliefs and practices based on fear and credulity (often including belief in the power of omens, signs, charms, and the like) have degenerated into the field of superstition. . . . Among almost all primitive peoples there are many superstitious beliefs and practices. Even among the supposedly enlightened of modern times much of the same degenerate form of belief and worship prevails. Examples of superstitious beliefs and practices found in modern churches include the use of charms, worship of images, revering of relics, baptism of unborn fetuses, the supposed appearances of spirits and personages to children and others, the presumed changing of the sacramental elements into

the literal flesh and blood of Christ, and many other things.[23]

Gifts of the Spirit

The restoration of the true gift of the Holy Ghost back to the earth through priesthood authority has also restored the appendage "gifts of the Spirit." Some of these gifts are listed by Paul (1 Corinthians 12), by Moroni (Moroni 10:8–18), and by Joseph Smith (D&C 46:9–31). Elder Bruce R. McConkie suggested that in the fullest sense, they are infinite in number and endless in their manifestations. He also felt that testimony is the first and greatest of all the gifts given by God to mortals.[24] There is a branch of Christianity (Pentecostal in nature) that accentuates certain gifts of the Spirit that act as evidence that the believer has been born of the Spirit. Their seemingly real experiences of speaking in tongues and miraculous healings are used to validate their spiritual status. The term "gift of tongues" in Mormon history has been applied to basically three kinds of phenomena:

1. Glossolalia, or the uttering of unintelligible words, usually in a church meeting, followed by a message or interpretation.
2. Divinely assisted acquisition, or Spirit-enhanced ability in a foreign language that one is learning or using.
3. Supernatural comprehension, or the spontaneous ability to comprehend the message of an utterance in a language which one has not learned. We sometimes refer to this as the interpretation of tongues.

The earliest known accounts of Mormon glossolalia were found in branches of the Church in Ohio and Pennsylvania in 1831. The first appearance of glossolalia was dismissed as a manifestation of the devil. The Prophet Joseph Smith was aware of the inherent danger of these so-called spiritual operations and spoke out against extreme abnormal exercises.

It was not until September of 1832 that Joseph Smith said he had heard the gift of tongues among the brethren for the first time. When Joseph called upon Brigham Young to close a meeting with prayer, Brigham spoke in tongues during the prayer. After the prayer, the other brethren questioned Joseph about the validity of Brigham's glossolalia. Joseph told them that it was the pure Adamic language and was of God. With this endorsement, the practice began to spread rapidly. In spite of the widespread popularity of this phenomenon between the years of 1832 and 1837, the practice of glossolalia was not without its problems. In response to some members' more energetic experiences and manifestations, Joseph received a revelation, now published Doctrine and Covenants 50, counseling the Church against so-called spiritual phenomena, some claiming to receive visions and revelations.

In July, 1833, when the citizens of Jackson County produced their anti-Mormon manifesto, they listed the practice of glossolalia as one of the offenses committed by the Mormons. The practice also became a problem in Kirtland. Church leaders thus began to curb the practice of speaking in tongues in church meetings.

By the end of the 1830s, Joseph Smith's earlier attitude of enthusiasm had turned to one of caution and reservation. In 1839, he publicly discouraged the use of the gift in meetings, asserting the gift was "given for the purpose of preaching among those whose language is not understood for any man that has the Holy Ghost can speak of the things of God in his own tongue, as well as to speak in another." Both Joseph Smith and Brigham Young taught that the gift of tongues was never an appropriate method to govern the Church or members within.[25]

During the Nauvoo era, evidence of glossolalia continued in both public and private gatherings of the Saints, but in a lesser degree. An editorial appeared in the *Times and Seasons* which labeled the gift of tongues "the smallest gift perhaps of the whole."[26]

There Are Many Kinds of Voices

There is great emphasis in Mormonism to be directed of the Spirit. There may be some despair among those members who feel they do not meet this challenge. A worthwhile study of the many ways in which the Spirit can manifest itself in our lives is to be found in *Preach My Gospel*, a guide to missionary service, and in the LDS Topical Guide under the topic: "Holy Ghost, Mission of." The fruits of this study should confirm that as a "chosen and peculiar people of the Lord," we are the blessed recipients of his Spirit—not only prophetically but as each person receives the spirit of prophecy and revelation. The angel reminded John the Revelator that "the testimony of Jesus is the spirit of prophecy" (Revelation 19:10). We follow the example of our Savior to be baptized by immersion in water for the remission of sins (see 2 Nephi 31:5–10). By the same token, we must also be baptized by and immersed in the Spirit of the

Lord, "and then cometh a remission of your sins by fire and by the Holy Ghost" (2 Nephi 31:17). As we continue to "walk in the way of the Lord" (see Micah 4:5; Colossians 2:6; Mosiah 6:6; D&C 136:4) by honoring our baptismal covenants and immersing ourselves with the influences of the Holy Ghost, we qualify ourselves to become sanctified by the blood of Christ and justified through the Holy Spirit (see D&C 20:30–31; Moses 6:60). We become fully justified when our course in life is in harmony with the mind and will of God.[27] This state of being is confirmed to each individual by the Spirit. It can also come as a revelation as it did to Nephi, the brother of Lehi. The Lord spoke to Nephi and said:

> Blessed art thou, Nephi, for those things which thou has done; for I have beheld how thou hast with unwearyingness declared the word, which I have given thee, unto this people, . . . [thou] has sought my will, and to keep my commandments.
>
> And now, because thou has done this with such unwearyingness, behold, I will bless thee forever; . . . for thou shalt not ask that which is contrary to my will (Helaman 10:4–5).

It doesn't necessarily mean that every action and behavior is a result of being prompted by the Spirit. In reality, we are fallen men and women living in a mortal world. We might not have the presence of the Holy Ghost with us every second of every minute of every hour of every day. Strong, dramatic spiritual impressions do not come to us frequently. However, the Holy Ghost can tarry with us much, if not most, of the time—and certainly the Spirit can be with us more than it is not with us. As we become ever more immersed in the Spirit of the Lord, we should strive to recognize those spiritual impressions in the mind and in the heart and what those impressions are testifying of and directing us to do.

The ancient people of Corinth lived within an environment bustling with the energy of commerce, politics, social drama, and religion. In Corinth you could find the cults of the gods of Egypt, Rome, and Greece. The temple of Aphrodite, the goddess of love, stood atop the Acrocorinth. In Paul's epistle to the Corinthians, he warned them that "there are, it may be, so many kinds of voices in the world, and none of them is without signification" (1 Corinthians 14:10). This same warning can be returned to each of us no matter in what city we place our residence. God counsels each of us to "be still and know that I am God" (D&C 101:16). Elder Packer reviewed a story from the life of John Burroughs in order to teach of the importance of training yourself to listen to the Spirit.

> Many years ago John Burroughs, a naturalist, one summer evening was walking through a crowded park. Above the sounds of city life he heard the song of a bird. He stopped and listened! Those with him had not heard it. He looked around. No one else had noticed it. It bothered him that everyone should miss something so beautiful. He took a coin from his pocket and flipped it into the air. It struck the pavement with a ring, no louder than the song of the bird. Everyone turned; they could hear that! It is difficult to separate from all the sounds of city traffic the song of a bird. But you can hear it. You can hear it plainly if you train yourself to listen for it.[28]

Our challenge is to clear away the sounds of the world and listen to the still, small voice of the Spirit (D&C 85:6; 1 Kings 19:12; 1 Nephi 17:45) and to give place so that "my Spirit shall be in your hearts" (D&C 84:88). A spirit of reverence invites revelation. Each son and daughter of God should determine the times and places where they are most likely to receive these spiritual promptings. We can do no better than to immerse ourselves within the holy scriptures. As spiritual impressions come, write them down. As we perform this task and repeatedly return to these documented sources of inspired thoughts and feelings, this process becomes a portal to enhanced and greater manifestations. There is a caveat* to the illumination that can be received through personal revelation. God and His Spirit are not pleased with blabber mouths. We must hold sacred these thoughts and feelings. Only when the Spirit prompts should these manifestations be shared in sacred moments or company—moments not to aggrandize oneself or boost one's spiritual ego. The Lord reminded Oliver Cowdery to "trifle not with sacred things" (D&C 6:12). The Lord cautioned the Church in Kirtland: "Remember that that which cometh from above is sacred, and must be spoken with care, and by constraint of the Spirit" (D&C 63:64).

The Liahona was an interesting device which appeared outside Lehi's tent one morning during his family's travel in the wilderness. They soon determined that it was a physical object that could help provide inspired direction for their travels. Alma, a later Book of Mormon prophet, described the Liahona as a shadow or type (see Alma 37:38–45), the implication being that the Liahona represented symbolically how each of us should respond individually to the direction of the Holy Ghost. It worked according to the principles of faith and diligence. As Elder David A. Bednar described it, it also became a "physical instrument that served as an outward indicator of their inner spiritual standing before God."[29] Surely such an object in our lives would become like a two-edged sword: a spiritual gift or an incriminating reprimand.

Roadblocks to receiving this wonderful influence in our lives are many: personal sin, expressions of anger and contention, extreme physical stress, busyness, worry, fret, and apathy. We are well served by the Spirit when we acknowledge God's hand in our lives. The opposite is true when we see life through lenses of self-centeredness, pride, and arrogance. Spiritual deafness describes the state of those who are lacking in spirituality, whose spiritual ears are not attuned to the whisperings of the still small voice of the Spirit. Similarly, spiritual blindness is the identifying mark that singles out those who are unable to see the hand of God manifest in the affairs of their lives. Such have "unbelief and blindness of heart" (D&C 58:15); "they are hard in their hearts, and blind in their minds" (3 Nephi 2:1). It is important, then, to not only recognize when the Spirit is with us but to also be able to recognize at what times and from which behaviors the Spirit withdraws. By avoiding the latter, the frequency in which the Spirit can be manifested will be enhanced.

The differences between the male and female genders seem to be well documented and publicized in the modern world. However, in the scope of the plan of happiness within the restored gospel, each person has equal access to the inspired promptings of the Holy Ghost if the prerequisites are in place. In Mormonism we give special credence to apostolic testimony and the testimony expressed by the Seventy. These brethren have received a divine calling to be especial witnesses of Jesus Christ and of his ministry and resurrection to the world at large (see D&C 27:12; 107:25). These men may have received miraculous manifestations, but they also bear solemn witness that their primary source of "knowledge" of the truth of the Savior's life and ministry is from the still, small voice of the Spirit which "whispereth through and pierceth all things, and often times it maketh my bones to quake while it maketh manifest" (D&C 85:6). Of this, President Wilford Woodruff testified:

> What is revelation? The testimony of the Father and Son. How many of you have had revelation? How many of you have had the Spirit of God whisper unto you—the still small voice? I would have been in the spirit world a great many years ago if I had not followed the

> promptings of the still small voice. These were the revelations of Jesus Christ, the strongest testimony a man or a woman can have. I have had many testimonies since I have been connected with this Church and kingdom. I have been blessed at times with certain gifts and graces, certain revelations and ministrations; but with them all I have never found anything that I could place more dependency upon than the still small voice of the Holy Ghost.[30]

When a man and a women seal their bond of love in a marriage covenant, one of the natural consequences of that relationship is the privilege of bearing and rearing children. This gift simulates the powers of heaven resident within our own heavenly parents. This phase of our laboratory of life certainly necessitates the need to call upon the guidance of the Holy Spirit. God implored Adam and Eve, after he personally performed their marriage union, to become one. In relation to accessing the Spirit, the challenges faced by men and women may bear inherent differences. Let's use my wife and myself as examples, though we might not be representative examples of each gender. I have a tendency to process life through linear reasoning, logic, and experimental problem-solving. EvaKay tends to experience life more intuitively, through her heart. We have learned to recognize these inherent differences. Though in continual need of reminders, we open ourselves to the combined spiritual perspective we each bring to circumstances needing clarity and direction. In this process, we try to become one synergistically.* This means that as we pool together all of our spiritual proclivities* as resources, the total effect of our spiritual togetherness is more than the effect of each of us individually.

There are times when I have suggested courses of action that seemed very logical and right. Conversely, EvaKay, at times, had strong feelings about different directions. I have learned to pay special attention to those deep feelings. There are also times when I have had no particular feeling about a situation, but she sensed a deep concern. I have learned it is wise to attend to her concerns. Other times, I may have felt directed to pursue a course having "studied it out in my mind" and felt a guiding hand in the logic and conviction of that decision. During those times, even if EvaKay had some emotional concern, she was a strong supporter of the course I had proposed. As a result and to the extent we are successful, our lives and the lives of our family have been blessed with this guidance and direction which comes from a marriage "blessed by heaven." The ideal environment in which to raise the sons and daughters of God in mortality is in the homes of a husband and wife who have had their marriage sealed within temple covenants. Then, working together with all the energies of their souls, they apply the principles of the gospel to realize their goal of being led by the Spirit and having their marriage sealed by the Holy Spirit of Promise (D&C 132:18, 20). Oftentimes in raising children the ideal cannot be realized and individuals find themselves alone with this tremendous challenge. It then becomes their individual challenge to also work with all the energy of their soul to live the principles of the gospel and receive the blessings of partnership with the Spirit which will guide, reveal, comfort, and help to heal the wounded soul.

1. Roberts, *History of The Church of Jesus Christ of Latter-day Saints*, 4:42.
2. Ibid.
3. Durham, *The Discourses of Wilford Woodruff*, 5
4. Watson, *Manuscript History of Brigham Young 1801-1844*, 529–31.
5. Joseph Smith, *Teachings of the Prophet Joseph Smith*, 190.
6. McConkie, *Doctrinal New Testament Commentary*, 1:739
7. Joseph Fielding Smith, *Doctrines of Salvation*, 1:49–50.
8. Joseph Fielding Smith, *Answers to Gospel Questions, 2:147*
9. McConkie, *Mormon Doctrine*, 359.
10. Joseph Fielding Smith, *Answers to Gospel Questions, 2:147.*
11. Rause, "Searching for the Divine," 141–145.
12. Ibid.
13. McConkie, *The Promised Messiah*, 208–9.
14. Cannon, *The Gospel Truth*, 1:321.
15. Joseph Fielding Smith, *Doctrines of Salvation*, 1:47.
16. Spencer W. Kimball, in an Area Conference address, Munich Germany, 1973.
17. Dallin H. Oaks, "Revelation," *New Era*, Sept. 1982, 38.
18. Ezra Taft Benson, "Seek the Spirit of the Lord," *Ensign*, Apr. 1988, 4.
19. Gerald N. Lund, from a BYU devotional address, Dec. 2, 1997.
20. Gerald N. Lund, "Is it Revelation?" *New Era*, July 2004, 44.
21. Dallin H. Oaks, "Eight Ways God Can Speak to You," *New Era*, Sept. 1982, 46.
22. Gerald N. Lund, "Revelation" *New Era*, Sept. 1982, 46.
23. McConkie, *Mormon Doctrine*, 772.
24. McConkie, *A New Witness for the Articles of Faith*, 371.
25. Watson, *Manuscript History of Brigham Young*, 60–61.
26. Much of this material on the gift of tongues and glossolalia was taken from an unpublished manuscript by Robert S. Clark entitled "The gift of tongues in the Church today: Cloven tongues as of fire or smoldering ashes?" Brother Clark was a fellow colleague and instructor at the Ogden Institute of Religion.

27. Joseph Smith, *Lectures on Faith*, 3:38.
28. Boyd K. Packer, "Prayers and Answers," *Ensign*, Nov. 1979, 19.
29. David A. Bednar, "That We May Always Have His Spirit to Be with Us," *Ensign,* May 2006.
30. Watt, *Journal of Discourses,* 21:195–196

CHAPTER FOUR

Transforming Testimony into Christlike Behavior

I pray thee, O God, that I may be beautiful within. – Socrates

People cannot change truth, but truth can change people. – Author unknown

One of my favorite classes during my undergraduate studies at Utah State University as I pursued a degree in psychology was "Motivation." This interest lead me to pursue a master's degree in counseling and guidance. I have always been interested in understanding why people do the things they do. This educational choice was probably an outgrowth of trying to understand my own behavioral complexities. I was introduced to reward-reinforcement theory, Maslow's hierarchy of needs, behavioral modification theories, and counseling paradigms* that offered unique approaches intended to initiate desired behavioral changes. As I immersed myself in this secular nectar of learning, I overlooked investigating this same subject matter from a religious perspective using sources from our LDS standard works.

Obviously, some modes of behavior can be elicited through conditioning or through coercive or controlling means. Some behavior is a product of negative or positive reinforcement schedules. In terms of moral behavior, desired behavior is Christlike behavior freely given from within the individual. Moroni spoke of behavior or "gifts" originating out of ulterior motives in the closing pages of the Book of Mormon. He taught: For behold, . . . a man being evil cannot do that which is good; for if he offereth a gift . . . except he shall do it with real intent it profiteth him nothing. For behold, it is not counted unto him for righteousness. For behold, if a man being evil giveth a gift, he doeth it grudgingly; wherefore it is counted unto him the same as if he had retained the gift; wherefore he is counted evil before God (Moroni 7:6–8).

I continued my education, and then, after my doctoral diploma had hung on the wall for several years, I heard a fascinating statement from Elder Boyd K. Packer. He said: "True doctrine, understood, changes attitudes and behavior. The study of the doctrines of the gospel will improve behavior quicker than a study of behavior will improve behavior. Preoccupation with unworthy behavior can lead to unworthy behavior. That is why we stress forcefully the study of the doctrines of the gospel."[1]

Some time later, I became acquainted with the following statement by President Ezra Taft Benson: "The Lord works from the inside out. The world works from the outside in. The world would take people out of the slums. Christ takes the slums out of people, and then they take themselves out of the slums. The world would mold men by changing their environment. Christ changes men, who then change their environment. The world would shape human behavior, but Christ can change human nature."[2]

It was then that I put my academic training on the back burner as I sought to understand the steps through which the Lord would initiate behavioral change. The results of my study produced what I call "The Lord's Method of Behavioral Modification." The essential steps of this methodology begin with acquiring an understanding of true principles and doctrines. These principles are massaged within a Know-Do-Feel experiential modality. From this dynamic emerges the basis of our value orientation. It is from our base of values that our assumptions and perceptions are formed and the attitudes and feelings undergirding our behavioral manifestations are influenced. Consider these following steps:

1. Principles and Doctrines
2. Know-Do-Feel
3. Formation of values
4. Formation of assumptions and perceptions
5. Formation of attitudes and feelings
6. Manifestation of behavior.

Principles and Doctrines

If Mormon theology is based upon restored gospel principles and those principles are incorporated into our actions, then model Mormon behavior should bear the fruit of that knowledge. Christ admonished his followers to be the "light of the world" and the "salt of the earth." An understanding of how a knowledge of principles translates into desired Christlike behavior is essential if we are to be judged by the standard of "by their fruits ye shall know them" (see Sermon on the Mount, Matthew 5–7). In this discussion, we are interested in good, productive, and potentially Christlike behavior. However, this same paradigm (using negative principles) is useful to understand environments that produce paradigms of hate, bigotry, and secret combinations. Joseph Smith taught of causal relationships when he said: "There is a law, irrevocably decreed in heaven before the foundations of the world, upon which all blessings are predicated—And when we obtain any blessings from God, it is by obedience to that law upon which it is predicated" (D&C 130:21–21).

Good behaviors emanate from correct principles. Evil behaviors emanate from evil and sordid principles. Remember Elder Packer's powerful first line: "True doctrine, understood, changes attitudes and behavior."

The Process of Converting Principles into Values: Know, Do, and Feel

KNOW: The first essential phase in the Lord's process is the teaching phase. It emphasizes cognitive recognition. Therefore, the head is the symbol for this phase. In this phase, true principles and doctrines need to be taught. This is true whether the desired behavior is sought within the corporate business world, on the domestic front within homes, or in other venues. Paul spoke to the Romans about the importance of receiving correct saving knowledge: "How then shall they call on him in whom they have not believed? And how shall they believe in him of whom they have not heard? And how shall they hear without a preacher?" (Romans 10:14).

Obviously, exposure to a knowledge of correct principles can come from formal instructional settings. It is also possible to learn of these principles indirectly by observing behavior in the lives of significant others. However, it is not always easily apparent through observation to come to an understanding of the principles that have a causal relationship to specific moral behavior.

The Book of Mormon prophet Enos had been taught by his father concerning the principles of eternal life. He finally desired to have a personal knowledge of these principles. This desire prompted his retreat into the forest, where he received personal divine insight and confirmation (see

Enos 1:1–9). As a young boy, the Prophet Joseph had been schooled by his parents concerning the Christian way. From his reading of the Bible, he felt impressed to personalize his search and go directly to God in humble prayer (see James 1:5; Joseph Smith—History 1:10–15). Adam performed his acts of obedience by offering sacrifice without knowledge of its purpose. An angel of the Lord appeared to Adam and Eve and provided this important instruction (Moses 5:5–12).

The importance of declaring true and correct principles that will bless the inhabitants of this earth is foundational to the motives of Latter-day Saint missionaries. "And how shall they preach, except they be sent? as it is written, How beautiful are the feet of them that preach the gospel of peace, and bring glad tidings of good things!" (Romans 10:15).

Mormonism places great emphasis upon the pursuit of education, religious and secular. A fundamental scripture often quoted is found in Doctrine and Covenants 93:36: "The glory of God is intelligence." A history of our emphasis upon establishing educational experiences, both formal and informal, parallels the history of our Church. Joseph Smith's first vision was actually a teaching moment. His initial annual interviews with the angel Moroni were for the purpose of receiving instruction and training (Joseph Smith—History 1:53–54). It was important that early church leaders were given proper instruction and training, which took place in a setting termed the "school of the prophets" (D&C 88:127–141; 90:7, 13; 95:10; 97:3). A university charter was secured during the Nauvoo era. Schools and academies were organized throughout the territory of Deseret and in Mormon colonies. Special educational investment was made in central America and in the south Pacific to help educate LDS Latin and Polynesian children. The Church currently maintains three collegiate institutions: BYU-Provo, BYU-Idaho, and BYU-Hawaii. The emphasis of BYU's continuing education program is captured on a stone monument located at the entrance of BYU-Provo: "The world is our campus." Campus Education Week, begun in 1922, is a program unique to adult continuing education in the United States. It is believed to be the largest continuing education program of its type.[3] Mormons take very seriously the following command:

> And I give unto you a commandment that you shall teach one another the doctrine of the kingdom.
>
> Teach ye diligently and my grace shall attend you, that you may be instructed more perfectly in theory, in principle, in doctrine, in the

> law of the gospel, in all things that pertain unto the kingdom of God, that are expedient for you to understand.
>
> Of things both in heaven and in the earth, and under the earth; things which have been, things which are, things which must shortly come to pass; things which are at home, things which are abroad; the wars and the perplexities of the nations, and the judgments which are on the land; and a knowledge also of countries and of kingdoms" (D&C 88:77–79).

Do: The know-do-feel process may seem similar to the three pillars of testimony previously discussed. In this current context, however, we are interested in how these principles are converted into Christlike behavior. The "Do" domain is the action domain. The symbol for this domain is the hand. The Savior said, "No man, having put his hand to the plough, and looking back, is fit for the kingdom of God" (Luke 9:62). The implication of this passage is the importance of staying on a steady course of correct and productive actions. It is one thing to know, but certainly it is another thing to do, and we usually know more than we do. There is a powerful access to understanding from personal experience that far surpasses a simple cognitive understanding. My grandmother, Eliza Zollinger, proudly held that she was a graduate from the university of hard knocks. My personal motto in life stems from my participation in the Future Farmers of America (FFA) program at the Bear River High School. Our motto in FFA stated:

> Learning to Do, Doing to Learn
> Learning to Live, Living to Serve

The first line stresses the importance of the "Do." As cited earlier, the Savior promised, "If any man will do his will, he shall know of the doctrine" (John 7:17). In his New Testament epistle, James, the Lord's brother, stressed the importance of works as well as faith. The apostle Paul is known for his emphasis on the importance of faith. These two are not contradictory to each other, but each wrote to very different audiences. Paul wrote to a Jewish audience who had been steeped in the importance of living the law of Moses. Salvation, as determined by Jewish doctrine, was obtained through their obedience to Mosaic laws and regulations as they interpreted them. Therefore, they were "saved" according to their works. Paul desired to convert them to Christ, who was the original author of the Mosaic law. This law had been given initially as a preparatory law to bring them to Christ. Symbols of Christ's life and his sacrifice were replete* throughout the ceremonies and festivals within Mosaic law. Paul warned them against their "dead works" and counseled them to exercise their faith in Christ, who was the whole object of the law. He taught that it was "by grace [that] ye are saved through faith; and that not of yourselves: . . . Not of works, lest any man should boast" (Ephesians 2:8).

James, on the other hand, wrote to individuals who had already made baptismal covenants and were now members of the Church. James felt that in addition to faith, it was needful to put forth works of righteousness, for "faith without works is dead," and to be "doers of the word, and not hearers only" (James 2:26; 1:22).

When the world audience investigates model Mormon actions, whether those that are sponsored through the Church's institutional programs, those coming from personal service orientation, or those found within the common day-to-day experience, we are often described as being "different," "unique," and "exemplary." This, we feel, is a by-product of incorporating the doctrines of the Restoration into our daily lives, and it fulfills the prophetic description given of the Lord's people: "But ye [are] a chosen generation, a royal priesthood, an holy nation, a peculiar people; that ye should shew forth the praises of him who hath called you out of darkness into his marvellous light" (1 Peter 2:9. see also Deuteronomy 14:2). On the other hand, we must acknowledge our imperfection. There are too many scenarios that illustrate the fact that some Latter-day Saints are in need of correction and repentance. Our prophets continue to admonish us to "do a little better" and eventually "to be as the salt of the earth," and "to be the light of this people (3 Nephi 12:13–14.) When we can collectively fulfill this command, we can truly be the "city that is set on a hill [that] cannot be hid."

Feel: The "feel" domain is the affective domain. The symbol for this domain is the heart. The heart has long been used in literature as the symbol for the seat of feelings and emotions. Emotions are often blamed or credited as the primary motivation behind behavior, some of which is irrational or illogical. In our know-do-feel trilogy, the importance of the affective domain, however, is when the spirit of the Holy Ghost testifies of truth. This type of witness is "sure" and "steadfast." It penetrates to the very core of our being.

This witness of the Spirit interacts within the other two domains to testify when one hears of truth and further confirms when one participates in the application of true principles. Through this know-do-feel process, our values are formed. Utilizing this process even from a worldly paradigm still produces core values. Individuals are exposed to and process ideas within their environment. They practice or implement those ideas into their lives. As they gain cognitive recognition and practical experience, their emotions filter through this stimuli and assign an affective investment or a detachment. Thus core values are established. Values are determined personally and then shared within a culture or society. Elder L. Tom Perry spoke of the importance of shared cultural values:

> Every healthy society needs a common core of values based on the divine law of the Lord. This core of values should be a fundamental upon which all laws governing human conduct are based. Societies which have governed themselves on this fundamental set of values have found peace, prosperity, joy, beauty, morality and fulfillment. Societies which have thought themselves beyond these basic principles have literally destroyed themselves.[4]

Assumptions and Perceptions

Our personal core values mold our life's assumptions and develop our unique perceptions. An assumption is that which is taken for granted. Perception is the process of becoming aware by means of the senses or intuition. If our assumptions are based on incorrect values or principles, then the way we perceive reality is skewed through that lens. The behavior that emanates from those incorrect assumptions is often unproductive or counterproductive, if not in error. Eden Ryl developed a training video entitled, "You Pack Your Own Chute." She stressed the importance of establishing correct assumptions in life. Of this importance, she said: "Behavior comes about because of assumptions. When you bring about a change in assumptions, you bring about a change in behavior. Your assumptions, your premises are what you believe to be true when you behave as you do. If you make faulty assumptions, you handicap yourself —you make mistakes. You won't reach your goals."[5]

Let me present an example of how incorrect assumptions can negatively affect a simple problem-solving exercise. Imagine I am in front of a white board. You are one of my students. I write on the white board the following Roman numerals: IX. I than ask anyone in the class to come and use the marking pen to add just one line to this number and change its value to 6. When I perform this exercise in my classes, I rarely find anyone who solves the puzzle—unless they have either been made aware of the answer beforehand or they have changed their frame of reference by changing their assumptions. The number IX seems to orient the observer to a Roman numeral mode of numbers. Obviously, it is not possible to add one line to change its value to 6. But by changing our assumption of Roman numerals to Roman letters, we can easily add a line (and I didn't say a straight line) that forms the letter S. Putting an S in front of the letters IX produces a word that equates to the value of 6.

This observation by Alberta Siegel, a professor of psychology and an expert in child development at Stanford University, is worth remembering: "Every civilization is only twenty years away from barbarism. For twenty years is all we have to accomplish the task of civilizing the infants . . . who know nothing of our language, our culture, our religion, our values, or our customs of interpersonal relations."[6]

Our society can become quickly polarized when the next generation moves away from time-tested traditional values as they become educated from sources who have rejected these assumptions and core values. Elder Neal A. Maxwell warns of this social dilemma:

> If one thinks about it at all, it becomes quickly and abundantly clear that the differing assumptions about the nature of man, the purpose of life, and the nature of God will produce polarization.
>
> True, much of society once shared approximately the same assumptions about God and life with resulting traditional values. True, also, that many who are not outspoken still cling to those traditional assumptions. But alas, departures from traditional values concerning the role of the family—what is and what is not sin, one's duties to God and to his fellowmen—lead to a growing divergence. Regrettable as this is, it is.
>
> Those who are intent on building the secular City of Man will be increasingly impatient with those who build the City of God! Brotherhood pursued in such circumstances is a real test of our love as well as of our capacity to articulate. But so it is.[7]

Whether dealing with husband-wife relationships, parent-child relationships, social, business, national, or international relationships, it is imperative to understand the assumptions and frames of reference of those with whom we are seeking cooperative relations, compatibility, and peace. This understanding leads to solutions requiring selfless service, compromise, or sacrifice in order to establish trust and deepened relations.

From a psychological perspective, our assumptions and how we perceive ourselves and others we interact with is influenced by acquired genetics and chemical and hormonal influences in the brain. Because of these inherent influences, some people see the bucket as half empty and have a natural disposition to a degree of pessimism. These same factors can produce the opposite: a natural tendency toward optimism or viewing the bucket as half full. All of this works together to create our attitudes, which is the next phase in understanding why people behave the way they do.

Attitude

A very successful NBA basketball coach was asked which he valued most in his player athletes—skill or attitude. Quickly came his reply: "Attitude!" Many an inspiring story of rags to riches success or of the indefatigable* athlete with modest skill becomes the script for successful Hollywood movies. Remember the proverb, "as he thinketh in his heart, so is he" (Proverbs 23:7).

Charles Swindoll, an evangelical Christian pastor, educator, and radio preacher made famous this statement:

> The longer I live the more I realize the impact of attitude on life. Attitude, to me, is more important than facts. It is more important than the past, than education, than money, than circumstances, than failures, than successes, than what other people think or say or do. It is more important than appearance, giftedness or skill. . . . The remarkable thing is that we have a choice everyday regarding the attitude we will embrace for that day. We cannot change the past. We cannot change the fact that people will act in a certain way. The only thing we can do is play on the one string we have, and that is our attitude. I am convinced that life is ten percent what happens to me and ninety percent how I react to it. And so it is with you. We are in charge of our attitudes.[8]

The significant influence of attitude toward success or failure is well documented in the plethora of quotable quotes found on the internet. The following represents a small sampling:

- Attitude is a little thing that makes a big difference. –Sir

Winston Churchill

- The only disability in life is a bad attitude. –Olympic skater Scott Hamilton
- Could we change our attitude, we should not only see life differently, but life itself would come to be different. –Katherine Mansfield
- Excellence is not a skill. It is an attitude. –Ralph Marston
- The greatest discovery of my generation is that a human being can alter his life by altering his attitudes. –William James

Our attitude is the last link in the process of producing behavior. Productive or unproductive behavior, good or bad behavior, Christlike or self-centered behavior—all are the result of acquired attitudes. Our attitude is formed from how we perceive our environment and our base of assumptions. These assumptions rise up out of our core value system, which is a result of our cognitive, affective, and practical life experiences.

Implementing "The Lord's Method of Behavioral Modification"

Let's see how this model can be implemented in an international setting. One of the current fears for international peace comes from religious conflict. Parties within the Islamic nation of Iraq are at war with one other. The United States has led the Western world to become an integral player in this conflict. There are many interests at play that fuel this international tension. The economic, political, and religious baggage of each of the players weigh down the ability to see much hope for peaceful resolution. There seems to be an unending supply of people who operate from a "natural man" perspective and a set of assumptions seeking power, wealth, and control. Can military power bring peace to the Middle East? No! Military power has only been useful in historic conflicts to depose despots and attempt to restore a condition of natural rights and freedom. The Book of Mormon is replete with examples of differing paradigms for those who instigate and those who participate in war. Despots and tyrants use war to satisfy selfish interests. Citizens with honor and integrity participate in war to secure and enhance personal and national freedoms and inalienable rights and to defend the safety of citizenry.

The Book of Mormon provides a successful paradigm where a previously warlike people were changed into peace-seeking and covenant-making citizens. Alma taught: "And now, as the preaching of the word had a great tendency to lead the people to do that which was just—yea, it had had more powerful effect upon the minds of the people than the sword, or anything else, which had happened unto them—therefore Alma thought it was expedient that they should try the virtue of the word of God" (Alma 31:5).

Through the ministry of Alma the Younger and the four sons of Mosiah, thousands of Lamanites turned from their former false traditions, assumptions, and value systems to become a peace-loving and a righteous people—many covenanting to never take up the sword again.

The only complete resolution to establish peace in the Middle East or peace on earth is to integrate the Prince of Peace into world politics and economy. Our missionary force of ambassadors for Jesus Christ are equipped with the power of the "word." Within the "word" are the true principles and doctrines needed to change the mind-set of individuals and nations. As these principles become accepted and lived, the Spirit of the Holy Ghost can change hearts and turn tendencies away from "natural man" instincts. People will change how they view each other, their assumption base, and their perceptions. Brotherly and sisterly love replaces greed, avarice, and vice. Gender roles and status are clarified to achieve equality and enhance gender uniqueness. Freedom becomes more valuable than control or repression. An attitude of cooperation and peaceful exchange are driving economic motivators. Personal desires are cradled within the needs of others in family, community, national, and international settings.

What has just been described is called a Zion society. A pessimist may doubt that such a society could exist. In fact, this society has been accomplished. Reference is made within scripture to the Zion society of Enoch and his people. The Saints of the early Christian Church held "all things in common" in order to take care of the needs of the poor, the widows, and fatherless. The Nephite society that developed after Christ's visit to the American continent following his Resurrection achieved a level of righteousness where there was "no contention in the land, because of the love of God which did dwell in the hearts of the people. And there were no envyings, nor strifes, nor tumults, nor whoredoms, nor lyings, nor murders, nor any manner of lasciviousness; and surely there could not be a happier people among all the people who had been created by the hand of God" (4 Nephi 1:15–16).

These Nephites lost their political labels of distinction where there were no "manner of–ites, but they were in one, the children of Christ, and heirs to the kingdom of God" (4 Nephi 1:17). The irony of such a society is that their economic position prospered more so during that period than at any other time. The greatest potential for economic prosperity comes when the resources of the community or nation are shared for common benefit and not to enhance the wealth of individuals. Though the capitalistic system has been extremely successful to produce a very high standard of living for many, it would pale in comparison to the society that completely incorporated the principles of the United Order into its economic and social system.

The Sermon on the Mount is a wonderful teaching model of how this process works to bring about such Christlike behavior and a Zion-like society. This sermon was delivered by Christ to an assembled group of disciples and interested citizens on a lovely hill overlooking the beautiful Sea of Galilee. It was repeated to those Nephites who had survived the devastating destruction that occurred in America preceding the Savior's visit after his Resurrection. The citizens who heard these teachings in the Old World failed to experience Zion. The Nephites who incorporated these principles into their personal as well as public lives enjoyed a Zion-like society for a time. The choice is a personal as well as a community decision.

The Sermon on the Mount is a teaching paradigm for world peace. This, the greatest of all sermons, describes the process a person goes through to "come unto Christ and be perfected in him" (Moroni 10:32). As followers of Christ understand and live the doctrines of Christ, they will not seek for social or political control, but will seek for control over all aspects of their lives that lead them to perfection. Through the grace and atonement of Christ, we can achieve full perfection as commanded by our Savior (Matthew 5:48; 3 Nephi 12:48).

Christ began his sermon by identifying a set of progressive conditions that brings a person from out of the "world" into a covenant relationship. This relationship enables that individual to develop and achieve a Zion-like attitude. These conditions have historically been called the Beatitudes (Latin, beatus: to be happy, blessed). With the help of the Latin word beatus, we can rephrase each Beatitude to indicate "Oh how happy are . . ." Italics represent significant additions found within the 3 Nephi account.

Blessed (oh how happy) are the poor in spirit *who come unto me.*	Without the influence of the Holy Ghost in our lives, we live in a fallen and a miserable state. The poor in spirit suffer from the enticements of the natural man. The natural man is not a happy man but he experiences superficial joy. The key to this disparaging situation and our only complete resolution is to "come unto Christ."
Blessed are they that mourn.	As we come to recognize our natural man state of being, we lament this miserable condition and seek for something better.
Blessed are the meek.	Recognizing our needs for betterment, we open our hearts and our minds to become receptive to a better solution. As we hear the gospel message, our spirit senses this truth that is found within the "word of God." We recognize a need to submit our will to Christ to gain his uplifting influence, his grace.
Blessed are all they who do hunger and thirst after righteousness, for they shall be filled *with the Holy Ghost.*	As we learn of the gospel of Christ and the plan of happiness, we discover answers that had been missing to the critical questions of life. We begin to change our base of assumptions and perceptions of how we view ourselves. Instead of products of evolution in which only the strong survive, we come to know ourselves as children of Divine Parents who have a vested interest in helping us achieve our divine potential. Our thirst for gospel knowledge becomes almost insatiable. We feel a desire to come into the fold and receive the gift of the Holy Ghost.

Blessed are the merciful.	Through baptism and the ordinance of confirmation, we are now covenant members of the kingdom of God on earth. We are grateful for God's mercy in forgiving us of our sinful past and feel inclined to express that mercy to others. We tend to forgive rather than hold resentment.
Blessed are the pure in heart.	As we deepen the values of edification in our lives, our disposition to do evil changes to a guileless state—a state in which we can be offended by no one. Our hearts become pure and we void ourselves of pride.
Blessed are all the peacemakers.	We are confident in our own divine self-esteem and seek to respond with appropriate and non-defensive action instead of defensive retaliatory reaction. With a pure heart, we are not reactionary but act to establish peace and harmony.
Blessed are all they who are (reviled) and persecuted for my name's sake . . . for ye shall have great joy (rejoice) and be exceedingly glad . . . for so persecuted they the prophets who were before you.	An incorrect base of assumptions and poor self-esteem among people of the world prompt them to persecute, mock, and tear down true Christian people to their level. To be persecuted has always been the lot of God's covenant people.

As we come unto Christ, we are given a charge to be a light and an example unto the world. We are also charged to be as salt—or to enhance the appeal of the gospel message and to preserve Abraham's covenant that all the earth will be blessed through his seed.

The rest of the Sermon on the Mount represents conceptually what Christ lived personally—a man of complete control, commitment, and eternal perspective. Thus, his charge to all of us: "Therefore, what manner of men ought ye to be? Verily I say unto you, even as I am" (3 Nephi 27:27). He also issued the ultimate personal challenge: Therefore I would that ye should be perfect even as I, or your Father who is in heaven is perfect" (3 Nephi 12:48).

Areas of life that Christ requires us to control include our emotions, thoughts, actions, language and judgments. We are also expected to develop a willingness to forgive, to serve, to love (even our enemies), and to share our possessions without a desire for public recognition. As a disciple of Christ, our prayers and devotions to God become genuine and sincere, without hypocrisy. In this state, we become candidates to receive personal revelation and guidance. Thus, persons of Christ will, by their actions, bear the image of Christ in their countenances.

Christlike Qualities	References	As Cited in the Sermon on the Mount
Control Emotions	Matthew 5:21–26; 3 Nephi 12:21–26	Don't kill or even be angry without a cause (righteous indignation). Diffuse tension by agreeing with thine enemy; attempt reconciliation.
Control Thoughts	Matthew 5:27–28; 3 Nephi 12:27–28	Don't commit adultery or look with lustful eyes.
Control Actions	Matthew 5:13–14; 3 Nephi 12:13–13 Matthew 5:29–30 Matthew 7:12; 3 Nephi 14:13 Matthew 7:21–23; 3 Nephi 13:21–23 Matthew 7:20; 3 Nephi 14:20	Be a light (example); be as salt to enhance the gospel's message by example and act to preserve the blessings of Abraham's covenant within the covenant people. Right eye/hand offend: eliminate small sins immediately before they grow to enslave the whole body. Live the Golden Rule.

Christlike Qualities	References	As Cited in the Sermon on the Mount
Control Language	Matthew 5:33–37; 3 Nephi 12:33–37	Righteous actions speak truer than professed belief. Avoid hypocrisy. We are judged by our fruits (actions). Perform thy oaths: Keep your word.
Control Premature Judgment	JST Matthew 7:1–5; 3 Nephi 14:1–5	Judge righteous judgments.
Forgive Willingly	Matthew 5:38–39; 3 Nephi 12:38–39	Take a little slack, forgive willingly.
Serve Willingly	Matthew 5:41; 3 Nephi 12:41	Go the extra mile.
Love Willingly	Matthew 5:43–44; 3 Nephi 12:43–44	Use love to turn an enemy into a friend.
Share Willingly	Matthew 5:40, 42; 3 Nephi 12:40, 42	Share possessions. Perform godly acts of service (alms) in secret.
Attend to Prayer & Inspiration	Matthew 6:1–4; 3 Nephi 13:1–4 Matthew 6:5–13; 3 Nephi 13:5–13	Prayers should be humble, sincere and full of gratitude; not sanctimonious. Seek personal revelation and direction. Fast without ceremonial attention.
Attend to Devotions	Matthew 7:7–8; 3 Nephi 14:7–8 Matthew 6:16; 3 Nephi 13:16	Serve one master, keep your eye single to God.

Christlike Qualities	References	As Cited in the Sermon on the Mount
Maintain Priorities	Matthew 6:19–24; 3 Nephi 13:19–24	Seek first the kingdom of God.
	Matthew 6:33; 3 Nephi 13:33	

We live in a complex world. Personal behavior is more public than ever before. Our lives are not confined to one spot of geography. We have access to an almost unlimited knowledge base. Our individual actions and behavior can affect community, national, and international relations now more than any other time in human history. What behaviors will make a difference and contribute to a better world? President Ezra Taft Benson commented on this dynamic and historic world condition. He said:

> Each day the forces of evil and the forces of good enlist new recruits. Each day we personally make many decisions showing the cause we support. The final outcome is certain—the forces of righteousness will win. But what remains to be seen is where each of us personally, now and in the future, will stand in this battle—and how tall we will stand.
>
> Great battles can make great heroes and heroines. We will never have a better opportunity to be valiant in a more crucial cause than in the battle we face today and in the immediate future. Some of the greatest battles we will face will be fought within the silent chambers of our own souls.[9]

1. Boyd K. Packer, "Little Children," *Ensign*, Nov. 1986, 17.
2. Ezra Taft Benson, "Born of God," *Ensign*, Jul. 1989, 2.
3. A history of the LDS Church's investment in weekday religious instruction for high school and college-age youth can be found in *A Miracle of Weekday Religious Education*, by William E. Berrett.
4. L. Tom Perry, "As a Man Soweth," *Ensign,* May, 1976, 63.
5. Ryl, "You Pack Your Own Chute," video exerpt.
6. Siegel, *Violence and the Media*, 279.
7. Maxwell, *We Will Prove Them Herewith*, 96.
8. http://thinkexist.com/quotes/charles_r._swindoll/
9. Ezra Taft Benson, *In His Steps*, Ensign, Sept. 1988, 2.

CHAPTER FIVE

What is Religion?

Pure religion and undefiled before God and the Father is this, To visit the fatherless and widows in their affliction, [and] to keep himself unspotted from the world. – James 1:27

I have dedicated a great effort in my life to studying the tenets of the LDS Church. Possessing an investigative mind, I have also felt it necessary to examine the tenets of major alternatives in Christianity, as well as other religious beliefs, philosophic thought, and empirical positioning (for example, atheism, agnosticism and humanism). What else is out there? Is there another paradigm that offers more: intellectually, spiritually, socially, physically? Can I find reasonable doubt for every other paradigm? Will my search challenge or actually vindicate the convictions gained from my isolated study and experience within Mormonism?

Critical analysis of religion must necessarily examine the very heart or prime element of religion: the existence of God. But before addressing the question of God's existence, a definition of the essence of religion is germane to this analysis. Religious literature is replete with suggestions:

> Religion is a mental faculty or disposition, which independent of, nay in spite of, sense and reason, enables man to apprehend the Infinite under different names and under varying guises. —Max Muller[1]

> Religion is the recognition of all duties as divine commands. —Immanuel Kant[2]

> Religion is morality touched by emotion. —Matthew Arnold[3]

> The essence of religion is the feeling of absolute dependence. —Schleiermacher[4]

> Religion rests, above all, upon the need of man to realize a harmonious synthesis between his own destiny and the opposing influences he meets in the world. —Albert Reville[5]

> Religion is the consciousness of the highest social values. —Edward Scribner Ames[6]

> Religion, therefore, as I now ask you arbitrarily to take it, shall mean for us the feelings, acts and experiences of individual men in their solitude, so far as they apprehend themselves to stand in relation to whatever they may consider the divine. —William James[7]

> Religion is the appreciation of an unseen world . . . , and religion is also whatever seems clearly to be moving toward such an appreciation, or to be returning from it. —G. W. Stratton[8]

> By religion is meant the life of man in his superhuman relations; that is, his relation to the power on which he feels himself dependent, the authority to which he deems himself responsible, and the unseen being with whom he is capable of communing. In the ideal of religion, dependence, responsibility and communion belong together. —Williams Adam Brown[9]

> Religion is the chief differentiating characteristic of man. In the history of mankind there never has been a tribe of men without some form of religion. Religion has been one of the most powerful factors in human history. Religion gives to a person what he can obtain from no other source—a confidence in the outcome of life's struggles through a personal connection with the superior Power or powers in the world. —Rome E. Hume[10]

These statements come from philosophers, psychologists, and social scientists. They all contain some element included in the definition of religion provided by Webster:

> Religion: 1. a) a belief in a divine or superhuman power or powers to be obeyed and worshiped as the creator(s) ruler(s) of the universe b) expression of such a belief in conduct and ritual; 2. a) any specific system of belief, worship, conduct, etc., often involving a code of ethics and a philosophy b) any system of beliefs, practices, ethical values, etc. resembling, suggestive of, or in state likened to such a system; 3. the community; 4. any object of conscientious regard and pursuit.[11]

Religion addresses man's inner striving toward a superhuman power. Religion defines moral behavior and social values. Religion defines appropriate dependence and personal responsibility and helps to reconcile oneself against the opposing forces in the world. Religion addresses the existence of our pre- and post-mortality. Finally, religion forges emotional confidence to sustain us through the trials and tribulations that pave our path through mortality.

Elder John A. Widtsoe said that "religion, under its wide definition, is the philosophy of life, by which we regulate our conduct.[12] James, one of Jesus' siblings and an officer in the Jerusalem Church supported this element of religion by stating that "pure religion and undefiled before God and the Father is this, To visit the fatherless and widows in their affliction, and to keep himself unspotted from the world" (James 1:27).

The prophet Joseph Smith stated that the Book of Mormon was the keystone of the Mormon religion. Hume suggested that "the sacred scriptures furnish the only uniform basis for reporting the various religions. In every one of the eleven living religions of the world the supreme seat of authority is located in, or connected with, their respective sacred scriptures.[13] In Mormonism, the seat of revelatory authority resides in the Word of ancient as well as modern-day prophets, seers, and revelators.

Hume also states that "religion is the chief differentiating characteristic of man?"[14] Is religion uniquely human? Not to be farcical,* but do animals have religion? A serious analysis of this question requires an understanding as to the characteristics of mankind that identify him as a unique creation from animals. First, mankind (a generic term including both the male and female gender) possesses self-awareness that transcends time. We are aware that we are aware of ourselves. We ponder our existence from the perspective of the three domains of time and within the realm of the space-time continuum. Second, mankind not only shares agency (volition of choice) with others in the animal kingdom, but has been endowed with the burden-blessing of moral agency, the principle of accountability exercised through the parameters of rightness and wrongness. The agency exercised within the animal world is based primarily upon the laws of survival and procreation. No moral consequence is pondered. Mankind bases its choices not only upon survival but also upon the scales of moral virtue. Our self-awareness and our moral agency truly separate us from all other life forms and characterize our human uniqueness. Has evolution evolved such a being? or is this condition a result of a power greater than nature and stellar accidents? William Wordsworth penned this poetic answer entitled, "Ode: Intimations of Immortality."

> Our birth is but a sleep and a forgetting:
> The soul that rises with us, our life's star,
> Hath had elsewhere its setting, and cometh from afar:
> Not in entire forgetfulness, and not in utter nakedness,
> But trailing clouds of glory do we come from God, who is our home:
> Heaven lies about us in our infancy!
> Shades of the prison-house begin to close upon the growing boy,
> But he beholds the light, and whence it flows, he sees it in his joy;
> The youth, who daily farther from the east must travel,
> Still is Nature's Priest,
> And by the vision splendid is on his way attended;
> At length the man perceives it die away,
> And fade into the light of common day.

Three references located in LDS scripture attest to the divine origins and unique creation of men and women with these simple statements: "Let us make man in our image, after our likeness . . . male and female created he them" (Genesis 1:26–27; Moses 2:27; Abraham 4:27). The origins of humanity come not from swamp pools or extra-terrestrial gene pools, but from God and our heavenly home. This imprint of the divine translates into man's need for religion.

1. Muller, *Introduction to the Science of Religion*, 13.
2. Kant, *Literature and Dogma*, 46.
3. Ibid.
4. Hume, *The World's Living Religions,* 7.
5. Ibid.
6. Ames, *Psychology of Religious Experience,* vii.
7. James, *Variety of Religious Experience*, 31.
8. Stratton, *Psychology of Religious Life*, 343.
9. Brown, *Christian Theology in Outline*, 29.
10. Hume, *The World's Living Religions* 3–4.
11. Webster's, 9th Ed. s.v. "Religion."
12. Widtsoe, *Evidences and Reconciliations*, 303.
13. Hume, *The World's Living Religions,* 11.
14. Ibid., 3.

CHAPTER SIX

The Existence and Character of God

A man can no more diminish God's glory by refusing to worship Him than a lunatic can put out the sun by scribbling the word, 'darkness' on the walls of his cell. – C.S. Lewis, *The Problem of Pain*

I cannot imagine how the clockwork of the universe can exist without a clockmaker. – Voltaire

God exists whether or not men may choose to believe in Him. The reason why many people do not believe in God is not so much that it is intellectually impossible to believe in God, but because belief in God forces that thoughtful person to face the fact that he is accountable to such a God. – Robert A. Laidlaw

The Idea of God's Existence

Joseph Smith taught that in order to develop perfect faith in God, one must start with the assumption or the "idea" of God's real existence. Let us now examine this idea. If there is no supreme power having a vested interest in man, then religion is a unique product of the human mind. We might be best served to just give reverential respect to our position within natural and cosmic forces. Without God, there cannot exist a "true" religion. All truth would be based upon situational relevancy. Therefore, moral accountability would also be based around situational ethics. The legal premise forming the foundation of a moral society would emanate from those laws or rules of conduct accepted by society as historically binding as well as those coerced upon society by dogmatic despots. But if there is a God who is responsible for the human condition and has a vested interest in us, then there must be some historical evidence and design of that fact and a modality in which God reveals himself.

Theistic Paradigms of God

Obviously, attempts to describe or characterize the entity of God or his existence have varied significantly down through the history of mankind. The following is a simple listing of historical theistic paradigms of God.

- **Pantheism.** This is the view that everything is of an all-encompassing immanent God, or that the universe, or nature, and God are equivalent.
- **Deism.** A belief in the existence of a God on purely rational grounds without reliance on revelation or authority. Deism of the seventeenth and eighteenth centuries suggested that God created the world and its natural laws, but takes no further part in its function and intervention.
- **Pandeism.** This is a kind of pantheism that incorporates a form of deism, holding that the universe is identical to God but also that God was previously a conscious and sentient force or entity that designed and created the universe.
- **Polytheism.** A belief in or worship of many gods, or more than one god.
- **Henotheism.** A term coined by Max Müller to mean devotion to a single "God" while accepting the existence of other gods. Simply monotheism in principle and polytheism in fact.
- **Dualism.** Within Zoroastrianism, as an example, there are two opposing forces: the force of good or light is Ahura Mazdā; the force of evil or darkness is Ahriman.
- **Monotheism.** A belief in one supreme entity who created all things (Judaism: Lord God Jehovah; Jehovah's Witnesses: Jehovah God; Christian Science: Father/Mother Entity; Islam: Allah; Bahá'í: One supernatural being).
- **Trinitarianism.** A unity of three supernal manifestations (Father,

Word, and Holy Spirit) into one metaphysical essence.

- **Arianism.** God is the only self-existing entity. Christ (Word) was created by God before time but is not of the same substance as the Father. Christ is exalted above all other creations of the Father.
- **Unitarianism.** God exists in only one person. The divinity of Jesus Christ is rejected but his teachings as found in the Gospels represent the highest moral standard. Each person is born with a spark of divinity and must seek for that inner light through which God reveals himself individually to each person. Unitarians are liberal, rational, tolerant, and by conservative Christian definition outside of the Christian religion.

In addition to these theistic definitions, the terms "atheist" or "agnostic" commonly convey a rejection of the existence of God or a belief that the human mind cannot know whether there is a god or an ultimate cause. Atheism, technically, does not mean a denial of the existence of God. It means literally a denial of the theistic definitions of God. That is to say, theism is not what God is but rather what human beings have decided that God is. Human definitions of God can die without God dying.

It is generally asserted that Hindu religious texts were the oldest known literature that contained the ideas of pantheistic doctrine. Judaism introduced a monotheistic supreme entity. The early Greeks and Romans were polytheistic with their menagerie of Olympian gods. After the Greek state failed to uphold its military might and suffered conquest from Macedonian and Roman power, their allegiance to the Greek Olympian gods declined. Rome, however, came to the rescue and all but absorbed the Greek gods into their pantheon while giving them new names. The writings of Socrates, Plato, and Aristotle indicate a shift away from mythological polytheism.

- Socrates: He rejected the ancient polytheistic faith in the Olympian gods. He felt there was no hope or real reward in the ancient religion. He believed in one God, and hoped in his modest way that death would not quite destroy him, but he knew that a lasting moral code could not be based upon so uncertain a theology. If one could build a system of morality absolutely independent of religious doctrine, as valid for the atheist as for the pietist, then theologies might come and go without loosening the moral cement that makes of wilful individuals the peaceful citizens of a community. "How can a society be saved, or be strong, except it be led by its wisest men?"[1]

- Plato: A nation cannot be strong unless it believes in God. "A mere cosmic force, or first cause, or *élan vital,* that was not a person, could hardly inspire hope, or devotion, or sacrifice; it could not offer comfort to the hearts of distress, nor courage to embattled souls. But a living God can do all this and can stir or frighten the self-seeking individualist into some moderation of his greed, some control of his passion. All the more so if to belief in God is added belief in personal immortality: The hope of another life gives us courage to meet our own death, and to bear the death of our loved ones. We are twice armed if we fight with faith."[2]
- Aristotle: "God is the prime mover, a being incorporeal, indivisible, spaceless, sexless, passionless, changeless, perfect and eternal. He is pure energy, not so much a person as a magnetic force. He is activity so pure that he never acts and his sole employment is the contemplation of himself and the essence of things."[3]

With the advent of Christianity and its theistic evolution, its monotheistic god was given a new twist: three entities within one essence. All the notable medieval philosophers developed arguments for the existence of God, but attempted to wrestle with the contradictions God's attributes seemed to imply. As Christian theologians retained philosophic credentials, they labored over the vexing problem of whether God's existence could be proven. One attempt to prove the existence of God is called the ontological argument for God's existence:

> The existence of the idea of God necessarily implies the very existence of God. Thus, by the notion of God we mean something so great that nothing greater can be conceived. Something so great must exist, because that which does not exist, but which in other respects is greater than anything else which can be conceived, can never be as great as something than which nothing greater can be conceived, exists. God, being that something, must consequently exist.[4]

Philosophically, the ontological argument may make sense but adds little to the "truth" of understanding God's character and person. A primal truth of religion addresses the very existence of God. Everything springs from this point of singularity. In the Lectures on Faith, prepared primarily by Joseph Smith to be taught to a school of elders in Kirtland, he stated that "faith could not center in a Being of whose existence we have no idea, because the idea of his existence in the first instance is essential to the exercise of faith in him."[5]

He goes on to clarify the following:

> Three things are necessary in order that any rational and intelligent being may exercise faith in God unto life and salvation. First, the idea that he actually exists. Secondly, a correct idea of his character, perfections, and attributes. Thirdly, an actual knowledge that the course of life which he is pursuing is according to his will. For without the acquaintance with these three important facts, the faith of every rational being must be imperfect and unproductive; but with this understanding it can become perfect and fruitful, abounding in righteousness, unto the praise and glory of God the Father, and the Lord Jesus Christ.[6]

The Trinity—Traditional Christian Definition of God

As we move from the first premise of the existence of God, the *summum bonum** assumption of all religion, the next requirement in our quest for faith is to gain a true understanding of God's origin, nature, characteristics, and purpose. A firm mooring as to the legitimacy of any religious belief lies within the scope of this answer. The beliefs of Catholics and Protestants can only be understood within the context of how they view their origins and their relationship to the divine. The same can be said of religions originating in south Asia, east Asia, and southwest Asia. For example, most Christians of Catholic or Protestant orientation describe God as an uncreated, eternal, all-powerful and everywhere present entity. Though the adjectives used to provide word labels for this essence have generic associations, the Christian god is void of specific form and gender orientation, having no body or parts and no human passions. This essence has always existed, is infinite, and is all-knowing of itself in its state of perfection. The essence of its being is "absolute," meaning it is unconditional and unrelated to anything outside itself. To use philosophic nomenclature:

> An 'absolute' being would be unconditioned in the sense that whatever qualities were possessed by him would be possessed unconditionally, there being no conditions, for instance, upon his goodness, his creative power, his thought processes, or his will. Such an absolute being would necessarily be unrelated, because if he were genuinely related to anything outside himself, that object or event would in effect constitute a condition upon him.[7]

It is not my purpose to give a detailed clarification of the relationships of the three modalities of the Trinity. Even Catholic and Protestants agree to the mystery of the Trinity. Furthermore, the Vatican Council defined that the Christian faith contains mysteries strictly so called. Their theologians admit that "the doctrine of the Trinity is of the number of these. Indeed, of all revealed truths this is the most impenetrable to reason. Hence, to declare this to be no mystery would be a virtual denial of the canon in question."[8] St. Jerome says, in a well-known phrase: "The true profession of the mystery of the Trinity is to own that we do not comprehend it."[9]

One Catholic apologist did attempt to explain the relationship between the three who compose the Trinity: God is a supreme, infinite, and eternal essence that expends itself within a triune unity known as the Father, Son, and Holy Spirit. The Son modality of this Trinity is the infinite, eternal idea of himself and was incarnated* into the man Jesus of Nazareth. God, as an infinite, eternal entity has an infinite love of himself. Since his creations are finite, he can only express love to them perfectly. This infinite love of himself is actually the Holy Spirit which proceeds from the Father.[10] Though this apologist used generic terms of manliness, it should be recognized that the Trinitarian definition in no way incorporates any inclusion of human form, passion, gender, or sexual orientation.

Many historical interpretations have developed pertaining to the dual nature of Jesus—of his humanness, and of his divinity. The reconciliation of Christ's humanness with his divinity was the major agenda item for the first four ecumenical councils participated in by both eastern and western Christianity. A product of these councils produced the Niceno-Constantinopolitan Creed and the Symbol of Chalcedon. A later creed emerged, the origin of which is uncertain. It bears the name of St. Athanasius, but is not accredited to this bishop of Alexandria. A reading of the Athanasian Creed, using the simple tool of reason, adds legitimacy to my confusion concerning the God of traditional Christianity. For example, one line of the Athanasian Creed reads, "And in this trinity none is afore, or after other: none is the greater or less than another. But the whole three Persons are co-eternal together, and co-equal." How, then, is the statement made by Jesus as recorded in the gospel of John reconciled: "I go unto the Father: for the Father is greater than I" (John 14:28). Though they claim the Trinity is and will always remain a "mystery not comprehended by man," I prefer to follow the scriptural admonition found in John 17:3. "And this is life eternal, that they might know thee the only true God, and Jesus Christ, whom thou has sent." For me, scripture trumps tradition—but such is not so in Roman Catholicism. A copy of the Athanasian Creed is contained in Appendix B. A summary of other false interpretations of Christ is included as Appendix C.

We need to continue to clarify man's relationship to God from a traditional Christian perspective. At some point within its self-existence, the supreme essence desired to create entities outside itself. Traditional Christian dogma labels these entities as angels with rank. However, these angels are genderless, a fixed population who never have nor ever will become "mortal" (except in Jehovah's Witnesses tradition). They exist only to serve God and to give him praise and glory.[11] God having created these beings, he then created "the heavens and the earth." God is responsible for the existence of all stellar forces which were created *ex nihilo*,* or out of nothing. This divine fiat* produced the world where nothing had previously existed. As God is the creator of the universe, creating all reality except himself, where before there was nothing but himself, then the universe is totally subservient to him, and there is no object or event in it that is not fully under his dominion. He is the Prime Mover. He is the force before the Big Bang.

> Under this doctrine God creates the universe in accordance with laws and prescriptions which are of his own making. There is no law or principle beyond himself which he must respect or be subject to in his creative act. Independently of the world's coming into being by the divine fiat, only one thing can be said about existence, that 'God is.' Moreover, his creation of man and the world is not necessary; that is, in creating them he wills freely, for he could will to not create them.[12]

With earth now in existence, Christianity follows the biblical story of Adam and Eve. Each human being is actually a creation of God, also created *ex nihilo* whose soul is produced by the "breath of God" either at conception or at some point before the moment of birth. The ultimate purpose of the creation of mankind is to return to some heavenly environment in a blessed state and to sing praise and glory to this essence forever. Many denominations in Christianity actually reject a literal or physical heaven, substituting instead a state of mind or a spiritual state of being. The fate of individuals who reject allegiance to this Trinity results in conditions of either annihilation or eternal damnation and physical punishment forever. Traditional Christianity is truly an either or phenomenon. A past tradition with Roman Catholics allowed for a side scenario called limbo, a place for unbaptized or unsaved children. As of this writing, the Roman Church has now disengaged itself from this historical teaching. A more complete treatment of limbo is found in Chapter Eight.

This form of "absolutism" to define the existence of God produces a conundrum concerning the existence of evil. Since the universe (all reality) is totally a product of God's creation, all reality is therefore utterly contingent upon God and is under God's dominion and power. God, then, is the First Cause from which everything and everyone emanates. This First Cause exists in a state of perfect knowledge and virtue. The conundrum, then, is simply stated through two questions. First, what is the origin of evil if all things are a creation of God, who is wholly good? Second, if God is wholly good from which no evil can emanate, then what is the origin of Lucifer, who was one of the archangels of heaven and is considered wholly evil? The doctrine of free will is also hotly contested within traditional Christianity. There has been much theological effort expended to justify the absoluteness of God's power with his vindication of all responsibility for those elements in his creation that are not compatible with his absolute goodness. The Mormon resolution to these issues will be woven into the discussion of Mormon theology which follows. This Trinitarian doctrine seems not only puzzling but fails to support the principle of faith in such a being.

Eastern religions also have a creation story. Shrouded in myth and developed over time, these religions generally define God as the Prime Mover, a supreme essence, the Ultimate Reality. All life was created from eternal elements. Life forces either advance or degenerate around the wheel of life through reincarnation. The goal or grand achievement is to strip oneself of all independence to return to an ego-free peace in Brahman* or in nirvana.* Nirvana is the only permanent reality—a reality of nonexistence. In religions of the Orient, the purpose of life is to live harmoniously in a secular society or to live in harmony with the kami (native Japanese gods) in this life. There is no well-defined sense of life beyond death, for life is to be lived for the present moment.

Nature and Character of God—LDS

The restoration of truth about the nature of God through the Prophet Joseph Smith, as well as complete and correct details of a plan of happiness, presents a paradigm of life that to me has no parallel. It is magnanimous,* robust, complete, internally consistent, and forms a holistic harmony of self-actualization. This is a strong position I now wish to defend.

To understand the Mormon plan of happiness and salvation we turn once again to religion's core—the nature and character of God. The Mormon God is not an essence, "a mystery of which cannot be known." Truly, we believe that "this is life eternal, that they might know thee the only true God, and Jesus Christ, whom thou has sent" (John 17:3). Latter-day scripture adds clarity to biblical canon to reveal a Godhead that is knowable yet exalted and glorified. Once we have a correct understanding of God, this knowledge percolates throughout the plan and dramatically impacts the whole of Mormon theology. In analogous terminology, when a person's view of life is framed around a belief in a personal, loving God in whose image we are created, that person's 20/20 vision interprets evidence of God in all scenarios. This analogy can be read within this scientific observation:

> In order to explain the [chemical] reaction [of burning], it becomes necessary to invent molecules and atoms. These tiny denizens of the world of the very, very small can never be seen, not even with the highest power microscope. . . . During the past forty years, we have leaned to "look" inside the atom and discover its structure. This is not done, as has been pointed out, by the use of the microscope; but man has learned to see the invisible by interpreting the messages which come out of the interesting atomic structures.[13]

Though God does not necessarily appear in form in our everyday life, he has been seen, he has communicated to prophets, and he reveals himself to each person who has eyes to see and ears to hear. Let's begin our understanding of who God is with a scripture from the Doctrine and Covenants, which states that "the Father has a body of flesh and bones as tangible as man's; the son also; but the Holy Ghost has not a body of flesh and bones, but is a personage of spirit" (D&C 130:22).

That the Father and the Son have tangible bodies is a doctrine that Trinitarian Christians seem to agonize over the most. The ramification of this doctrine smacks in the face of most doctrines associated with Trinitarian Christianity, including the issue of salvation, the doctrine of pre-existence, the character and nature of God, and the familial relationship of Christ with human beings.

Elder M. Russell Ballard said of the plan: "It seems clear to me, as this great work continues to roll forth, that the leaders of the Church at every level . . . need to understand God's plan for his children and then teach these principles to their people . . . . In my judgment, the greatest motivator that we have in the Church is to have Church members understand the plan of salvation."[14]

The doctrines associated with this grand design, this plan of salvation, are linked to sources from biblical canon, modern-day scripture, and teachings of Latter-day prophets and apostles. I, however, will keep them to a minimum. Let me paint a word description of this very significant epoch. A graphic model of the LDS plan of salvation is found in Appendix D.

The Plan of Salvation

The State of Intelligence

"A long, long time ago in a galaxy far, far away. . ." This is the way the epic movie Star Wars begins. In reality, time is measured only by man. God dwells in a state where he can perfectly comprehend the past, present, and the future. But there was a time when our God was not God. The primal existence of all matter and being lies in a domain referred to as the realm of "intelligence." "Man was also in the beginning with God. Intelligence, or light of truth, was not created or made, neither indeed can be" (D&C 93:29). Though an essential doctrine, the Lord has not revealed to ancient or modern prophets the details of this state of existence. There continues among LDS scholars, ecclesiastical leaders, and Church members a varied discussion as to the degree to which agency and individuality exist in this state of being. The ramifications of these issues are interesting but outside the purview of this treatise.

Spirit Birth and Premortal Existence

Doctrines of the gospel are truths associated with the plan of salvation.

A basic doctrine of Mormonism is the doctrine of premortal existence. We were brought into this realm through the procreative powers of divine and exalted parents. We became children of this heavenly couple, thus forming a heavenly family. Abraham learned through the Urim and Thummim that there is an infinite variety of spirits within this heavenly family (see Abraham 3:19). Each individual is unique. Elder Neal A. Maxwell, master of symbolism, phrased it this way: "As snowflakes, though different, are of the same substance, so it is with man. We are the begotten spirit children of our Father in heaven with endless variety in the configurations of our personalities. But the thing that we have in common is that we are the spirit offspring of our Father in heaven."[15]

In A.D. 553, the Roman Emperor Justinian coerced Virgilius, the Bishop of Rome and head legate of western Christianity at the time, to reject the doctrine of premortal life and exorcize* that doctrine from Christian faith by an edict known as the "Anathemas against Origin." The pope consented only under extreme duress.[16] It is an interesting observation that among the eleven living world religions, Christianity alone fails to identify a pre-earthly existence for mankind. All other world religions incorporate some form of premortal existence into their dogma.

Plato, the second of the great triune philosophers, also recognized these seemingly divine origins. He states: "Let us declare the cause which led the Supreme Ordainer to produce and compose the universe. He was good, and he who is good has no kind of envy. Exempt from envy, he wished that all things should be as much as possible like himself. Whosoever, taught by the wise men, shall admit this as the prime cause of the origin and foundation of the world, will be in the truth."[17]

Note the similarity in the thought of the Greek philosopher and the thought of America's first prophet, Joseph Smith. Plato says that the Supreme Ordainer wished that all things should be as much as possible like himself and therefore He produced and composed the universe. Joseph declared that "God, in the beginning, surrounded with spirits and glory, saw proper to institute laws whereby the rest might have a privilege to advance like Himself."[18] Before the era of the great philosophers, this same knowledge of a pre-existence of man co-existing with God was held by the ancient Egyptians. In essence, this Egyptian belief held that "Pharaoh was conceived by his father when there was as yet no heaven, no earth, nor people, nor were there any dead. And every individual existed when the plan of the ancient Lord of heaven was not yet formulated."[19]

The eminent LDS scholar Hugh Nibley quotes a pharaoh from an ancient pyramid text: "I existed before I was born, when the gods did not exist, when as yet there was no bird trap, when the cattle were not yet lassoed. I was formerly; I was of yesterday, a great one among the great and noble ones.[20] In a related text called the coffin text, Nibley cites this statement: "Before I was born by hand or born of woman, he created me in the midst of his perfection, which caused jubilation to those who shared in the secrets."[21] "That's the creation hymn," Nibley said, "and it's often referred to in these Egyptian writings."

Divine parents who were omniscient, omnipotent, and possessed perfection of mind, body, and virtue were empowered to embody elements of the "intelligence" domain to create innocent spirit bodies of children possessing gender characteristics. Each spirit body resembled the form and likeness of its parents. This is an eternal law. Its ramification ripples throughout the natural world. Like begets like. Acorns inherit the genetic code to achieve, in maturity, the status of the oak tree from which they sprang.

The Lord revealed through Joseph Smith that "every spirit of man was innocent in the beginning" (D&C 93:38). This innocence refers to the initial phase of a child's spirit development when he is not fully accountable for the rightness and wrongness of decision making. But this initial phase of innocence gave way as the full ramifications of agency matured within this spirit realm. We were part of an extended spirit family. The eldest and firstborn of all of our Heavenly Parents' children was Jehovah, who was to become Jesus of Nazareth and Jesus Christ, a title of extreme significance. (See Appendix F for a discussion of the title "Jesus Christ.")

Jehovah, then, is our eldest brother. This realm of premortality was a progressive realm where we acquired knowledge and developed proclivities, talents, skills, virtues, and even vices. These traits passed through the veil at birth and provided a spiritual genetic endowment that helps influence the development of each person in this mortal domain. Therefore, within the realm of child development theories, Mormonism adds a third dimension to the nature versus nurture formula: our spirit genetic inheritance developed in and brought from our premortal environment.

The Eternal Law of Justice

Eventually in this world of spirits, there came a historic moment of family and personal crisis. This crisis required each individual to make an irrevocable decision. A family council was held and presided over by the grand patriarch of this family. In order for each spirit son and daughter of God to achieve their full potential of self-actualization, an earthly, mortal experience was a necessary second act of a three-act progressive drama. But there were laws governing this mortal experience. One of the great governing laws of heaven is called the Law of Justice. Our Heavenly Parents were, of themselves, a successful product of this great and eternal law, and they were also members of an extended "family of the gods." The Law of Justice, in actuality, guarded the perpetuity of this divine family. There could be no allowance for intelligences who, traveling the path toward Godhood, would gain omnipotent power without also acquiring perfect virtue and omniscient knowledge. A person of omnipotent power lacking integrity and virtue would introduce catastrophe into the great plan. A human analogy of this caricature is played out in the character called "Q" in the Star Trek franchise.

The term god, in Mormonism, refers not only to a person but also to a status or achievement. One of the conditions associated with this exalted state of being is experienced within the role of parent. Gods can and do perpetuate their species. Spirit children are not born *ex nihilo*. As mentioned earlier, this creative process follows eternal parameters. The actions of divine and heavenly parents must be consistent with not only maintaining their existence but also perpetuating their existence—they cannot act to bring about disorder or chaos. Elder Neal A. Maxwell comments on this state of being:

> The ultimate models for us are, of course, God the Father and Jesus Christ. Joseph Smith advises us in his Lectures on Faith that God has perfected each of the attributes that make him God. That is, he is perfect in knowledge, power or faith, justice, judgment, mercy, truth, and love. As the prophet describes his perfection in each of these attributes, we can readily see that if he were not perfect in each of them he could not be God. Perfect knowledge without perfect love would be a dangerous condition. To be absolute in power without perfect mercy would be insufferable, and to be perfect in love without being perfect in truth could give us unchecked sentimentality. Any leader on the proximate, mortal scale who does not seek to work on these same attributes, cannot be fully effective or fully safe in terms of the power he possesses to influence and to direct the lives of others.[22]

The Doctrine of Theosis

A central tenet of Mormonism is the doctrine of theosis* or of man's deification.* Joseph Smith taught of this truth to the early Church. Lorenzo Snow restated it in a famous couplet: "As man now is, God once was; as God now is, man may be."[23] This doctrine is vehemently rejected in western Christianity. A critical study of the writings of the Church leadership from the second through the fourth century supports the fact that this indeed was a doctrine taught and believed in by the early Church. In one of his letters, Athanasius, a fourth century defender of the faith, made his famous statement that the Son of God became man "that he might deify us in himself."[24] In his great work, *On the Incarnation*, he wrote similarly that Christ "was made man that we might be made God."[25] This is the doctrine of theosis, also known as deification, divinization, or, as some prefer, participation in God. Though almost unknown to western Catholicism's members as well as theologians, it is a central tenet in Eastern Orthodoxy. "It is not too much to say that the divinization of humanity is the central theme, chief aim, basic purpose, or primary religious ideal of Orthodoxy."[26]

The doctrine of theosis as defined in Eastern Orthodoxy does not actually project that it is possible for humans to achieve Godhood status. The Greek Fathers taught that in the Fall, humanity lost the likeness but retained the image. In their view, according to G. L. Bray,

> The Christian life is best conceived as the restoration of the lost likeness to those who have been redeemed in Christ. This is a work of the Holy Spirit, who communicates to us the energies of God himself, so that we may become partakers of the divine nature (2 Peter 1:4). The energies of God radiate from his essence and share its nature; but it must be understood that the deified person retains his personal identity and is not absorbed into the essence of God, which remains for ever [sic] hidden from his eyes.[27]

I have in my library a copy of a master's thesis written by a non-LDS student enrolled at the University of California, Berkeley. He was intrigued with this LDS doctrine and the opposition to it by mainstream Christianity. The question of whether or not this doctrine was taught in the early Church became the basis of his thesis. In his concluding statements, he said:

> Yet what was meant to be a term of ridicule has turned out to be a term of approbation, for the witness of the Greek Fathers of the Church

> . . . is that they also believed that salvation meant "becoming a god." It seems that if one's soteriology* cannot accommodate a doctrine of human divinization, then it has at least implicitly, if not explicitly, rejected the heritage of the early Christian church and departed from the faith of first millennium Christianity. However, if that is the case, those who would espouse such a soteriology also believe, in fact, that Christianity, from about the second century on, has apostatized and "gotten it wrong" on this core issue of human salvation. Thus, ironically, those who would excoriate Mormons for believing in the doctrine of exaltation actually agree with them that the early church experienced a "great apostasy" on fundamental doctrinal questions. And the supreme irony is that such persons should probably investigate the claims of the LDS Church, which proclaims that within itself is to be found the "restoration of all things." If the Latter-day Saints were inclined to do so, they could point out that they alone, among contemporary followers of Jesus, seem to possess the ancient Christian doctrine of theosis.[28]

God has achieved a state of being in which every thought and action of his being maintains order and maintains the possibility that every form and level of life has the potential to fill the measure of its creation. This potential extends to all things that "act and are acted upon" (2 Nephi 2:14). Joseph Smith taught that "God himself, finding he was in the midst of spirits and glory, because he was more intelligent, saw proper to institute laws whereby the rest could have a privilege to advance like himself. He has power to institute laws to instruct the weaker intelligences, that they may be exalted with himself, so that they might have one glory upon another."[29]

It is God's perfection and his perfect moral nature that maintains order in the universe. God cannot allow anything to conflict with the laws upon which he (or the Gods) exists. Tad Callister, an Area Seventy of the Church, stated it this way:

> There are certain laws of the universe that are immutable, that are without beginning of days or end of years. They were not created by an intelligent being, nor are they the product of moral thought, rather they are eternal, co-existing realities with the intelligences of the universe. These laws are immutable in that they cannot be altered or modified in any form. They are unchangeable from eternity to eternity. They are self-existing, self-perpetuating laws to which even God himself is subject.[30]

God cannot go contrary to the laws that govern the achievement of any blessing. If this was so, chaos would be the result. The Law of Justice governs the gods and their offspring who possess moral agency with its attendant accountability. If God transgressed the moral law which sustains his being, he would cease to be God. Because human beings are gods in embryo dwelling in a probationary and mortal state of existence, they also are subject to the Law of Justice of which the sole aim is to maintain the order of existence and the race of Gods. Therefore, the Law of Justice demands the reconciliation of any behavior which transgresses the moral laws that make up the divine nature of man and God. The Law of Justice is a law of checks and balances. It demands a reconciliation for each act of transgression of divine law. There must be a full and complete reconciliation. A complete reconciliation of mankind's transgressions must be equated to the comprehensiveness of payment or the demands of the Law of Justice would not be met. This must be to maintain order and perfection in the universe. Lehi taught this to his children: "And because that they . . . have become free forever . . . to act for themselves and not to be acted upon, save it be by the punishment of the law at the great and last day, according to the commandments which God hath given" (2 Nephi 2:26).

The Law of Mercy

The Law of Justice is not discriminatory but is concerned with proper payment. The Law of Justice is bound to the principle that each and every sin and transgression is reconciled. Our successful progression through the plan of happiness rests upon the correct use of the eternal gift of agency, especially in the first two acts of our existence. The misuse of this agency in the mortal, or "probationary," act introduces another law called the Law of Mercy. This law helps to resolve the dilemmas of disobedience. The Law of Mercy exhibits power through the life and Atonement of Jesus Christ. This law allows for a payment by someone within the species of the Gods other than the transgressor to provide reconciliation. But if it be a single act of atonement, then it must be infinite in its scope and eternal in its reach. Only a God has the physical and emotional capacity to provide the legal tender* for an infinite number and variety of physical and emotional transgressions committed by mankind. Since the Father dwells in a state of physical resurrection where the body and spirit are "inseparably connected," this task must fall upon one of God's offspring who could receive a physical body as offspring of a mortal mother but also receive the seeds of immortality from the genetics of an immortal and Divine Father. Christ became that "Only Begotten Son" of the Father, also inheriting flesh, bone, and blood from his mortal mother. He became the foreordained sacrifice to provide nothing short of an infinite and eternal atonement or payment to satisfy the demands of the Law of Justice which held fallen mankind in ransom. Therefore, Christ was made to suffer "both body and spirit" in order to provide proper reconciliation (See Alma 34:12).

The Atonement of Jesus Christ also reconciles all transgressions performed in ignorance of the law or those beyond a sense of accountability. "For the atonement satisfieth the demands of his justice upon all those who have not the law given to them" (2 Nephi 9:26). "For behold that all little children are alive in Christ, and also all they that are without the law" (Moroni 8:22).

At one end of the law is mercy in all its compassionate splendor; at the other end of the law is justice in all its stern reality. The Atonement of Jesus Christ stands alone in the grand sum of human actions that demonstrated the maximum mercy, yet never robbed justice of one ounce of payment. The Atonement runs the full gamut of the law, end to end, mercy to justice. Christ's suffering was the only legal tender in the universe sufficient to both pay the debt of justice and unlock the door of mercy.

Evil and the Law of Opposites

Agency is, in this life, one of life's greatest gifts and comes as a two-edged sword. Through its proper use, blessings and happiness are realized. Through its misuse, pain, disappointment, and sorrow are its outcome. The correct uses of this power were nurtured in our pre-existent life. When the time came for our spirit family to prepare for the laboratory of mortal life, our Father was approached by Lucifer to consider a different option than that which had been eternally in place. The scriptures describe Lucifer's attempt to introduce an alternative course (compare Moses 4:1–3; D&C 29:36–37; 76:25–27; Abraham 3:27–28). Thus, this heavenly realm became a staging area for discourse, discussion, and opposing ideas. How does this idea of opposition in our pre-existence fit within the unfolding story of our evolutionary spirit development? An understanding of the law of opposites is crucial to gain a correct understanding of the full parameters of the plan of salvation, including the origins of Satan and of evil. Lehi taught his children that "there must be an opposition in all things" (2 Nephi 2:11). A similar though not exact parallel doctrine is found in the concept of the yin and yang, correlative opposites, a tenet of the Tao* or the Way of Taoism.

Lucifer was one of the early "sons of the morning." The name Lucifer means "light bearer" in Latin and is a translation of the Hebrew *Heylel ben Shakhar*, which means "herald son of dawn" or "morning star"[31]. He also was a spirit offspring of our Heavenly Parents. He, apparently a person of significance and with possible authority, received the attention of Father's spirit family. He presented an alternate plan based upon the element of pride which dominated his spiritual development. He was jealous of God's power and had a proud heart. His plan would severely restrict freedom of choice from the mortal experience. Lucifer cunningly suggested that he would come to earth as a savior and as "thy son" (Moses 4:1). His role, however, would be to force all into obedience of divine law. His plan suggested that all would return back to heaven without the taint of disobedience and violation of the Law of Justice. It was a plan offering universal salvation, but without personal accountability. In his twisted mind and because all would be saved or returned back to the realm of heaven, an act associated only with the divine power of the gods, he must be credited with this success. He sought for God's glory and power without subscribing to the conditions upon which that power and status was protected. For many, this shortcut back to heaven seemed enticing.

Even in mortality, this same temptation is present. People desire the reward without giving heed to the requirements within the process. They seek for satisfaction without bearing responsibility. During one of Jesus' teaching moments, he denounced both adulterers and sign-seekers as wicked (Matthew 12:39; D&C 63:7–14). I long pondered what these two types of sinners had in common. The scriptures speak of Lucifer as being the "father of all lies" (Moses 4:4). With this idea as a backdrop, it became clear. Adulterers and sign-seekers both seek an outcome without bearing responsibility. They both desire the reward without giving heed to the proper process. Adulterers want sex without responsibility. Sign-seekers want proof without giving head to pondering with a sincere heart, with real intent, and having faith in Christ. A third of the heavenly family supported Lucifer and his plan for whatever reason. Too many in mortality continue to be deceived.

The action of Lucifer and his followers provoked rebellion. Prime motivators were greed, power-seeking, and pride. These vices are not just realities of mortality but are inherently associated with the spiritual origins of mankind since we have always been endowed with the gift of agency. Evil, then, is any action through the exercise of moral agency which damns our spiritual development. Any exercise of our agency—in any domain of our evolutionary spiritual development—that moves us away from realizing our embryonic and true potential as Gods, is evil. When Lucifer first sought to follow his inclination to gratify his pride and vain ambitions, he tainted himself with evilness. When Cain, one of Adam's early children, sought to gratify his pride and vain ambitions, he too developed an evil disposition. In this state, Cain became a vehicle of evil influence on other offspring of Adam and Eve. The mortal state in which the "natural man" resides seems to be especially receptive to evil tendencies. When we in mortality seek to gratify our pride and our vain ambitions, when our actions are prompted out of greed, power-seeking, and fulfilling lustful passions, we are evil and are following the paradigm of the "natural man." There is one biblical verse that seems to ascribe evil to God. "I form the light, and create darkness: I make peace, and create evil: I the LORD do all these things" (Isaiah 45:7). In the sense that we all are creations of our Heavenly Parents and have the capacity to use our agency in actions that violate divine law, we then, as God's creations, become evil. Joseph Smith observed:

> Satan was generally blamed for the evils which we did, but if he was the cause of all our wickedness, men could not be condemned. The devil could not compel mankind to do evil; all was voluntary . . . . God would not exert any compulsory means, and the devil could not; and such ideas as were entertained [on these subjects] by many were absurd.[32]

Evil actions are always preceded by evil thoughts. One of the battlefields in which to fight this potential for evil is in the dynamics of the mind. Control the thought processes and you control the person. It is in this domain that the power of God is our greatest advocate. Only God has the power to read our minds. We, on the other hand, have the responsibility to control our own thought processes. The king of Israel, during a military campaign against Syria, sought out Elisha, the prophet, for council and guidance. At that time, Syria had encompassed the city with a host of men and chariots. When Elisha's servant reported this situation to the prophet with fear and concern, Elisha answered, "Fear not: for they that be with us are more than they that be with them. And Elisha prayed, and said, Lord, I pray thee, open his eyes, that he might see. And the Lord opened the eyes of the young man; and he saw: and behold, the mountain was full of horses and chariots of fire round about Elisha" (2 Kings 6:16–17).

Our Father has made available to his mortal children a "mountain full" of spiritual forces that can inspire and purify our mind. But, we must use our agency to open ourselves up to these influences. God will not violate the agency of man and force this cadre* of defense upon us.

Because of Lucifer and his followers' rebellion against God and their attempt at circumventing* the eternal plan of happiness, they were removed from that heavenly environment. They were cast out. Any priesthood authority held by Lucifer and any of his followers was surely removed. This same pattern exists in God's earthly kingdom. When any priesthood holder acts in open rebellion to priesthood authority or participates in the dissemination of incorrect doctrine and fails to repent, he is excommunicated from the Church. Lucifer and his hosts, then, were excommunicated from heaven. With their dismissal from heaven and by following the dictates of the evil that was within them, they also lost any remnant of priesthood power and the influence of the Holy Spirit (D&C 121:35–38). They dwell in "outer darkness." In this state of hell, any progression toward fulfilling their embryonic potential has been dammed—stopped. They have no divine power within themselves and have removed themselves from the benefits of the Atonement. Elder John A. Widtsoe felt that "wicked spirits have their bounds, limits, and laws by which they are governed or controlled, and know their future destiny; hence, those that were in the maniac said to our Savior, 'Art thou come to torment us before the time?' "[33]

The only influence they have is that which is inherent between one spirit to another. Brigham Young taught this same idea: "Take a spirit that has gone into the spirit world, does it have control over corruptible bodies? No. It can only act in the capacity of a spirit. As to the devils inhabiting these earthly bodies, it cannot control them, it only controls spirits."[34]

At times, there are attempts by these evil spirits to bind our physical bodies. Joseph experienced this phenomenon within the sacred grove. Missionaries report receiving this same type of experience. But by calling upon the power of God, these attempts surely end in failure. Only God has the power to massage our minds and our hearts. And God will only express this power based upon the laws which govern that power. The primary influence of God's Holy Spirit is to illuminate our minds with truth and bring peace to our heart. Brigham Young taught:

> The volition of the creature is free; this is a law of their existence and the Lord cannot violate his own law; were He to do that, He would cease to be God. . . . This is a law which has always existed from all eternity, and will continue to exist throughout all the eternities to come. Every intelligent being must have the power of choice, and God brings forth the results of the acts of his creatures to promote his kingdom and subserve his purposes in the salvation and exaltation of his children.[35]

Appendix G contains a collection of scriptural references and statements documenting the idea that evil thoughts originate not from the devil as is popularly held but from the "natural man" side of our dual nature.

Enticements of the Natural Man and of God

The eternal plan of happiness allowed for a mortal experience where our spirits would be clothed in bodies of flesh, bone, and blood. A prime purpose of this mortal experience, other than to gain mortal bodies, was to also determine if we could maintain our divine self-concept and obediently submit to divine law. As such, we would use our agency to further our spiritual progression. We would learn how to limit the evil enticements that come in this "natural man" state and how to benefit from the good enticements placed here by our Father. The consequence of our agency would continue to bless us or damn us. King Benjamin gave one of the greatest sermons ever recorded, the contents of which he received from angelic instruction. As his people gathered around the temple tower, he taught these supernal truths:

> For the natural man is an enemy to God, and has been from the fall of Adam, and will be, forever and ever, unless he yields to the enticing of the Holy Spirit, and putteth off the natural man and becometh a saint through the Atonement of Christ the Lord, and becometh as a child, submissive, meek, humble, patient, full of love, willing to submit to all things which the Lord seeth fit to inflict upon him, even as a child doth submit to his father (Mosiah 3:19).

A careful reading of this verse reveals significant truths. The method of putting off the natural man is by (1) yielding to the enticement of the Holy Spirit and (2) becoming a saint through the Atonement of Christ the Lord. As a result, we come to acquire those godly qualities often ascribed to meek and submissive children.

Joseph taught that our Father's plan enabled the Spirit to give "light to every man that cometh into the world: and the spirit enlighteneth every man through the world, that hearkeneth to the voice of the Spirit, and every one that hearkeneth to the voice of the Spirit cometh unto God, even the Father" (D&C 84:46). The Lord further declared through the Prophet Joseph, "God having redeemed man from the fall [of Adam], men became again, in their infant state, innocent before God" (D&C 93:38). Sometime between our conception and the moment of our birth, our spirit enters into the little fetal body ready to receive our first breath of life. From that time, we are allowed a few years of innocence "before God." We are protected from the enticement of the natural man through a halo of spiritual protection. As we develop in the process of physical maturation, the enticements of the natural man start to assert themselves. The natural man is fueled by the fire of pride, selfishness, carnality, and sensuality. These motivators, if attended to, prompt rebellion against divine origins toward being self-centered and alien to God's existence. The companionship of the gifts of the Spirit withdraws to be replaced by the companionship of other persons with similar disposition. The personification of this evil state is in the person called Lucifer, the devil, or Satan. The ultimate fate of those who persist in this state of rebellion is described in Doctrine and Covenants 76. They receive the classification as "sons of perdition." A discussion of the dynamics of sin and the sins of those who will become sons of perdition is discussed in Chapter Seven.

God is aware of the enticements originating within our natural man environment. However, he has instituted a time of innocence, a buffer time, wherein these enticements are not manifest within children. During this phase, the sweet Spirit of the Lord helps instill a divine conscience, an inherent knowledge of right from wrong. Then comes the age when our cognitive abilities begin to comprehend choice and consequences. The developing child becomes aware of the consequences of his actions in the future and connects currents actions with events of the past. Children's physical bodies are also maturing and developing. Lehi taught:

"Wherefore, the Lord God gave unto man that he should act for himself. Wherefore, man could not act for himself save it should be that he was enticed by the one or the other" (2 Nephi 2:16).

Thus the scene is set for the great drama of life. The natural man offers enticements of selfishness, carnality, sensuality, giving into pride, vain ambition, power-seeking, and so on. The result of giving in to these enticements produces evil and secret combinations, designing individuals, despots, corrupt industries motivated out of greed, power seeking, and work at the proliferation of their selfish and immoral aims. God, who is faithful, does not allow for such a one-sided paradigm. Through his resources, alternative enticements are provided to combat the natural man and enable us to progress toward a full realization of our divine inheritance. These enticements begin with the Spirit of the Lord and build with the influence and gift of the Holy Ghost, spirit gifts, and the Atonement of Jesus Christ.

The Apostle Paul recounts a list of those actions that stem from the natural man: "Now the works of the flesh are manifest, which are these; adultery, fornication, uncleanness, lasciviousness, idolatry, witchcraft, hatred, variance, emulations, wrath, strife, seditions, heresies, envying, murders, drunkenness, revellings, and such."

Paul then proposes a second list describing the fruits enjoyed by those responding to the enticements of the Spirit: "But the fruit of the spirit is love, joy, peace, longsuffering, gentleness, goodness, faith, meekness, and temperance" (Galatians 5:19–22).

The forces of the natural man produce a plethora of supporting media, literature, and opportunities intended to indulge in selfish ambition. On the other hand, God has made available sacred canon, prophetic council, Sabbath observance, nurturing parents, compassionate and service-oriented leaders and teachers, inspired bishops, supportive church organizations and agencies, CES teachers and classrooms, inspiring literature, media, and entertainment, opportunities for service, fathers' and priesthood blessings, and the list goes on.

What Is Man's Nature: Good or Bad?

One of the great debates in philosophy focuses on man's inherent nature. Is man's nature evil, or is it good? There seems to be ample support for each view. The debate continues, especially within religious circles. Traditional Christianity views mankind as inherently evil, a state inherited by man through Adam's transgression. In this fallen state, mankind possesses no power of his own to do good works. The Catholic tradition teaches that the grace of God can be received through the sacraments of the church, which help to empower individuals to do good and enable them to gain spiritual salvation. Those of the Protestant orientation feel that once a person accepts Christ as their personal Savior, they are ushered into a "saved" condition. A consequence of this saved condition produces the good works individuals will perform. These works are evidence of this saved condition. Once a person is so saved, they will not fall out of this condition. How does Mormonism answer this philosophic and religious query? Does the Restoration provide greater illumination and a more reasonable scenario? I think so.

First, a humorous anecdote* is in order.

> A Question for a Zebra by Shel Silverstein
>
> I asked a Zebra:
> Are you Black with White stripes—or,
> are you White with Black stripes?
> And the Zebra asked me:
> Are you good with bad habits—or,
> are you bad with good habits?
> Are you noisy with quiet times—or,
> are you quiet with noisy times?
> Are you happy with some sad days—or,
> are you sad with some happy days?
> Are you neat with some sloppy ways—or,
> are you sloppy with some neat ways?
> And on and on and on and on and on he went . . .
> I will never ask a Zebra about stripes again!

Within LDS theology, it is not an either-or conundrum. From what I have presented thus far, the answer should be obvious. We possess a dual nature. Which of the two natures wins out is a result of our own decision making. The picking up of a stick or pencil has great theologic implications. As one grasps one end of the pencil, with certainty, the other end follows. If a person gives in to the enticements of the natural man, that person becomes "an enemy to all righteousness." He gives up a realization of his true embryonic potential, a mess of pottage for his birthright. On the other hand, if we invite our Father's enticements into our lives, we can not only limit the power of the natural man, but we can be "born again" to receive the "image and countenance of our Savior." Our thoughts and our emotions will become cleansed and purified, and our minds a receptive vessel for even greater manifestations of God's goodness and mercy. Joseph Smith gave us this insight:

> As man approaches God he is enlightened. We consider that God has created man with a mind capable of instruction, and a faculty which may be enlarged in proportion to the heed and diligence given to the light communicated from heaven to the intellect: and that the nearer man approaches perfection, the clearer are his views, and the greater his enjoyments, till he has overcome the evils of his life and lost every desire for sin; and like the ancients, arrives at that point of faith where he is wrapped in the power and glory of his Maker and is caught up to dwell with Him. But we consider that this is a station to which no man ever arrived in a moment: he must have been instructed in the government and laws of that kingdom by proper degree, until his mind is capable in some measure of comprehending the propriety, justice, equity, and consistency of the same.[36]

The principles of justification and sanctification are tangent to this discussion. Simply stated, as we purify our minds and our hearts to become vessels in which the spirit can freely act, our actions become justified of the spirit. That which we do is right before the Lord. Ideally, we realize the sacramental promise of "always having his spirit to be with us." Nephi, a resident of Zarahemla, received confirmation of his state of justification through this inspired communication from the Lord:

> Blessed art thou, Nephi, for those things which thou has done; for I have beheld how thou has with unwaryingness declared the word, which I have given unto thee, unto this people. And thou hast not feared them, and hast not sought thine own life, but hast sought my will, and to keep my commandments.
>
> And now, because thou hast done this with such unwearyingness, behold, I will bless thee forever; and I will make thee mighty in word and in deed, in faith and in works; yea even that all things shall be done unto thee according to thy word, *for thou shalt not ask that which is contrary to my will.* (Helaman 10:4–5; emphasis added)

In strict terms, any action that God directs to a faithful servant through revelation, no matter if such an action conflicts with a prior command of God, it is justified and becomes right. Such was the dilemma of Nephi when he was directed by the Spirit to take Laban's life in order to recover the plates of brass. Fortunately, the scriptural narrative provides us this insight to resolve the "why?" "It is better that one man should perish than that a nation should dwindle and perish in unbelief" (1 Nephi 4:13).

The second principle in this discussion is sanctification. In our fallen state within mortality, we have not the power to totally redeem ourselves from our fallen condition. Paul reminded the early saints that all of us "sin and come short of the glory of God" (Romans 3:23; Gal. 33:22). To be sanctified is to be cleansed from the taint of sin. This cleansing comes only in and through the atoning blood of Jesus Christ. These principles have been taught within the gospel framework even from the genesis of our human family. An angel taught these principles to Adam and Eve soon after their eviction from the Garden of Eden (Moses 5:6–9). The Lord taught these principles to Enoch, who passed them on to the citizens of his city when he said:

> By reason of transgression cometh the fall, which fall bringeth death, and inasmuch as ye were born into the world by water, and blood, and the spirit, which I have made, and so became of dust a living soul, even so ye must be born again into the kingdom of heaven, of water, and of the Spirit, and be cleansed by blood, even the blood of mine Only Begotten; that ye might be sanctified from all sin, and enjoy the words of eternal life in this world, and eternal life in the world to come, even immortal glory;
>
> For by the water ye keep the commandment; by the Spirit ye are justified, and by the blood ye are sanctified (Moses 6:59–60).

Previously, I alluded to the Christian concept of fallen man. This concept comes out of the great drama inside the Garden of Eden. Again, the interpretation of these Edenic events have great ramification on primary doctrine and belief. Most outside of Christianity and many within view this story as myth possessing allegorical value. The Restoration, once again, helps restore the veracity of this real event and enables a true understanding of the doctrines and principles coming from its script.

The Garden of Eden and the Atonement of Christ

A correct understanding of the garden account develops from a correct understanding of the Atonement of Christ. Ted Callister presented a wonderful review of the Atonement in his book *The Infinite Atonement.* He identified the purposes of the Atonement, the conditions in the Garden of Eden before and after the Fall, and misunderstandings taught and not taught concerning the Atonement.

Three principle purposes of the Atonement are:

1. To restore all that was lost by the Fall of Adam.
    a. It brings about the resurrection for all men, thus overcoming physical death (1 Corinthians 15:21–22)
    b. It will restore all men to the presence of God for the purpose of being judged, thus overcoming what the scriptures call a first spiritual death (see Helaman 14:16; D&C 29:41).
2. To provide for the possibility of repentance so that men might be cleansed from their individual sins and by so doing overcome what the scriptures call a second spiritual death (see Helaman 14:18).
3. To provide the power necessary to exalt us to the status of a god (see D&C 76:69).

These three purposes are designed to help us permanently return to God's presence and become like Him. Now let us look at the conditions that existed in the garden before the fall of Adam and Eve:

1. Adam and Eve were immortal, not subject to pain, disease, or death.
2. Adam and Eve walked and talked in the presence of God. "God conversed with him [Adam] face to face. In his presence he was permitted to stand, and from his own mouth he was permitted to receive instruction. He heard his [God's] voice, walked before him and gazed upon his glory, while intelligence burst upon his understanding."[37]
3. Adam and Eve were in a state of innocence, without a full knowledge of good and evil, and thus unable to experience a fulness of joy. John Fiske, a Harvard philosopher, grasped this

dilemma: "Clearly, for strong and resolute men and women an Eden would be but a fool's paradise. How could anything fit to be called character have ever been produced there?"[38]

4. Adam and Eve would have had no children (2 Nephi 2:23), no joy in a posterity.

It should be noted that each of the four conditions before the Fall were reversed after the Fall. There are also many misunderstandings, confusing beliefs, and doctrinal heresies associated with the Atonement. These include:

1. Adam and Eve would have had children in the Garden of Eden if they had been allowed to remain.
2. Adam and Eve were not in a state of innocence in the Garden, but rather were experiencing unparalleled joy.
3. The Fall was not part of God's master plan, but rather a tragic step backwards. It was a stumbling block, not a stepping stone in man's eternal journey.
4. If Adam had not fallen, all of Adam's children would have been born in a state of bliss, to live "happily ever after" in Edenic conditions.
5. Because of the Fall, all infants are tainted with original sin.
6. Grace alone can save (ensure life everlasting) us, regardless of any works on our part.
7. The physical resurrection of the Savior was merely symbolic; we will be resurrected as spirits without the "limitations" of a physical body.
8. The Atonement does not have the power to transform us into gods; in fact, such a thought is blasphemous.

In addition to misunderstandings, there are key points of the Atonement that are present in LDS theology, but are not correctly taught by other Christian religions. These include:

1. Christ took upon himself all sins and likewise assumed all pains, infirmities, and sickness inherent in the mortal experience.
2. The power of the Atonement reaches those who have no law.
3. The power of the Atonement is retroactive upon the saints of not only pre-meridian times but all of God's children on all of the earths created by the "power of mine only Begotten."
4. The power of the Atonement transcends the grave and redeems spirits in the postmortal realm.
5. The power of the Atonement is infinite and eternal in its implication.

It is important to understand the reasons why the Atonement is infinite in its nature:

1. Infinite in the divineness of the one sacrificed. Jesus as the Divine Redeemer is the consummate expression of godliness.
2. Infinite in power. The Savior went from grace to grace until he "received all power, both in heaven and on earth" (D&C 93:17).
3. Infinite in time. It applies retroactively and prospectively through time immemorial.
4. Infinite in coverage. It applies to all God's creations and all forms of life thereon.
5. Infinite in depth. "The Son of Man hath descended below them all" (D&C 122:8).
6. Infinite in the degree of suffering endured by the Redeemer which caused "even God, the greatest of all, to tremble because of pain, and to bleed at every pore" (D&C 19:18).
7. Infinite in love. The Atonement of Jesus Christ is the grandest demonstration of love this world has ever known. His motivation was not duty or glory or honor or any temporal reward. It was love in the purest, deepest, most enduring sense.
8. Infinite in the blessings it bestows. Blessings of:

a. The resurrection.

b. Repentance.

c. Peace of mind.

d. The succoring (healing, calming, restoring) power of Christ.

e. The power of motivation, to draw all men to Christ.

f. Being "added upon" to raise mortal man to a higher and nobler state.

g. Overcoming weaknesses, inadequacies, and shortcomings.

h. Freedom from sin, sorrow, ignorance, and death in order for men to have power to "act for themselves" rather than being "acted upon" (2 Nephi 2:26); internally motivated rather than externally driven.

All these blessing are woven into the concept of Christ's grace. "We know that it is by grace that we are saved, after all we can do" (2 Nephi 25:23). In the aggregate, the effect of this event so blesses our lives in a multiplicity of ways, both known and yet to be discovered.[39]

The Garden of Eden Paradox *

There is some discussion within Mormonism as to the perceived contradiction of God giving two seemingly conflicting commandments to Adam and Eve: (1) multiply and replenish the earth and (2) do not partake of the fruit of the tree of knowledge of good and evil. At first glance, it doesn't appear possible to be faithful to both of them. They had to break one in order to keep the other. Restoration scriptures make it quite clear that God does not—indeed, cannot—contradict himself. As Alonso Gaskill states, "There is not a single example in scripture, outside of the story of the Fall, which supports the notion that God ever gives us commandments which require the breaking of other commandments in order for us to be obedient to the first."[40] It is contrary to the nature of God to place us in a position where we cannot possibly be obedient (1 Nephi 3:7). Gaskill cites supporting references, then provides this summary statement:

> God was quite clear with Adam and Eve that they had a choice—and that choice was not which of the two contradictory commandments they would keep. On the contrary, the two options given them

> were as follows; If they wanted to stay in Eden, then the fruit of knowledge of good and evil was forbidden. However, if they wanted to leave, they would have to partake of that fruit. The first couple would have been quite clear on what their options were and what the repercussions of either choice would be.[41]

Let us pursue this idea of a paradox. Paradoxes are situations that seem to present a logical self-contradiction. There are evidences of several God-ordained paradoxes recorded in scripture. Matthew 23 describes two such paradoxes. Jesus declared in verse 11 that "he that is greatest among you shall be your servant." In verse 12 he states that "whosoever shall exalt himself shall be abased; and he that shall humble himself shall be exalted." Another is found in Matthew 10:39: "He that findeth his life shall lose it: and he that loseth his life for my sake shall find it." It is important, however, to note that these paradoxes are God-ordained and not man-ordained. Instances of paradoxical situations in the scriptures which are God-ordained also show them to be tests of obedience given by direct revelation. For instance, in Genesis 22, the Lord commands Abraham to sacrifice Isaac. This is a true paradox because Abraham was forbidden during his early life in Ur of Chaldea to follow that pagan custom. Now, on top of Mount Moriah God is seemingly commanding Abraham to disregard the commandment against human sacrifice and to obey him and sacrifice Isaac, his only covenant son. Surely, our first parents did some pondering as to how they were to obey each of Father's commandments. In retrospect, they would have had no children unless they became mortal, which was achieved by partaking of the forbidden fruit—hence a paradox. These paradoxical situations are connected to the concept of obedience. With Abraham, his willingness to obey God's current injunction passed a divine test and Isaac was spared. Adam, after Eve had partaken of the forbidden fruit, seemed to sense that they must disobey the second command in order to stay together and fulfill the first.

God, in his wisdom, created a "garden paradox" wherein mankind, through its primal parents, ushered itself into a fallen environment. But God, in his perfect mercy, made it safe for Adam and Eve to "transgress" one of God's directives in order to be obedient to a moral imperative. In addition, while in mankind's fallen and mortal state, God provided a Savior who would reclaim all of fallen man through the power of the Resurrection. He would also redeem all of fallen man who would be obedient to the requirements of the Atonement.

Concerning God-ordained paradoxes, Joseph Smith taught:

> That which is wrong under one circumstance, may be, and often is, right under another. God said, "Thou shalt not kill;" at another time He said, "Thou shalt utterly destroy." This is the principle on which the government of heaven is conducted—by revelation adapted to the circumstances in which the children of the Kingdom are placed. Whatever God requires is right, no matter what it is, although we may not see the reason thereof till long after the events transpire.[42]

Long after Adam and Eve, we can now see the significance of the Lord placing them in their unique paradoxical circumstances. He did so not only to test their obedience but also to create for our benefit a probationary, albeit, fallen world through their transgression. Elder Dallin H. Oaks identified the distinction between Adam's "transgression" and "sin." He stated:

> Some acts, like murder, are crimes because they are inherently wrong. Other acts, like operating without a license, are crimes only because they are legally prohibited. Under these distinctions, the act that produced the Fall was not a sin—inherently wrong—but a transgression—wrong because it was formally prohibited. These words are not always used to denote something different, but this distinction seems meaningful in the circumstances of the Fall.[43]

Man-made paradoxes characteristically follow a very different course, not being used as a divine testing agent. Man-made paradoxes are usually rooted in some biased or prejudiced opinion of a group or individual. The early Christian Church went from being the persecuted in the early Christian centuries to become the persecutor during the Dark and Middle ages. The Puritans came to America for religious freedom, but failed to allow that same principle to those of other religious persuasions who lived within their colonies.

The idea of sacrifice is also usually present in God-ordained paradoxes, not as much in the sense of a physical sacrifice as in a sacrifice of our will in submission to God's will. Though the official name of our church in Arabic doesn't include the word Islam which means submission or to submit, the message of the gospel of Jesus Christ and the power of the Atonement makes it safe for each of Heavenly Father's children to submit their will, in fact their agency, to become obedient followers of Christ—disciples from which the word *discipline* originates. In exchange, our Father distills upon us His love and peace, His Holy Spirit, all of the blessings associated with each principle of the gospel and in the end, a fulness of joy and true happiness. Pretty good exchange. Elder Boyd K. Packer came to this momentous decision point in his life when he found it safe to give up his agency. Of this experience he said:

> I knew what agency was and knew how important it was to be individual and to be independent, to be free. I somehow knew there was one thing the Lord would never take from me, and that was my free agency. I would not surrender my agency to any being but to Him! I determined that I would give Him the one thing that He would never take—my agency. I decided, by myself, that from that time on I would do things His way. That was a great trial for me, for I thought I was giving away the most precious thing I possessed. I was not wise enough in my youth to know that because I exercised my agency and decided myself, I was not losing it. It was strengthened!
>
> I learned from that experience the meaning of the scripture: "If ye continue in my word, then are ye my disciples indeed; "And ye shall know the truth, and the truth shall make you free" (John 8:31–32).[44]

The Prophet Joseph recorded this declaration:

> A religion that does not require the sacrifice of all things never has power sufficient to produce the faith necessary unto life and salvation; for, from the first existence of man, the faith necessary unto the enjoyment of life and salvation never could be obtained without the sacrifice of all earthly things. It was through this sacrifice, and this only, that God has ordained that men should enjoy eternal life.[45]

Both men and women of the Church are called to this holy commitment. Ours is not an easy church—a church for the lackadaisical, a church for the complacent, a church for the those who are lukewarm. Of these type of members the Lord warned, "I know thy works, that thou art neither cold nor hot: I would thou wert cold or hot. So then because thou art lukewarm, and neither cold nor hot, I will spue thee out of my mouth" (Revelation 3:16). Male members of the church are invited to make priesthood covenants which empower us to use Christ's divine authority to serve and bless others. There is not one priesthood ordinance which allows a priesthood holder to serve himself. Priesthood service is sacrificial in nature. Priesthood service attempts to emulate the sacrificial nature of Christ. But within the oath and covenant associated with the Melchizedek Priesthood comes this promise: "And also all they who receive this priesthood receive me, saith the Lord; for he that receiveth my servants receiveth me; and he that receiveth me receiveth my Father; and he that receiveth my Father receiveth my Father's kingdom; therefore all that my Father hath shall be given unto him. And this is according to the oath and covenant which belongeth to the priesthood" (D&C 84:35–39). The existence of paradoxes, therefore, is part of a divinely ordained plan for our eternal progression.

The Purpose of Life—A Worldly Perspective

Of the three great questions in life—Where did I come from? Why am I here? Where am I going?—it is the second question which has been deliberated most by philosophers and religionists. What is the purpose of life? How do I fit into the grand scheme of things? What is the meaning of life? For some, the ramifications to these questions are so ominous that avoidance is the acknowledged solution. Eventually, however, each person seeks or is forced to some type of resolution.

The father of existential* psychology, Viktor Frankl, found his resolution crammed in a small cubicle located in a Nazi concentration camp at Auschwitz, Germany. Even within the degradation and misery of this terribly repressive environment, Frankl discovered what to him was the most important part of his humanness: his freedom to determine his own attitude and spiritual well being. In his landmark book written during his imprisonment, he wrote: "Ultimately, man should not ask what the meaning of his life is, but rather must recognize that it is he who is asked. In a word, each man is questioned by life; and he can only answer to life by answering for his own life; to life he can only respond by being responsible."[46]

"Cogito ergo sum." This Latin form of a popular statement is attributed to René Descartes (1596–1650), a French philosopher and mathematician who is called "the father of modern philosophy." Because he wanted to eliminate the uncertainties in philosophy, and make it more like the "certainties" of mathematics, he proceeded to discard all preconceived philosophic notions and started from what he conceived to be a rock solid foundation. The only thing Descartes found certain was the fact that he was thinking. He further felt that thought was not a thing in itself, and so he had to proceed from somewhere (viz., cause and effect); therefore, since he was thinking the thoughts, he existed—by extension. Hence, "thought" and "extension" were the very beginnings from which all things proceeded, "Cogito ergo sum" or, "I think therefore I am." His scrapping of previously accepted philosophies marked the beginning of the belief in the human-centered universe which currently drives Western thought.

Frankl and Descartes are only two of a vast array of well-known "thinkers" who have deliberated the meaning of our existence. Somewhere on the continuum are those who are more negative about life's existence: nihilist, fatalists, and pessimists. Nihilism is the belief that there is no meaning or purpose in existence. Nihilists deny the existence of any basis for knowledge or truth and generally reject customary beliefs of morality and religion. Fatalism is the belief that all events are determined by fate and are inevitable. Pessimism is the belief that the existing world is the worst possible; the bad in the world outweighs the good. Pessimists tend to expect misfortune or the worst outcome in any circumstance.

The purpose of life within some eastern religions is focused on escaping the reincarnation wheel of life and losing individuality into nirvana. A humorous anecdote places this mode of life in a whimsical setting.

> What does reincarnation mean? A cowpoke asked his friend.
> His pal replied, "It happens when yer life has reached its end.
> They comb yer hair, and warsh yer neck, and clean yer fingernails,
> and lay you in a padded box away from life's travails.
>
> The box and you goes in a hole, tha's been dug into the ground.
> Reincarnation starts in when yore planted 'neath a mound.
> Them clods melt down, just like yer box, and you who is inside.
> And then your just beginnin' on yer transformation ride.
>
> In a while the grass'll grow upon yer rendered mound.
> Till some day on yer moldered grave a lonely flower is found.
> And say a horse should wander by and graze upon this flower
> That once wuz you, but now's become yer vegetative bower.
>
> The posey that the hoss done ate up, with his other feed,
> Makes bone, and fat, and muscle essential to the steed.
> But some is left that he can't use and so it passes through,
> And finally lays upon the ground this thing, that once was you.
>
> Then say, by chance, I wanders by and sees this upon the ground,
> And I ponders, and I wonders at, this object that I found.
> I thinks of reincarnation, of life, and death, and such,

> And come away concludin': "Slim, you really ain't changed—
> all that much."[47]

Religions that possess an attachment to biblical authority stress within their purpose of life the importance of submitting to and serving God. In general, most denominations within Christianity accentuate the "badness" or the evil that resides within humans. The only way to counter that inherited condition is to accept Christ. From then, their purpose in life is to perform acts which return back to God praise and glory in an attempt to express appreciation.

Mormonism's Plan of Happiness

How is this germane question answered within Mormonism? The prophet Lehi taught a simple doctrine to his son Jacob: "men are, that they might have joy" (2 Nephi 2:25). The prophet Joseph Smith reiterated this perspective with this succinct summation: "Happiness is the object and design or our existence."[48] Thankfully, the religion of Mormonism reintroduces the attainment of happiness as a central theological principle and our primary purpose of life. The attainment of happiness was integral to the philosophy of the early Greek philosophers. Aristotle taught that happiness is the meaning and the purpose of life, the whole aim and end of human existence. Socrates asserted that the highest good for any human being is happiness. Whatever action a man chooses is motivated by his desire for happiness. Knowledge, virtue, and wisdom are all the same, since man chooses an action according to what he thinks will bring him the greatest happiness. Therefore the more a man knows, the greater his ability to reason out the correct choice and to choose those actions that truly bring happiness to him. In contrast, Plato regarded happiness as a state of perfection hard to comprehend because the metaphysical presuppositions seemed both hazy and out of the realm of ordinary understanding.

Inherent within the Restoration of the gospel of Jesus Christ was the restoration of the significant details concerning the true plan of happiness. Because of our knowledge of true principles and our emphasis upon correct use of agency, Latter-day Saints should be among, if not, the happiest people on earth. President Lorenzo Snow taught: "No religion has in it such prospects as has the religion of the Latter-day Saints. Nothing was ever introduced to man equal to it in its grand and glorious advantages. We ought to enjoy our religion to such an extent as to be happy most all the time."[49] Couched within our focus upon happiness is also our focus upon expectations of perfection. Unfortunately, some Latter-day Saints have a difficult time harmonizing our emphasis upon achieving perfection verses the realistic balance of becoming a little bit better each day. Sometimes, that dissonance* creates feelings of depression, which rob the realization of a fully happy life.

Joy and happiness are only two aspects within the plan of happiness of Mormonism. The following represents a scriptural analysis of the purposes of earth life.

The Purposes of Earth Life:

Experience Joy

1. We are that we might have joy (2 Nephi 2:25).
2. Our assistance in the saving of souls brings "great joy" (D&C 18:15–16).
3. Our joy is made full through Jesus as our Savior (D&C 101:36).
4. Our joy will be full forever if we endure the crosses of the world (2 Nephi 9:18).

Develop Attributes of Godliness

1. We are commanded to become perfect as God is perfect (Matthew 5:48; 3 Nephi 12:48).
2. Improvement comes "line upon line, precept upon precept, here a little, and there a little" (2 Nephi 28:30; D&C 50:24).
3. The ordinances of the priesthood place the powers of godliness within our reach (D&C 84:19–23).
4. The measure of our creation, through God's grace, is godliness (Ephesians 4:12–13).

A Time of Testing

1. Mortal life is a probationary period, the time for us to prepare

to meet God (Alma 12:24; 42:4, 10; 34:32).

2. We are tested in mortality to show whether we will keep God's commandments and overcome sin and opposition (Abraham 3:25–25; D&C 98:14–15; 136:31; 124:55; Revelation 3:21).

3. The tests of mortality often take the form of persecution, tribulation, calamity, personal adversity, and loneliness (2 Timothy 3:12; 1 Peter 1:7; Romans 5:3–5; D&C 101:2–4; 121:1).

4. Those seeking to be obedient to God will not be tried or tested beyond their ability to bear (1 Corinthians 10:13; Alma 13:28–30; 38:5).

Tests of Mortality for Our Good

1. We taste the bitter fruits of life in order that we may grow and learn to prize the good (Moses 6:55; D&C 29:39; 2 Nephi 2:1–2, 11).

2. Mortality is our opportunity to live by faith in God (Galatians 2:20; 3:11; JST Romans 1:17; Habakkuk 2:4).

3. If we maintain faith in God, our trials in life will work together for our good and our eternal glory (D&C 90:24; 58:2–4; 121:7–8; 122:5–9; Romans 8:28).

Gain a Mortal Body

1. When combined, the spirit and the body compose the soul of man (D&C 88:15; Genesis 2:7).

2. A physical body is essential to our obtaining a fulness of joy (D&C 93:33; 138:17).

3. The body should be a temple in which the Spirit of God may dwell (1 Corinthians 3:16–17; 6:19–20; D&C 93:35).

4. The body is sacred and should be properly valued (Exodus 20:13; Genesis 1:26–27; 9:6; D&C 42:18–19).

Mormons are not pessimists or fatalists. They are positive about life. They view life through lenses of faith in God and hope in Jesus Christ. Trials, tests, and tribulations are positioned within the panorama of life's great adventure. President James E. Faust declared that trials and tribulation are the "refining fire which clears our vision and orders our priorities."[50] Unfortunately for some, God is blamed as the source of our trials in statements such as "why did God allow this to happen?" Within such a perspective, faith is weakened and undue blame placed on God. Without the expanding vision which comes from truth and is confirmed by the Holy Ghost, trials and tribulations in our life can become a condemnation to us (see D&C 35:8, 11; 58:2–6). To Latter-day Saints, trials are the refining fire that smelts out the impurities and helps to produce the purified gold that reflects the image of the Master. One of the purposes of earth life is to walk by faith, not by fear. Our faith sustains our knowledge that we have a loving Heavenly Father who provides peace and opportune direction, strengthens our courage, and has given us a plan of life in which trials aid in our pursuit of perfection on our path toward Godhood. Those with faith and an optimistic view of life interpret trials not as hardships but as stepping stones for character development and backdoor opportunities to serve others.

Even a casual observation of the human condition reveals scenarios where some individuals seem to have an inordinate number of trials and tribulations. Why is this so? What is the source of the trials we experience in this life? Do we have any control over their number and their magnitude?

Sources of Trials and Tribulations:

1. Cause and effect—consequences of our own decision making.
2. Cause and effect—consequences of the decisions of others.
3. Consequences of living in a wicked world.
4. Conditions of mortality (sickness and disease, handicaps, accidents, and so forth).
5. Interactions with Satan (Job's life and trials as acknowledged by the prophet Ezekiel [Ezekiel 14:14], the brother of Jesus [(James 5:11], and the Lord himself [D&C 121:10]).
6. Tests of obedience initiated by God (Abraham commanded to sacrifice Isaac).

My own experience in life has taught me that effective and inspired decision making can influence the occurrence of trials as well as their impact. My decision to live the Word of Wisdom has helped me avoid the trials associated with drinking, smoking, and drug addiction. Avoiding debt and living frugally has helped limit tribulations associated with financial indulgence. Decisions related to educational and vocational choices, selection of my spouse, home and work environment, and how I relate with others have all had an impact on the management of life's tribulations, whether coming from my own decision making, the decisions of others or the natural consequences of living in a mortal world. Though trials associated with items 5 and 6 above are out of my control, their occurrence can still be measured from within a divine perspective. That perspective helps provide parameters for the purposes of trials in our lives.

Purposes for Trials in Our Lives

1. We must taste the bitter fruits of life in order that we may grow and learn to prize the good (Moses 6:55; D&C 29:39; 2 Nephi 2:1–2, 11).
2. Mortality is our opportunity to live by faith in God (Galatians 2:20; 3:11; JST Romans 1:17; Habakkuk 2:4).
3. If we maintain faith in God, our trials in life will work together for our good and our eternal glory (D&C 58:2–4; 90:24; 121:7–8; 122:5–9; Romans 8:28).
4. "That the works of God should be made manifest in him" (John 9:1–3).
5. Trials experienced by others represent opportunities for us to extend love, compassion, and service.

The temptations we face in life do not necessarily translate into challenging trials. How we process each temptation is key to how each affects our lives. The Savior reminded the young Joseph Smith that "he suffered temptations, but gave no heed unto them" (D&C 20:22). After Jesus had retired into the wilderness he countered Satan's temptations with a scriptural perspective of who He was. The apostle Paul promised the Corinthian saints that "there hath no temptation taken you but such as is common to man: but God is faithful, who will not suffer you to be tempted above that ye are able; but will with the temptation also make a way to escape, that ye may be able to bear" (1 Corinthians 10:13).

As we come into partnership with God, we will be strengthened and fortified to successfully process life's trials and evil temptations. In the least, we can receive the peace that comes with understanding. With our eternal perspective and exercising faith, we can use trials to our advantage knowing that there will be "ways of escape" or that "all these things shall give thee experience, and shall be for thy good" (D&C 122:7). As we utilize the promptings of the Holy Spirit, we can be directed away from circumstances of portending but unnecessary evil or trials. President Harold B. Lee spoke of a childhood experience he had with the Spirit. One day he was playing alone while his father was working in the field. Across from a neighbor's barbed wire fence lay some broken down buildings and sheds. These presented an opportunity for exploring and discovery for young Harold. As he approached the fence to cross over, he felt a spiritual prompting warning him from this course of action. He heeded this warning but never did discovered what harm awaited him.[51] Though trials are a reality, through inspired, effective, and efficient decision making, they can be limited in quantity and degree.

We are taught from our primary years that one of the reasons for coming to this earth is to gain a physical body. We view our bodies as sacred and as an eternal inheritance eventually to receive glorified and resurrected status. The powers of procreation are a gift from God. When exercised within the "oneness" of a covenant marriage, sexual expression between a husband and wife is good, holy, and not only for the intent of producing children.[52] Commandments like the Word of Wisdom have both spiritual and physical ramifications. Not only can we be blessed to "run and not be weary" but we can access "wisdom and great treasures of knowledge, even hidden treasures" (D&C 89:19). As this commandment is a requirement for those desiring to participate in temple covenants, by obeying this principle the great treasure house of God's endowment is made available.

We bring clarity to our earthly existence through our knowledge of where we came from and what our eternal potential can be in the life to come. We are in the second act of a three-act play. During mortality, our greatest need is to discover God, then develop faith in his true character and person. It is not always easy to see the hand of God, either in the detail of our own lives or in the tapestry of living history. It may be easier to recognize God at work in the lives of the great prophets or in the dramatic miracles of the Exodus. His handiwork may be easily evident in people of renown like Francis of Assisi, in the heroic devotion of a Mother Theresa, or events like the Reformation. It is much more difficult to see God's hand in Europe's Black Death or the dropping of the bomb in Hiroshima or racial genocide like that of the holocaust. But it is wrong to confine God to the pleasant, the congenial, or the spiritually dramatic. The chorus in T.S. Elliot's play "Murder in the Cathedral" takes a wider view of God's activity in history. Contemplating all the pain and suffering of human existence, they conclude that "only in retrospection, selection, we say, That was the day. The critical moment that is always now and here. Even now in sordid particulars the eternal design may appear."[53]

The shadows as much as the sunlight, the agony as much as the ecstasy, are part of the divine purpose of mortality. In the tapestry of time, the hand of God weaves as many somber skeins as bright-hued silks. In our perceptions of history, we may see only the reverse side of things with all the muddle of loose strands, back-stitching, and over-worked patterns. On the underside, we see the hint of something of the design as it appears on the right side, but we never see it as it actually is. The clarity and beauty of the design as it appears face up are as yet denied to us. The Apostle Paul understood this truth when he admitted that "for now we see through a glass, darkly" (1 Corinthians 13:12).

The Prophet Joseph discounted our veiled view of God's handiwork, which at times lends to myopic* judgments, if not faltering faith, when he declared with certainty, "when the designs of God shall be made manifest, and the curtain of futurity be withdrawn, we shall all of us eventually have to confess that the Judge of all the earth has done right."[54]

We believe that God is the Lord of history in all its totality. Only at a future time are we promised, if we faithfully endure, a view of real history from the summit of God's throne, to appreciate how exactly the hand of God has been at work throughout life's processes.

> Yea, verily I say unto you, in that day when the Lord shall come, he shall reveal all things—
>
> Things which have passed, and hidden things which no man knew, things of the earth, by which it was made, and the purpose and the end thereof—
>
> Things most precious, things that are above, and things that are beneath, things that are in the earth, and upon the earth, and in heaven.

> And all they who suffer persecution for my name, and endure in faith, though they are called to lay down their lives for my sake yet shall they partake of all this glory.
>
> Wherefore, fear not even unto death; for in this world your joy is not full, but in me your joy is full (D&C 101:32–36).

In our pursuit of happiness, joy more than fun becomes the determinant. The fullness of joy lies not within hedonistic or selfish paradigms. True joy is found within eternal family covenants and relationships and a life full of service and good works. The Savior reminded Joseph and his companions that if in their labors they were successful only in bringing one soul unto the Lord, "how great shall be your joy with him in the kingdom of my Father! And now, if your joy will be great with one soul that you have brought unto me into the kingdom of my Father, how great will be your joy if you should bring many souls unto me" (D&C 18:15–16).

In this life, we will have arrived at a wonderful revelation when we view ourselves in a condition of happiness as "saviors upon Mount Zion" (Obadiah 1:2, D&C 103:9; 100:17–17) and co-participants in helping the Father "bring to pass the immortality and eternal life of man" (Moses 1:39; 1 Nephi 17:36; D&C 132:63).

1. Will Durrant, *The Story of Philosophy*, 9-10.
2. Ibid., 24.
3. Ibid., 57.
4. Bainton, *Christendom*, 186.
5. Joseph Smith, *Lectures on Faith*, 38.
6. Ibid.
7. McMurrin, *The Philosophical Foundations of Mormon Theology*, 10.
8. http://newadvent.org/cathen/15047a,htm#IV.
9. De Mysterio Trinitarus recta confessio est ignoratio scientiae—"Proem ad 1. xviii in Isai."
10. Taken from a videotaped panel discussion between Elder Gary Coleman and a Catholic apologist when Elder Coleman was a mission president in California.
11. *The Catholic Source Book*, 117–220.
12. McMurrin, *The Philosophical Foundations of Mormon Theology*, 10.
13. Carl F. Eyring, "The Atomic Bomb," *Improvement Era*, Sept. 1945, 502.
14. M. Russell Ballard, "The Kingdom Rolls Forth in South America."
15. Maxwell, *That My Family Should Partake*. 96.
16. Schaff, *Nicene and Post-Nicene Fathers*, 320.
17. Orson F. Whitney in *Conference Report*, Oct. 1907, 51.
18. Joseph Smith, *Teachings of the Prophet Joseph Smith*, 354.
19. Nibley, Hugh, *Ancient Documents and the Pearl of Great Price*, Lecture 3.

20. Ibid.
21. Ibid.
22. Maxwell, *A More Excellent Way*, 16–17.
23. Williams, *Teachings of Lorenzo Snow*, 2, 373.
24. Athanasius in *Nicene and Post-Nicene Fathers*, 575–578.
25. Athanasius in *Nicene and Post-Nicene Fathers*, 65.
26. Clendenin, *Eastern Orthodox Christianity*, 120.
27. Bray, *New Dictionary of Theology*, 189.
28. Vajda, "Partakers of a Divine Nature," (master's thesis, UC—Berkeley), 94–95.
29. Joseph Smith, *Teachings of the Prophet Joseph Smith*, 354.
30. Callister, *The Infinite Atonement*, 299–300.
31. Ludlow, *Encyclopedia of Mormonism*, s.v. "Devils."
32. Joseph Smith, *Teachings of the Prophet Joseph Smith*, 187.
33. Widtsoe, *Priesthood and Church Government*, 40.
34. Young, *Journal of Discourses*, 4:133.
35. Young, *Discourses of Brigham Young*, 62.
36. Joseph Smith, *Teachings of the Prophet Joseph Smith*, 51.
37. Joseph Smith, *Lectures on Faith*, 13.
38. Roberts, *The Truth, The Way, The Life*, 349.
39. These ideas were developed in Tad Callister's *The Infinite Atonement*.
40. Gaskill, *The Savior and the Serpent*, 13.
41. Ibid., 15.
42. Joseph Smith, *Teachings of the Prophet Joseph Smith*, 256.
43. Dallin H. Oaks, " 'The Great Plan of Happiness'," *Ensign*, Nov. 1993, 72
44. Boyd K. Packer, "Spiritual Crocodiles," *Ensign*, May 1976, 30.
45. Joseph Smith, *Lectures on Faith*, 58.
46. Frankl, *Man's Search for Meaning*, 172.
47. Wallace McRae, *Cowboy Curmudgeon*, 1992.
48. Joseph Smith, *Teachings of the Prophet Joseph Smith*, 256.
49. Lorenzo Snow, *Conference Report*, Oct. 1900, 63.
50. James E. Faust, "Refined in our Trials," *Ensign*, Feb. 2006, 3.
51. Harold B. Lee, "The Way to Eternal Life," *Ensign*, Nov. 1971, 17.
52. An excellent treatise on the importance of sexual intimacy within marriage is *And They Were Not Ashamed: Strengthening Marriage through Sexual Fulfillment*, by Laura M. Brotherson.
53. Dowley, *Erdman's Handbook to the History of Christianity*, 12.
54. Joseph Smith, *Teachings of the Prophet Joseph Smith*, 217–218.

CHAPTER SEVEN

Religion—A Gift from God or a Product of Man?

We believe that religion is instituted of God; and that men are amenable to him, and to him only, for the exercise of it, unless their religious opinions prompt them to infringe upon the rights and liberties of others. – D&C 134:4

I would now like to return to two questions I raised earlier. Is religion a gift from God, or is religion a product of man? In my study of religion and religious history, I have observed that most college text books on religion are written by social scientists. They represent attempts to develop an understanding of the origin and histories of religion and religious beliefs in the world. From one of these books I take a representative quote: "A study of religion from a historical, analytical and impersonal perspective equates religion as a product of man's need to deal with issues outside of his phenomenal world."[1] These social scientists view the phenomenon of religion as rising up out of an inherent need in the human condition. According to them, religion is the product of man's inner spiritual drive. This same book continues:

> Each religion provides definition to the nature of man. The realities of human existence lead most people to conclude that there is within us a struggle concerning choices about good and evil. Outside forces influence us; there are inner inclinations toward good and evil. Each individual ultimately bears the final responsibility for their choices.[2]

The thesis of developmental religion, as well as a developmental concept of God, is not confined to social scientists, however. Henry

Emerson Fosdick, a well-known and popular Baptist minister of the early twentieth century with congregations in the New York area, dedicated an entire book to this thesis. Fosdick maintained that the character of the God of the Hebrews evolved over time. At first, this god was a mountain god. It then become a storm god displaying violent exhibitions of nature's power, then evolved into a god of war. This god received a name, Yahweh, and became a tribal god, bringing his people into a covenant relationship. Eventually, Yahweh came to possess anthropomorphism, humanlike characteristics. Finally, it was a territorial god assigning to his covenant people a special possession of geography. Fosdick maintained:

> This idea [Yahweh, a god of the sky], at the beginning, doubtless coexisted with earlier and more mundane conceptions; it was thought by a few before it was held by many; it was conceived by many before it became practically operative in their daily religion. At last, however, it occupied the minds and imaginations of the people and tended inevitably toward universalism. A god who, as the Eighteenth Psalm put it, 'bowed the heavens' was escaping from the limited ideas by which his earlier followers had conceived him.[3]

Religion, then, is a product of man—from Fosdick's point of view. It is not surprising for people of this mind-set to observe many similarities of belief within religions which are born within the same culture. The religions of south Asia (Hinduism, Jainism, Buddhism, and Sikhism) hold that humanity's goal is to gain some form of unity with an impersonal divine principle. This is monism, a belief that god, mind, and matter are not different. In contrast, the religions of southwest Asia (Judaism, Zoroastrianism, Islam, and Christianity) are monotheistic, or believe in one God who is personal, worthy of adoration, and separate from the world but continuously active in it. In none of these scholarly studies is the question posed: Is there a true religion that has been established directly by a real, existing, supreme being?

Religious Myopia

Each religion delineates its position and its parameters. Here are some possibilities:

- **Agnostic/atheistic.** "All religions are the outcome of superstition, bigotry, heredity, or ignorance. I propose to define religion as 'A sum of scruples which impede the free exercise of our faculties.'"[4]

- **Christian myopia.** "The Christian religion is altogether good. The false systems cannot be regarded as progressive steps toward the true. Christianity is the absolute religion; that is, it is wholly free from error."[5]
- **Biblical myopia**. "All the religions, save Christianity and the religion of Israel, belong to the natural stage. Biblical religion is the only purely moral religion."[6]
- **Religious egalitarian.*** All religions contain some good. "Each religion has its own mission in the world, is suited to the nations to whom it is given, and to the type of civilization it is to permeate."[7]
- **Religious elitist.** All religions contain some good, but unequally. "In studying Western civilization I have felt that there is something wanting. This something India has. If we want to avert all future wars, even the possibility of war, we must humbly sit on a prayer-rug, instead of always rushing about in motor-cars."[8]
- **Religious myopia**. The only true church is mine. "This is the usual point of view of a person who has studied neither the history of other religions nor the history of his own faith. This attitude is just as common among Hindus as among Christians."[9]

Unfortunately, there are also misinformed members of the LDS Church who likewise possess a sense of myopia. That is to say, many Church members label other religious faiths and beliefs as lying outside the handiwork of God. Here is a classic example. After Lehi experienced his tree of life vision, his son Nephi desired to know of its meaning. During his prayerful supplications, an angel appeared and gave to Nephi not only an expanded perspective of Lehi's vision but also included a view of many events in history. One of those events was the formation of a "great and abominable church." The angel then declared, "Behold there are save two churches only; the one is the church of the Lamb of God, and the other is the church of the devil; wherefore, whoso belongeth not to the church of the Lamb of God belongeth to that great church which is the mother of abominations; and she is the whore of all the earth" (1 Nephi 14:10).

In my classroom experience after reading this scripture, I usually ask the following questions: "What is the church of the Lamb of God?" What is the church of the devil?" In every occasion, the answer to the first question is, "The Church of Jesus Christ of Latter-day Saints." Most every time the answer to the second question is, "All other religions!" A more acceptable response is based on scripture, statements of the brethren, and some common logic.

First, I reject the idea that religion is totally a product of man, but I do give some credence to the observations by social scientists: there do exist recognizable similarities among religions rising up out of a common culture; religions seem to possess marks of human thought and intrigue; they do incorporate cultural bias and influence; they do develop from personal interpretation; and religious laws and mores do serve social and personal needs. From these observations, one might conclude that there really is no personal, absolute God who has revealed to any specific entity a "true religion" containing absolute truths.

Let's see how we can reconcile the idea, then, that religion really is a gift from God and that Mormonism really is God's gift to all mankind.

Religion: A Gift of God to Man

After Alma and the four sons of Mosiah successfully preached the gospel among the Lamanites, Alma stated a dynamic truth: "For behold, the Lord doth grant unto all nations, of their own nation and tongue, to teach his word, yea, in wisdom, all that he seeth fit that they should have: therefore we see that the Lord doth counsel in wisdom, according to that which is just and true" (Alma 29:8). This is one of the most doctrinally significant scriptures in all of the standard works. Let's break this verse down word for word and phrase for phrase.

For behold	A scriptural term that begs the attention of the reader; something important is coming.
the Lord	Not just any lord but the Lord.
doth	A scriptural way of referring to an act, or an action of.
grant	Permit as a right, privilege, or favor; to bestow or transfer.
unto all	Not just a few or many, but all.

nations	Historic entities of people of geographic, cultural, or ethnic identity.
of their own nation and tongue	God is cognizant of each nation, culture, and language and raises up individuals accordingly.
to teach	Instruct, convey, edify.
his	The antecedent of "his" is "the Lord."
word	Inspired instruction.
yea, in wisdom all that he seeth fit that they should have	Inspired instruction is measured out according to God's wisdom.

Down through the ages, the Lord has blessed every nation through sages, wise men, and prophets of the people. Each of these nations was given essential truths which would bless and uplift its people. On February 15, 1978, the First Presidency—consisting of Spencer W. Kimball, N. Eldon Tanner, and Marion G. Romney—issued the following statement: "The great religious leaders of the world such as Mohammed, Confucius, and the Reformers, as well as philosophers including Socrates, Plato, and others, received a portion of God's light. Moral truths were given to them by God to enlighten whole nations and to bring a higher level of understanding to individuals."[10]

Latter-day Saints can allow the Analects of Confucius, the Koran of Mohammed, and scriptures of other lands such as the Tripitaka, Granth, Tao Te Ching, and the Zend-Avesta as evidence of God's commanding "all men in the east and in the west, and in the north, and in the south. . . . I shall also speak unto all nations of the earth and they shall write it" (2 Nephi 29:11–12). Elder Carlos E. Asay supports this idea in yet another way:

> How very fortunate for mankind that God's word was given in diverse ways to the people of India, of Persia, of Babylon, of Arabia, of China, of Greece, of Rome, and of America. Each spark of inspiration, each revealed law, and each guideline for living was an expression of

> God's limitless love for the family of Adam. It mattered not whether the word came in high or low places. . . . What mattered was that saving truth was received by man from God.[11]

Remember the words of Moroni:

> Wherefore, all things which are good cometh of God. . . .
>
> But, behold, that which is of God inviteth and enticeth to do good continually, wherefore, every thing which inviteth and enticeth to do good, and to love God, and to serve him, is inspired of God.
>
> Wherefore, take heed, my beloved brethren, that ye do not judge that which is evil to be of God, or that which is good and of God to be of the devil (Moroni 7:12–14).

One of my cherished possessions is a Bible that my oldest daughter found in a used book store and presented to me as a Christmas gift. It is a World Bible. Within its pages are selections from the sacred canon of all eleven major world religions. There is much inspired writing within these pages. The Lord, however, has placed caveats on sacred and secular literature of the world. This "reader beware" caveat is best explained in Doctrine and Covenants 91. Joseph had been working on a revision of the Bible to clarify those passages that had become corrupt or to restore content that had been lost. He and his scribe wondered what to do with the Apocrypha,* that collection of Catholic canon which was part of the King James Bible Joseph had purchased from E. B. Grandin, the printer who published the first edition of the Book of Mormon. Section 91 is the revealed answer of Joseph's query to the Lord.

> Verily, thus saith the Lord unto you concerning the Apocrypha—There are many things contained therein that are true, and it is mostly translated correctly; there are many things contained therein that are not true, which are the interpolations of men. . . . Therefore, whoso readeth it, let him understand, for the Spirit manifesteth truth; and whoso is enlightened by the Spirit shall obtain benefit therefrom; and whoso receiveth not by the Spirit, cannot be benefited (D&C 91:1–6).

For Latter-day Saints, the bull's eye of true and inspired writings are the four standard works of the Church: the Book of Mormon, the Doctrine and Covenants, the Pearl of Great Price, and the Holy Bible (as far as the Bible is translated correctly; see Articles of Faith 1:8). On most dart boards, there is a red spot in the very middle of the bull's eye that possesses the highest point value. For Mormons, in that centered position are the teachings, proclamations, and officials writings of our prophets, seers, and revelators. One of the purposes for these men is not only to establish truth but also to guarantee the perpetuation of the same. Unfortunately, the collection of the world's sacred writings and great literature has not had that vouchsafed oversight. President Ezra Taft Benson always reverenced those who before him held the high and holy calling of prophet, seer, and revelator. Of them he said:

> The most important prophet, so far as we are concerned, is the one who is living in our day and age. This is the prophet who has today's instructions from God to us today. God's revelation to Adam did not instruct Noah how to build the ark. Every generation has need of the ancient scripture plus the current scripture from the living prophet. Therefore, the most crucial reading and pondering which you should do is of the latest inspired words from the Lord's mouthpiece.[12]

God, then, has granted the gift of religion within each culture and seeded religions with truths (though not a fulness) that would bless and uplift their lives. The opportunity of each individual to be blessed with a fulness of gospel principles will be provided in the spirit world if not on earth.

Mormonism: God's Gift to All Mankind

Now we need to address the question of "What is the Church of God?" Two years before the official organization of the Church of Jesus Christ of Latter-day Saints, the revelation now known as section 10 of the Doctrine and Covenants was received through Joseph Smith. The Lord said,

> And for this cause have I said: If this generation harden not their hearts, I will establish *my church* among them.
>
> Now I do not say this to destroy *my church,* but I say this to build up *my church*;
>
> Therefore, whosoever belongeth to *my church* need not fear, for such shall inherit the kingdom of heaven.
>
> But it is they who do not fear me, neither keep my commandments but build up churches unto themselves to get gain, yea, and all those that do wickedly and build up the kingdom of the devil— yea, it is they that I will disturb, and cause to tremble and shake to the center. . .
>
> Yea, and I will also bring to light my gospel which was ministered

> unto them, and behold, they shall not deny that which you have received, but they shall build it up, and shall bring to light the true points of doctrine, yea, and the only doctrine which is in me.
>
> And this I do that I may establish my gospel. (D&C 10:53–56, 62–63; emphasis added)

Notice the Lord said that "I do not say this to destroy my church." This may be a veiled reference to a broader interpretation than is common in most Sunday School discussions. It seems the Lord acknowledged in this revelation the existence of a "church" even two years before Joseph was instructed to organize the true Church back on the earth, which purpose was to "bring to light the true points of doctrine." In this revelation, the Lord may be recognizing a cumulative effort which he called "my church" within Christianity of those who sought for and practiced historic Christian truth. He encouraged them to not "fear," for the goal of members of that church had always been to seek truth. Members of this "church" were counseled to "not deny that which you have received." At this time Joseph had already been visited by the Father and the Son in the Sacred Grove and restored precious truths about the nature and character of the Godhead. The contents of the Book of Mormon were then being translated, which would help "establish my gospel." In addition, the Lord referenced other religionists who were not members of his "church" but were imposters attempting to build up churches unto themselves to get gain. It was these churches and their members that would shake and tremble and fight against true religion from God. These are they who had developed the creeds which "were an abomination in [God's] sight; [and] that those professors were all corrupt; that: 'they draw near to me with their lips, but their hearts are far from me, they teach for doctrine the commandments of men, having a form of godliness, but they deny the power thereof'" (Joseph Smith— History 1:19).

The Lord also proclaimed an interesting promise, "Whosoever belongeth to my Church need not fear, for such shall inherit the kingdom of heaven." Doctrine and Covenants 76 provides a wonderful paradigm to further our explanation of those who will inhabit the "kingdom of heaven." This section is known as "the Vision."

Three Degrees of Glory and Universal Salvation

Many have called the revelation contained in Doctrine and Covenants 76 the greatest vision ever given to man. Actually, it was received by both Joseph Smith and Sidney Rigdon simultaneously in February of

1832. In this vision we are given greater information concerning the three heavens Paul refers to in his letter to the Corinthians. In heaven, there are three degrees of glory: the celestial, the terrestrial, and the telestial. To simplify the depth and breadth of scriptural terminology used to describe these kingdoms, let me explain them this way.

Celestial Kingdom

The celestial kingdom is the abode of those who have made and kept sacred covenants. This is the abode for those who will be exalted, glorified, and who will eventually become gods and goddesses. In this kingdom, "all that the Father hath will be given unto [them]" (D&C 84:38). This is the reward for every human being from Adam and Eve down to the last children possessing this earth who are true and faithful to their covenants. These covenants emanate from priesthood power and keys. In every dispensation of time on this earth, prophets and patriarchs have held these priesthood keys. Associated with priesthood keys and covenant making has been the knowledge of the gospel of Jesus Christ which has been taught by these holy men called of God through revelation. The Father reigns supreme in this kingdom. Celestial inhabitants will enjoy the influence and presence of the full Godhead.

Terrestrial Kingdom

The terrestrial kingdom will be inhabited by those who are "honorable men [and women] of the earth, who were blinded by the craftiness of men" (D&C 76:75). These individuals led honorable lives on earth. They were moral, good neighbors, and faithful within the scope of truth they espoused, but for whatever reasons decided not to accept the covenants associated with celestial glory. The inhabitant of this kingdom were blessed with the light of Christ and promptings of the Holy Ghost to a lesser or greater extent. They will be judged according to the truth they received and lived. These inhabitants will receive the "presence of the Son, but not of the fulness of the Father" (D&C 76:77). The Savior provides jurisdiction in this kingdom and reigns over its inhabitants. The path of salvation to the terrestrial kingdom is a subject to be covered in greater detail in Chapter Nine.

Telestial Kingdom

The telestial kingdom is the lowest kingdom of glory. Keep in mind, these are kingdoms of glory and all are God's kingdoms and a heavenly reward. This kingdom, however, is reserved for "liars, and sorcerers, and adulterers, and whoremongers, and whosoever loves and makes a lie" (D&C 76:103). A year earlier in another revelation received by Joseph called "the law," the Lord condemned these same evil practices but expanded the list to include three additional types of sin: murder, stealing, and evil speaking (see D&C 42:18–27). These are they who "received not the gospel, neither the testimony of Jesus, neither the prophets, neither the everlasting covenant" (D&C 76:82). However, in due time, all these inhabitants will "bow the knee, and every tongue shall confess to him who sits upon the throne forever and ever" (D&C 76:110).

It seems that a significant difference between a telestial and a terrestrial candidate is how they view other people. Terrestrial people are good at heart, they basically desire to be good and to do good to others, but occasionally give in to temptation but still feel remorse of conscience. Telestial people, on the other hand, see others as objects that they can exploit. They are self-centered, greedy, and power seeking. They have given in to the lusts of the flesh. The Law of Justice will hold special grip on the sins of this group. They have rejected the Atonement in their lives, and by resisting the opportunity for repentance, they "must suffer even as I; . . . which suffering caused myself, even God, the greatest of all, to tremble because of pain, and to bleed at every pore, and to suffer both body and spirit" (D&C 19:17–18). These are they who will be "cast down to hell and suffer the wrath of Almighty God, until the fulness of times, when Christ shall have subdued all enemies under his feet, and shall have perfected his work; When he shall deliver up the kingdom, and present it unto the Father, spotless" (D&C 76:106–7).

Telestial candidates on earth, however, were blessed to a lesser or greater degree by the light of Christ, which is given "to every man who cometh into the world" (D&C 84:46). They will be judged according to the heed and diligence they gave to this venue of truth. The inhabitants of the telestial kingdom will be served by administering angels of the terrestrial realm sent by the Father as the inhabitants of the terrestrial realm are administered to by the celestial.

In this vision, the Lord teaches the grand doctrine of universal salvation (except for sons of perdition): "That through him all might be saved whom the Father had put into his power and made by him; Who glorifies the Father, and saves all the works of his hands, except those sons of perdition who deny the Son after the Father has revealed him. Wherefore he saves all except them" (D&C 76:42–44).

Either through repentance and partaking of the Atonement of Christ or through the process of self-atonement, the law of justice will be satisfied. All except sons of perdition will inherit a kingdom of glory. No other theology or philosophy offers such grand potential for all of God's children. The Lord added to Joseph's vision the final jewel to this most magnificent paradigm of all: "And thus we saw, in the heavenly vision, the glory of the telestial which surpasses all understanding" (D&C 76:89). If that is true of the lowest kingdom of glory, why not shoot for the grand prize?

The Dynamics of Sin

Throughout the scriptures the Lord reiterates His plea for all men and women to repent (see 1 Nephi 10:18; D&C 20:29; Acts 17:30; Moses 5:14). The command to repent is the most repeated command given by the Lord. As mentioned previously, some sins are classified as those which receive no forgiveness through the Atonement of Christ. Most, however, can be forgiven through the process of repentance and by partaking of the tender mercies of Christ and the great atoning act performed in our behalf by Christ during his Gethsemane experience. Let us now penetrate the dynamics of sin. Appendix E contains a simplified chart of these four domains of sin.

Forgivable Sins

Most sins fall within this category. The Law of Justice is reconciled for these acts of disobedience to divine law through the Atonement of Christ. Each individual must, however, participate in and complete the repentance process to access this redeeming grace and receive a forgiveness of sins. It is as if we provide a "down payment." The balance then, is paid in full by the Savior. Forgiveness is possible, but the extent of personal effort cannot be minimized. It requires full purpose of heart. Within this category of sin, rising to the top of seriousness are the sins of adultery, fornication, and other sexual perversions. Alma taught his son Corianton, who had left his missionary duties to seek satisfaction with a harlot, the seriousness of breaking the law of chastity. He taught, "Know ye not, my son, that these things are an abomination in the sight of the Lord: yea, *most* abominable above all sins save it be the shedding of innocent blood or denying the Holy Ghost?" (Alma 39:5; emphasis added). "These things" that Alma referred to specifically were adultery and fornication. The prophets down through the scriptural record have condemned all manner of sexual perversion, including same-sex relations, indulging in pornography, and other sexual deviancies. Unfortunately, even within Christianity there is no clear clarion position and firm resolution upholding a high standard of sexual fidelity. The continuum is wide ,with liberal, permissive Christianity allowing for "agreement" between partners, same-sex marriages, and even sexual deviancy among clergy. The more conservative denominations thankfully still hold to abstinence outside the bonds of marriage and holding in abeyance the passions of the flesh.

Modern Western civilization seems to have bought into a new morality (actually of old origins) of situational ethics, of verbal agreements without legal sanctions, and of relations between consenting adults. In the final analysis, it is still adultery and fornication. One of the great facets to the gem of the Restoration is the clear doctrine of chastity. Why is sexual perversion so serious in the sight of God and ranks next to murder and the unpardonable sin? Again, the answer ultimately reverberates back to our divine origins and our eternal potential. One of the divine powers inherent in our Heavenly Parents is the power of procreation. It is most sacred and essential to the perpetuation of the heavenly family. This power remains functional only with those who are exalted as gods and goddess. All other saved beings maintain their gender uniqueness but without functionality. Unfortunately, traditional Christianity has no doctrine supporting the concept of eternal families and the continuation of the power of procreation. In fact, traditional Christianity essentially strips saved beings from their gender characteristics and purports their existence in a genderless spirit state.

One of the "plain and precious" truths restored in this dispensation is that "the spirit and the body are the soul of man" (D&C 88:15). Elder Jeffrey R. Holland clarified this perspective:

> The body is an essential part of the soul. This distinctive and very important Latter-day Saint doctrine underscores why sexual sin is so serious. We declare that one who uses the God-given body of another without divine sanction abuses the very soul of that individual, abuses the central purpose and processes of life, "the very key" to life, as President Boyd K. Packer once called it. In exploiting his or her soul—one desecrates the Atonement of Christ, which saved that soul and which makes possible the gift of eternal life. And when one mocks the Son of Righteousness, one steps into a realm of heat hotter and holier than the

noonday sun. You cannot do so and not be burned.[13]

The ability of sexual reproduction is common to plant, animal, and human life. The motivating power of sexual procreation is characterized within the animal world as "seasonal." There are, however, many examples of animals and birds mating for life or establishing "family" units. Elder Boyd K. Packer, in his instruction to LDS youth, taught that human sexual urges are characterized as strong and more or less constant. He said that: "This power must be strong; for sometimes, except for the compelling persuasion of these feelings, men would be reluctant to accept the responsibilities of fatherhood. This power must be constant, too, because it is an important binding tie for family life."[14]

This is by divine design. Civilization's long and instructive lessons bear out the civility that needs to be associated with this aspect of the human domain. The historians, Will and Ariel Durrant have written:

> No man [or woman], however brilliant or well-informed, can . . . safely . . . dismiss . . . the wisdom of lessons learned in the laboratory of history. A youth boiling with hormones will wonder why he should not give full freedom to his sexual desires; but if he is unchecked by custom, morals, or laws, he may ruin his life before he . . . understands that sex is a river of fire that must be banked and cooled by a hundred restraints if it is not to consume in chaos both the individual and the group.[15]

It is ironic that in Western society there is great protection associated with the death process in contrast to the legal permissiveness associated with the process of producing new life. Fortunately, in the case of how life is terminated, most nations seem to be quite responsible. But in the significance of giving life, we sometimes find near-criminal irresponsibility.

The institution of marriage, the covenant relation between a man and a woman, provides the civil arrangement that can best govern the responsibilities that come with the primary product of sexual relations—children. In addition, sexual relations within a covenant relationship between husband and wife help produce the "oneness" encouraged by the Lord when He performed the first marriage in the Garden of Eden between Adam and Eve.

The marriage contract is sacred. The promises that underscore each marriage empower this relationship to endure through the troubled waters that naturally and inevitably arise in any intimate relationship. The long-term perspective introduced by an LDS temple marriage sets a marriage on a course "for time and all eternity." Within this conviction, and utilizing the power of the Atonement by each participant, every marriage can be successful. But when the enticements and motivations of the natural man are allowed a place within a marriage relationship, then the "oneness" ceases, and pride, vanity, selfishness, greed, and lust become the motivating powers. But such a total union within a spiritual paradigm, such an unyielding commitment between a man and a woman, can only come with the proximity and permanence afforded in a marriage covenant (especially a temple marriage covenant), with solemn promises and a solemn pledge of all they possess—their very hearts and minds in all their days.

Elder Holland characterized the mental conflict experienced when individuals violate the law of chastity and avoid God-ordained marital vows.

> Can you see the moral schizophrenia that comes from pretending you are one, pretending you have made solemn promises before God, sharing the physical symbols and the physical intimacy of your counterfeit union but then fleeing, retreating, severing all such other aspects of what was meant to be a total obligation? If you persist in pursuing physical satisfaction without the sanction of heaven, you run the terrible risk of such spiritual, psychic damage that you may undermine both your longing for physical intimacy and your ability to give wholehearted devotion to a later, truer love. You may come to that truer moment of ordained love, of real union, only to discover to your horror that what you should have saved you have spent, and that only God's grace can recover the piecemeal dissipation of the virtue you so casually gave away.[16]

The world needs a moral revolution away from permissiveness and back to our God who gave us life and the eternal plan, which allows us to participate in the miracle of creating life. Those who hold this power as sacred and protected by God's divine law will be empowered to carry this power into the eternities.

Pardonable Sins

Nephi taught that "the kingdom of God is not filthy, and there cannot any unclean thing enter into the kingdom of God" (1 Nephi 15:34). As stated earlier, each of the three kingdoms of God are kingdoms of glory: celestial, terrestrial, and telestial. All inhabitants of the Celestial kingdom take full advantage of the Atonement of Christ. The sinful behavior of the inhabitants of the other two kingdoms who reject the saving power of the Atonement will of necessity need to be pardoned through the process of self-atonement. They will be turned over to the buffetings of Satan in hell (D&C 104:10) until the uttermost farthing is paid (JST Matthew 5:27–28).

The Lord told Joseph Smith, "And, again, I say unto you, that whoso having knowledge, have I not commanded to repent?" (D&C 29:49). Innocent children and adults who are mentally challenged are without knowledge and are not considered accountable according to both civil law as well as divine law. The grasp that the Law of Justice has upon the inappropriate behavior of these individuals is pardoned through the tender mercies and loving arms of our Savior.

Unforgivable Sins

Generally, murder is consider the "unforgivable sin" in which forgiveness is not obtained in the world or out of the world. "Murder, the unlawful killing of a human being with malice, aforethought, or under such circumstances of criminality that the malice is presumed, 'is a sin unto death' " (1 John 5:16–17). Ofttimes in LDS discussions, murderers are automatically assigned a place in the telestial kingdom. A careful reading of the last chapter of 3 Nephi reveals a more merciful scenario. Moroni encourages all gentiles, meaning those who are outside the new and everlasting covenant of the gospel of Christ and who have never been taught or received gospel covenants, to "turn . . . from your wicked ways; and repent of your evil doings, . . . and come unto Christ" (3 Nephi 30:2). Included within his list of sins is that of being a murderer. He then recommends that all these individuals be baptized and receive the gift of the Holy Ghost. As such and by enduring to the end, the rewards associated with a covenant relationship through the gospel can be achieved. The damnation for murderers in the telestial kingdom seems to be associated with those who have once been enlightened by gospel truths and then reject its plan of salvation and willfully take the life of another person.

The unforgivable nature associated with second-offense adultery is tantamount* to the value placed not only upon chastity but upon the repentance process. Since adultery is considered to be "most abominable above all other sins (Alma 39:5), to return back to this behavior after having received full forgiveness through the blood of Jesus Christ is to make a mockery of Christ's suffering and His tender mercies. Joseph was taught this higher law by the Lord: "But he that has committed adultery and repents with all his heart, and forsaketh it, and doeth it no more, thou shall forgive; But if he doeth it again, he shall not be forgiven, but shall be cast out" (D&C 42:25, 26).

Unpardonable Sin

The clearest definition of blasphemy against the Holy Ghost was taught to Joseph Smith within the same revelation where he was introduced to the law of celestial marriage, including plural marriage. The Lord taught: "The blasphemy against the Holy Ghost, which shall not be forgiven in the world nor out of the world, is in that [1] ye commit murder wherein ye shed innocent blood, and [2] assent unto my death, [3] *after* ye have received my new and everlasting covenant, saith the Lord God" (D&C 132:27; emphasis and numbers added).

In the revelation known as "the Vision," Joseph received detailed information about the sons of perdition who commit blasphemy against the Holy Ghost and their eternal state of damnation. The Lord said of them:

> Having denied the Holy Spirit after having received it, and having denied the Only Begotten Son of the Father, having crucified him unto themselves and put him to an open shame.
>
> These are they who shall go away into the lake of fire and brimstone, with the devil and his angels—
>
> And the only ones on whom the second death shall have any power. Yea, verily, the only ones who shall not be redeemed in the due time of the Lord, after the sufferings of his wrath (D&C 76:35–38).

Because of the seriousness of this sin, neither Christ's Atonement nor self-atonement has the power to satisfy the demands of the Law of Justice. This is the fate of those members of the Church of the Firstborn (Christ's covenant Church down through the ages of time) who reject their eternal covenants and become anti-Christ, or those who fight against the Savior and desire to crucify him anew. They have been taught of the eternal plan of happiness. The Holy Ghost has burned the witness of the truth of the gospel and the veracity of the Father's plan into their very hearts and sinews. After this witness, they turn their allegiance against God and Christ and, in addition, willfully take human life. It seems clear that this knowledge and conviction is readily available to persons of both genders. However, the term for this state is called "sons of perdition."

The Multiple Modalities of Salvation

In many discussions between Mormons and those of other denominations, invariably the word salvation surfaces. The question, "Have you been saved?" is central to this query. If not careful, a tone of dissonance and tension may creep into even the most polite conversations. Roman Catholics, with their emphasis upon their sacraments, actually recognize the baptisms performed by most Christian denominations but have officially denounced baptisms performed by the LDS Church. This is due primarily to theological differences between their understanding of the Trinity and our concept of the Godhead. The Eastern Orthodox have historically proclaimed that they are the true custodians of Primitive Christianity and are "The One, Holy, Catholic, Apostolic Church" possessing the sure path of salvation. The protestant denominations of the Southern Baptists, the Jehovah's Witnesses, the Seventh-day Adventists, and the Lutheran Church–Missouri Synod are among those very conservative denominations who also claim a peculiar possession of true worship and a sure path to salvation.

In general, however, there are four approaches within Christianity dealing with the issue of salvation. One approach is that held by the Catholic family, which includes the Roman, Orthodox, and Anglican denominations and their subgroups. This family of denominations offers salvation through their church's administration of the seven sacraments. It is through five of these essential sacraments that the saving grace of Christ is extended to each member.

Another approach is held by those denominations coming out of the Reformation that are commonly called Protestant. Salvation is gained by confessing the name of Christ and believing in Him. They reject any intermediary church or saving sacrament or ordinance. Each person is his own priest. After a person confesses, he is saved—and once saved, always saved. As a sign of this saved condition, he will perform the acts of righteousness of a saved Christian. One cannot earn his way to salvation, for it is a gift from God. Some Protestants stress the need to follow Christ's example and be baptized; others are not as adamant. They participate in weekly or monthly sacramental services, which are generally viewed as memorial services—but incorporate no doctrine supporting a renewal of prior covenants.

A third approach is held by the more liberal denominations of Christianity. They are more humanistic in their theology. Each person has the spark of the divine within. Christ was a man whom God sent to represent the best of what humanity can achieve. However, Christ was a man who died on the cross and is still dead. Their emphasis is on living a good, moral, and socially productive life. The issue of salvation is more an issue of getting heaven into our hearts than for us to return to some hypothetical heaven.

The Mormon Doctrine of Salvation

The fourth and final approach is the Mormon doctrine of salvation. In Romans 10:9–10, the words "saved" and "salvation" signify a covenant relationship with Jesus Christ. Through this covenant relationship, we are assured salvation from the eternal consequences of sin if we are obedient. Every faithful Latter-day Saint is saved according to this meaning. Each member of the Church has accepted the restored gospel of Jesus Christ and has entered into a covenant relationship with the Son through the ordinance of baptism. By this covenant we take upon ourselves the name of Jesus Christ and accept him as our personal Savior. This covenant is renewed each time we partake of the sacrament.

There are other implications of the word saved that are important to understand. According to these, our answer to the question "Have you been saved?" will be either "yes" or "no." The following explanations outline six different meanings of the word salvation.[5]

Salvation from Physical Death

All people die. No one escapes from this ultimate fate of mortality. But through the Atonement and Resurrection of Jesus Christ, all human beings will be resurrected— saved from physical death.

Salvation from Sin

Sin is a consequence of wrongly exercising our agency by breaking the commandments of God. This condition comes from setting aside our divine self-concept and giving in to our natural-man instincts. We are cleansed from sin when we (1) have faith in Christ and accept him as our Savior; (2) experience the ordinance of baptism by immersion for the remission of sins and receive the gift of the Holy Ghost. Through this process, we have been conditionally saved from sin. We cannot be saved in our sins, but from our sins. As we progress in this life, we may fall back into a sinful state. As we continue to participate in the process of repentance, we reconcile our estrangement from God and return to this saved condition. Sin alienates us from God. The Atonement provides the process to be "at one" with God again. A key concept in this definition of salvation is the principle of "enduring to the end."

Being Born Again

The principle of spiritual rebirth appears frequently in the scriptures (see John 3:5, Mosiah 27:25–26, Alma 5:14). This rebirth is a process that occurs after we have been baptized and have received the gift of the Holy Ghost. It comes as a result of our willingness "to enter into a covenant with our God to do his will, and to be obedient to his commandments in all things that he shall command us, all the remainder of our days" (Mosiah 5:5).

Through this spiritual "rebirth" our hearts are changed. King Benjamin taught that we begin to take upon us the countenance of our Savior. Our disposition changes, we become peacemakers, our hearts are purified. We desire no more to rebel against our God. We lose the chains of pride that bind us to our sense of independence and rebellion. True repentance involves a "change of heart." Within the scriptures, every reference to God's forgiveness is always a forgiveness of *sins*, not *sin*. God is not concerned about a list of sins that we singularly check off, but the condition of our heart. When we truly repent, our heart is reconciled back to God and our "sins" are forgiven. In this condition, we return not again to those former behaviors.

The concept of repentance was one of the first principles within the apostasy to become corrupted. The etymology* of the word "repent" has Hebrew, Greek, and Latin origins. The Hebrew word for "repent" is *shuwb* (shoob), a verb meaning to return, go back, turn toward, or turn back (from evil). The Greek form is *metanoeo* (met-an-o-eh'-o), a verb meaning to change one's mind, to change one's mind for better, or heartily to amend with abhorrence of one's past sins. It was the Latin definition that turned the course of action against the true application of this gospel principle. The Latin verb *re-poenitere* introduced the ideas of self-reproach, being conscience-stricken, being penitent, and punishment. The Latin form became standard when the St. Jerome's Latin Vulgate Bible became the official Bible of the Roman Church during the beginning of the fifth century.

The Hebrew and Greek words referring to repentance involve the concept of turning from transgression and turning back to our loving Father in Heaven. It implies a desire to leave unhappiness, sorrow, regret, and despair behind and turn back to our Father's family. There we can find happiness, joy, and acceptance among his children. The Latin word, unfortunately, changed the meaning to imply hurt, punishment, whipping, cutting, mutilation, disfigurement, starvation, or even torture. The word "penance" is the common nomenclature used in the Catholic Church. Historically, Protestants substituted the word repentance for the word penance. The word "repentance" was actually an invention of William Tyndale, who was the first to translate the Bible into the English language using Greek and Hebrew texts. He recognized that the words from these ancient tongues meant more of a "change of heart" than of receiving punishment.

The steps of penance in the Latin Church before the thirteenth century, when the institution of penance was not a sacrament, included:

1. Contrition of the heart.
2. Aricular* (verbal) confession to the priest wherein all sins known must be confessed
3. Satisfaction or penance becomes the outward manifestation of sorrow and the necessary precedent to the forgiveness of sins. Penance is satisfied through the performance of outward works as prescribed by the Church (alms, fasts, prayers, pilgrimages, and so on).
4. Absolution (forgiveness of sins) and the release from punishment pronounced by the priest in the name of God. During the seventh century, satisfaction of penance by substituting pecuniary* compensation (money) began with the origin of indulgences. The practice of indulgences rested on the theory that Christ, Mary, and the saints had performed more good works than were needed for their own salvation. These surplus merits (contained in the "treasury of merit") were at the disposal of the pope and could be given or sold to sin-laden people. It is officially called the doctrine of supererogation.
5. All arrears* (unpaid or overdue debt) of temporal punishment are inflicted in purgatory, a place of punishment before the

> resurrection. Souls in purgatory can be delivered through masses, candle burning, intercessions, alms, and good works.

After the thirteenth century, when the institution of penance became a sacrament in the Latin Church, the order of events changed. This is the order now practiced within the Catholic Church.

1. Contrition of the heart.
2. Aricular confession to the priest wherein all sins known must be confessed.
3. Absolution. God forgives the guilt of the sins confessed and the eternal punishment. But the sinner needs to bear temporal punishment either in this life or in purgatory. The priest has the power to "remit" or forgive the penitent of their confessed sins. (Their scriptural support for this priestly power is found in John 20:23.)
4. Remittance of temporal punishment through a display of good works (indulgences). The heavenly reward cannot be received until the punishments of sin have been endured or payment made.

The practical value of indulgences consisted in the remission of penalties that were due after a person had received the absolution. At the time of Martin Luther, the popular idea prevailed that indulgences procured the forgiveness of sins as well as the remission of penalties. Sale of indulgences tended, therefore, to lead the people away from true repentance. These Catholic procedures and concepts document how far the simple truth had strayed. Unfortunately, punishment and penance have an unholy union in the Catholic tradition. Our struggle to repent may cost us agony of mind and spirit, but our commitment to our Heavenly Father to do his will, will make repentance possible and bearable. In our repentance, we should remember that the Lord does not punish us for our sins; he simply withholds blessings. We punish ourselves.

Salvation from Ignorance

John 8:31–32 states, "If ye continue in my word, then are ye my disciples indeed; and ye shall know the truth and the truth shall make you free." Many people live in a state of darkness, not knowing the light of the restored gospel. As one embraces the Restoration, one is brought back into the light of truth and saved from this condition.

Saved from the Second Death

There is mention within the scriptures of a "second death." This death is a spiritual death in which the individuals dwell in a final state of outer darkness. This second death will not occur until the Final Judgment and will come to very few (see D&C 76:31–37).

Eternal Life or Exaltation

This is the saved condition of those who have not only repented of their sins, been baptized by proper authority, and received the confirmation of the Holy Ghost, but have also made and kept sacred covenants, including eternal marriage, which is the crowning ordinance of the endowment process received within LDS temples. These are they who dwell with the Father and the Son forever and who will have kingdoms of their own as they gain the status of gods and goddesses. These are they who belong to the Church of the Firstborn.

1. Ludwig, *The Sacred Paths: Understanding the Religions of the World*, part 1.
2. Ibid.
3. Emerson, *A Guide to Understanding the Bible*, 17.
4. Reinache, *Orpheus: A General History of Religions*, 3.
5. Burrell, *Religions of the World*, 4.
6. *Non-Biblical Systems of Religion: A Symposium*, 199–200.
7. Besant, *Four Great Religions*, 7.
8. Maitra, *Hinduism, the World Ideal*, vii–viii.
9. Hume, *The World's Living Religions*, 11.
10. Palmer, *The Expanding Church*, v.
11. As quoted in *Mormons and Muslims*, Spencer J. Palmer, ed., 208.
12. Burton, *We Believe: Prophets, Seers, and Revelators*, 602.
13. Jeffrey R. Holland, "Personal Purity," *Enisgn*, Nov. 1998, 75.
14. Boyd K. Packer, "Why Stay Morally Clean," *New Era*, July 1972, 5
15. Durrant, *The Lessons of History*, 35–36.
16. Jeffrey R. Holland, "Personal Purity," *Enisgn*, Nov. 1998, 75.

CHAPTER EIGHT

Doctrinal Dilemmas within Traditional Christianity

If you board the wrong train, it is no use running along the corridor in the other direction. – Dietrich Bonhoeffer

That I am not a member of any Christian Church, is true; but I have never denied the truth of the Scriptures; and I have never spoken with intentional disrespect of religion in general, or of any denomination of Christians in particular. – Abraham Lincoln

Who does not see that the same authority which can establish Christianity, in exclusion of all other religions, may establish with the same ease any particular sect of Christians, in exclusion of all other sects? – James Madison

I have been asked which religion I would choose if I were not LDS. Though there is much to be valued within traditional Christianity—the Christmas spirit, expressions of charity and service, inspiring music, literature, and architecture—it has a dark downside with doctrinal dilemmas and contradictions, sexual abuse, clerical immorality, unforgiving persecution, dishonorable history, self-serving and power-seeking clergy, and lastly, religious intolerance. It is ironic that for the first three centuries in which the fledgling primitive Christian Church existed, it most desired the freedom to exercise, without restraint, its newfound faith. Then, after Constantine legitimized Christianity and

Theodosius made it the religion of the empire, that very freedom was withheld and the Church fought from that moment to exercise control over the religious mind of its citizens. This pattern was replicated in New England by the Puritans, in France through the Inquisition, and even in Germany and other high-country nations that adopted Lutheranism. But, alas, it may be in two doctrinal contradictions that I have the most trouble with traditional Christianity.

Salvation of Little Children

Salvation is the ultimate goal in Christianity. A saved condition offers eternal happiness, a beatific vision, and communion within God's presence. Unfortunately, there is little agreement on how that is to be accomplished. There are, however, two major camps. The Catholic camp offers saving grace through the sacraments of the Church and even through the acquisition of historic relics. This very fact held many a king hostage by the pope throughout the Middle Ages. In historic Catholic doctrine, however, there has been no salvation available for children who through no fault of their own died before the initial sacrament of baptism could be administered. Though the "unofficial" doctrine of limbo relegates children to a place that is neither heaven nor hell, this damning doctrine to me is irreconcilable.

In the fifth century, St. Augustine concluded that infants who die without baptism were consigned to hell. By the thirteenth century, theologians referred to the "limbo of infants" as a place where unbaptized babies were deprived of the vision of God, but did not suffer because they did not know what they were deprived of. Up until 2006, the Catechism of the Catholic Church stated simply that unbaptized infants are intrusted to God's mercy. In 2004, a commission headed by Cardinal Joseph Ratzinger (now Pope Benedict XVI) began studying the question of limbo in a systematic way. In a document published April 20, 2007, the commission stated that the traditional concept of limbo—as a place where unbaptized infants spend eternity but without communion with God—seemed to reflect an "unduly restrictive view of salvation."[1] This commission used phrases like "there is greater theological awareness today," "our conclusion is," and "we emphasize that these are reasons for prayerful hope, rather than grounds for sure knowledge." These phrases seem to contradict the process of original New Testament Christianity, which resolved doctrinal dilemmas through prophetic and apostolic declaration. The problem for the Catholic Church (in addition to the lack of prophetic direction) stems from its stand on original sin. Stated simply, Adam's sin (original sin) passes upon all who are born into mortality. As such there is need for the redeeming grace of Christ to remove original sin. The removal of original sin is performed through the sacrament of baptism. For such an important theological question as the salvation of unbaptized children, it seems self-condemning as an institution which proclaims to possess the true path of salvation to declare "it must be clearly acknowledged that the church does not have sure knowledge about the salvation of unbaptized infants who die." This commission concluded that there is "serious theologic grounds for hope that unbaptized infants who die will be saved and enjoy the beatific vision." It further stated that depriving innocent babies from heaven "does not seem to reflect Christ's special love for 'the little ones.'" So, if there is no limbo for unbaptized children, what happens to them? It is my recommendation that the Catholic Church read JST Matthew 18:11, which teaches this saving doctrine: "For the Son of man is come to save that which was lost *and to call sinners to repentance; but these little ones have no need of repentance, and I will save them*" (italics represents JST addition). That, my Catholic friends, is prophetic revelation.

Protestants hold no "official" hope for children (used here as an inclusive term for those individuals who possess a childlike mind, children who die before the age of accountability, and stillborn infants) who die and who haven't been saved. Though they aren't as condemning, their position is that God will somehow extend his mercy and issue salvation based solely on His grace, through the sacrificial Atonement of Christ. The age at which a child becomes accountable and needs to act on their own initiative to accept Christ is not standardized within Protestantism.

Protestants in general believe in salvation by faith only and would not accept baptism as necessary for salvation. Yet many of them will baptize their babies. Instead of baptizing the baby for the remission of sins, as the Catholics do, Protestants baptize babies as a promise that the parents will raise the child in a godly home and bring the child to church services. Infant baptism (also known as christening) is viewed as a sign or a pledge made by the parents to the child. Protestants who do baptize infants attempt to reconcile this practice with their interpretation of the term household as found in various New Testament scriptures (see Acts 11:14; 16:15, 33; 18:8; 1 Corinthians 1:16). Those who advocate infant baptism "assume" the word household as used in these scriptures includes babies (see 2 Peter 1:20–21 concerning private interpretation).

Many people—Catholic, Protestant, and Orthodox—have been baptized as infants. Protestant churches that practice infant baptism include most Lutheran, Presbyterian, Methodist, Episcopalian, Anglican, and Reformed churches. Protestant churches that only baptize adults or children who have repented include Baptist, Pentecostal, Nazarene, Charismatic, Wesleyan, Church of God, Assembly of God, and Adventist.

Historic positioning for Protestant interpretation goes back to their major Protestant icons. At the time of the Reformation, John Calvin (1509–1564) rejected the doctrine of limbo. He based his beliefs on the principle of predestination. He believed that God decides in advance which individuals will be eternally saved and which will be eternally lost. This would be true not only for adults but also for infants and children who had died before reaching the age of accountability. Some would go to be eternally tortured in hell while others would go to heaven.

Ulrich Zwingli (1484–1531) disagreed. He was opposed to the concept of the "necessity of baptism for infant salvation." With unusual generosity, he taught that "all elect children who die in infancy are saved whether they are baptized or not, whether pagan or Christian."[2]

The Westminster Confession[3] states "Elect infants, dying in infancy, are regenerated and saved by Christ." This seems to imply that there are elect infants who go to heaven and unelect who go to hell. The Presbyterian Church in the U.S. cleared up this confusion among its members by issuing a Declaratory Statement in 1903 that stated, in part, "We believe that all dying in infancy are included in the election of grace, and are regenerated and saved by Christ through the Spirit, who works when and where and how he pleases." Other Protestant leaders agree with the Presbyterian position:

> Presbyterian Charles Hodge, 19th century preacher: "The common doctrine of evangelical Protestants is . . . all who die in infancy are saved."
>
> Presbyterian Lewis Chafer: "It may be definitely asserted . . . that infants who die before accountability begins are saved."
>
> Baptist William L. Pettingill: "I am convinced that unaccountable children are saved by the blood of Christ."
>
> Brethrenite Harry Ironside: "Little ones who die go to be with Christ."

> Independent M. R. DeHaan: "Little children who die in infancy are [never] lost."

What does Mormonism offer to resolve this dilemma? Moroni teaches this glorious doctrine:

> Listen to the words of Christ, your Redeemer, your Lord and your God. Behold, I came into the world not to call the righteous but sinners to repentance; the whole need no physician, but they that are sick: wherefore, little children are whole, for they are not capable of committing sin; wherefore the curse of Adam is taken from them in me, that it hath no power over them. . . .
>
> I know that it is solemn mockery before God, that ye should baptize little children.
>
> Behold I say unto you that this thing shall ye teach—repentance and baptism unto those who are accountable and capable of committing sin; yea teach parents that they must repent and be baptized, and humble themselves as their little children, and they shall all be saved with their little children.
>
> And their little children need no repentance, neither baptism . . . .
>
> But little children are alive in Christ, even from the foundation of the world; if not so, God is a partial God, and also a changeable God, and a respecter to persons; for how many little children have died without baptism!
>
> Wherefore, if little children could not be saved without baptism, these must have gone to an endless hell.
>
> Behold I say unto you, he that supposeth that little children need baptism is in the gall of bitterness and in the bonds of iniquity; for he hath neither faith, hope, nor charity; wherefore, should he be cut off while in the thought, he must go down to hell.
>
> For awful is the wickedness to suppose that God saveth one child because of baptism, and the other must perish because he hath no baptism.
>
> Wo be unto them that shall pervert the ways of the Lord after this manner, for they shall perish except they repent (Moroni 8:8–16).

Salvation for Those Ignorant or without Opportunity

The second contradiction is a close cousin. In South and Central America, when the Spanish brought their supposed true religion to the "heathen" natives, the priests labored to convert the chiefs, assuming the rest of their people would follow. It was reported that one chief had the following conversation with a priest:

> "You tell me that if I, my family, and my people get baptized, we will be saved in heaven. Is this true?" The priest answered in the affirmative. "And heaven is the happiest and most peaceful place to go after we die?" The priest answered in the affirmative. "Then I want my forefathers who have already died to go also to this happy and peaceful place!" The priest asked if they had been baptized into the Catholic religion. "No!" the chief answered. "Then they will go into hell for all eternity," was the priest's reply. The chief pondered this answer briefly, then said, "Then to hell I will go also in order to be with my forefathers."

In principle, the historic use of indulgences for Catholics provided some relief in purgatory for the penalties associated with sin. "The faithful on earth, through the communion of saints, can relieve suffering of the souls in purgatory by prayer, fasting, and other good works, by indulgences, and by having Masses offered for them."[2] Indulgences could be earned through the saying of prayers, reading of scripture, reciting the rosary, and through the contribution of money (which was discontinued after the Council of Trent in 1567). It is possible in Roman Catholic theology to acquire indulgences on behalf of deceased individuals currently residing in purgatory. Purgatory is a place, in Catholic doctrine, where one absolves oneself from the temporal punishments associated with sins of mortality. It is a place of cleansing prior to one's eventual abode in heaven.

Protestants offer no doctrine related to work or salvation for the dead. What about the millions who existed in countries and cultures outside the Protestant definition of Christianity? What about the ages upon ages when and where the traditional Christian religion did not exist? Formal orthodoxy in Protestantism has no solution but the consignment of hell. However, personal interpretations of Protestants (often called "folk" religion) can't reconcile an all-loving God with the execution of such drastic injustice.

Again, the principles and doctrines of the restored gospel come to the rescue and provide an opportunity for the redemption of all, for the salvation of most, and for the exaltation of some. Joseph F. Smith, sixth President of the Church, was pondering over concepts taught by Peter concerning the dead being taught in the world of spirits (see 1 Peter 3–4). President Smith received a grand vision that helped clarify these original New Testament doctrines:

> As I pondered over these things which are written, the eyes of my understanding were opened, and the Spirit of the Lord rested upon me, and I saw the hosts of the dead, both small and great. . . .
>
> While this vast multitude waited and conversed, rejoicing in the hour of their deliverance from the chains of death, the Son of God appeared, declaring liberty to the captives who had been faithful.
>
> And there he preached to them the everlasting gospel, the doctrine of the resurrection and the redemption of mankind from the fall, and from individual sins on conditions of repentance.
>
> But unto the wicked he did not go, and among the ungodly and the unrepentant who had defiled themselves while in the flesh, his voice was not raised. . . .
>
> But behold, from among the righteous, he organized his forces and appointed messengers, clothed with power and authority, and commissioned them to go forth and carry the light of the gospel to them that were in darkness, even to all the spirits of men; and thus was the gospel preached to the dead (D&C 138:11, 18, 19, 30).

What a beautiful doctrine of mercy and of fairness. But one of the requirements after accepting the gospel message is the earthly ordinance of baptism (see Matthew 3:16, Mark 1:4; 16:16; John 3:5; 2 Nephi 31:5–10). Christ displayed his own obedience to this ordinance by submitting himself to the authority of John the Baptist and by being immersed in the waters of the Jordan river. Throughout the ministry of the early apostles, baptism followed investigators who converted to the Christian message (Acts 2:38; 10:48; 22:16). As the community of Christian believers expanded and the institutional church matured, it faced an additional dilemma. The death of friends or family members preempted opportunities for conversion and for baptism. One of the saving doctrines taught and practiced by the early church membership was baptism for the dead. Paul hints of this in his letter to the Corinthians (1 Corinthians 15:29).

Not surprisingly, the Christian world debates this passage and arrives at no common consensus. The Catholic tradition of baptism of desire evolved over time in an attempt to provide a solution to the dilemma of believers as well as nonbelievers who failed to receive this sacrament prior to their death.

> If they live up to the light that has been shown to them and would have embraced Christ and the gospel had they known about them, then they can be saved. Neither is their lack of baptism an obstacle. Scripture reveals that sometimes the graces that normally come through

> baptism are given early, to those who have not yet been baptized. Such people have what the Church terms "baptism of desire" and are united to God through their desire to do what he wants of them.
>
> In the case of those who have not yet heard the gospel or learned of God, but who nevertheless seek to follow the truth as they understand it, they have an implicit desire for God since they desire to follow the truth. They simply do not know that God is the truth. Consequently, they also can be saved through baptism of desire; therefore, a proxy baptism is superfluous, either before their death or after it. They are already united to God, even if they are not fully aware of it in this life.[4]

This may bear the appearance of a merciful doctrine but it violates the New Testament command: "Except a man be born of water and of the Spirit, he cannot enter into the kingdom of God" (John 3:5). Also, "He that believeth and is baptized shall be saved" (Mark 16:16). Finally, "baptism doth also now save us" (1 Peter 3:21). Joseph Smith shocked the Christian world with this revealed insight:

> It is sufficient to know, in this case, that the earth will be smitten with a curse unless there is a welding link of some kind or other between the fathers and the children, upon some subject or other—and behold what is that subject? It is baptism for the dead. For we without them cannot be made perfect; neither can they without us be made perfect. Neither can they nor we be made perfect without those who have died in the gospel also; for it is necessary in the ushering in of the dispensation of the fulness of times, which dispensation is now beginning to usher in, that a whole and complete and perfect union, and welding together of dispensations, and keys, and powers, and glories should take place, and be revealed from the days of Adam even to the present time. And not only this, but those things which never have been revealed from the foundation of the world, but have been kept hid from the wise and prudent, shall be revealed . . . in this, the dispensation of the fulness of times. (D&C 128:18)

Joseph further clarified:

> The ordinance of baptism by water, to be immersed therein in order to answer to the likeness of the dead, that one principle might accord with the other; to be immersed in the water and come forth out of the water is in the likeness of the resurrection of the dead in coming

> forth out of their graves; hence, this ordinance was instituted to form a relationship with the ordinance of baptism for the dead, being in likeness of the dead.
>
> Consequently, the baptismal font was instituted as a similitude of the grave, and was commanded to be in a place underneath where the living are wont to assemble, to show forth the living and the dead, and that all things may have their likeness, and that they may accord one with another—that which is earthly conforming to that which is heavenly (D&C 128:12–13).

Latter-day Saint temples are now beginning to "dot the earth" as has been prophesied.[5] They are not only architectural marvels built with superior craftsmanship and beauty but are also houses of worship, of service and covenant-making. Members of the Church feel an extended sense of familial relationship to all who are beyond the grave and who had never received the ordinance of baptism while in mortality. Hours and hours of personal time are sacrificed in order to provide the proxy for the names of all those of our Heavenly Father's family awaiting these blessings in the spirit world. The Church is the leading force in the world to gather and compile the genealogy of the human family. It is an orderly process utilizing the best of modern technologies. The doctrine of performing "work for the dead" does not take away or diminish the agency of those who exist in the spirit world. This doctrine only provides the blessing and opportunity of progression for those who have been taught in the spirit world and who accept the gospel of Jesus Christ. Again, is there anything comparable in the world of religion that offers a design of such love, mercy, service, and opportunity? I think not. I know there is not.

1. Thavis *Catholic News Service*, April 20, 2007
2. http://religioustolerance.org/limbo3.htm
3. Quoted in Peterson and Ricks, "Baptism for the Dead, Secrecy." *Offenders for a Word.*
4. See *Catechism of the Catholic Church*, 847–48, 1257–60.
5. See Richard O. Cowan's, *Temples to Dot the Earth.*

CHAPTER NINE

True Christianity

I believe in Christianity as I believe that the Sun has risen, not only because I see it, but because by it I see everything else. – C.S. Lewis

Earlier, I dismissed somewhat the legitimacy of Christianity. Now let me raise true Christianity back upon the doctrinal pedestal to which it belongs, having no equal. Let's place each of the eleven living world religions side by side and attempt to evaluate them with some objectivity. We will look at humanism independently.

World Religions: Side by Side

The eleven religions that I list as world religions are Judaism, Christianity, Islam, Buddhism, Sikhism, Jainism, Hinduism, Taoism, Confucianism, and Zoroastrianism. Within these religions, we find many categorical similarities. The following is a simplified list of commonalities they all share:

1. God(s), deities, divine beings or saviors, supreme reality, a world spirit.
2. Founders,[1] leaders, prophets, gurus.
3. Sacred writings, scriptures.
4. A definition of pre-earthly (Christianity excepted) and post-earthly existence.
5. Clergy, priests, monks, rabbis, holy men and women.
6. Doctrines, principles, commandments, ethics, morals.

7. Devotions, ceremonies, ordinances, vows.
8. Social structure, hierarchical organization.
9. A path of salvation, dharma,* Tao.
10. Ultimate rest and peace, heaven, nirvana, Brahman.
11. Code of accountability, karma,* law of harvest, cause and effect.

Humanism

The "religion" of humanism places an honorific status upon the dignity of the human position in which there is no hierarchical supreme entity other than the natural forces in the physical world. The philosophy of humanism rejects the supernatural and stresses an individual's dignity, worth, and capacity for self-realization through reason. The upside of humanism is a commitment of personal responsibility to help resolve social problems and contribute to society and ultimately to all of humanity. The downside is the lack of divine absolutes and the reliance on situational ethics. As such, humanists offer no insight into the theologic questions of "Who was I?" "Where did I come from?" "What can I become, ultimately?" and, "Where am I going?" The purpose of life for some is to experience pleasure. Those with more noble aspirations desire to participate in life in such a way as to make it better within the parameters of their moral and ethical construct. Their test of truth is pragmatism.* Simply, the proof of the pudding is in the eating. Their ethics are situational. Their commitment is for the present. They yield to no supernatural power or religious hierarchy.

The noted Reagan political scholar Charles W. Dunn described God's position within the humanistic paradigm.

> They [secular humanists] reject the idea that God has intervened miraculously in history or revealed himself to a chosen few, or that he can save or redeem sinners. They believe that men and women are free and are responsible for their own destinies and that they cannot look toward some transcendent Being for salvation. They reject the divinity of Jesus, the divine mission of Moses, Mohammed, and other latter-day prophets and saints of the various sects and denominations.
>
> The problems that humankind will face in the future, as in the past, will no doubt be complex and difficult. However, if it is to prevail, it can only do so by enlisting resourcefulness and courage. Secular humanism places trust in human intelligence rather than

> in divine guidance. Skeptical of theories of redemption, damnation, and reincarnation, secular humanists attempt to approach the human situation in realistic terms: human beings are responsible for their own destinies.[2]

To me, humanism, though couched in some lofty ideals, is still based upon pride and an egocentric view of life. It provides no access to divine guidance and truth. It yields no answers regarding prior existence or my life beyond death. It provides little fulfillment for the spiritual nature that is native to our mortality. Its moral foundation is as the shifting of sand or driven as the wind-tossed sea.

Savior or savior

From an objective perspective, what factor can elevate one religion above another? Each of these religions produce beautiful, moral, sacrificing, service-oriented, and devout individuals and societies. On the downside, from these religions have also come war, bloodshed, and persecution, being justified through a myopic interpretation of their sense of identity.

The Terrestrial Paths of Salvation

There is one factor, however, that creates significant separation. That factor lies within the word "savior." In ten of these religions, the responsibility for "salvation" lies within the parameters of individual decision-making and life choices. Within these religions there are various prescriptions or "paths" which, if followed, can lead each person to a "heavenly" reward. These paths are self-aligning. I am my own savior. When I fail to follow the prescribed "path" in my actions and thoughts, I receive the negative consequences of those choices and retrogress on the wheel of life or in my life. I must merely "get back on the path" to make course correction and continue my pursuit toward a heavenly hope. Incorrect choices equate to bad karma or a retrogression toward spiritual attainment. A brief synopsis of the paths of these ten religions follows:

Religions of South Asia

- **Hinduism.** The three "ways" of works, knowledge, and worship.
- **Jainism.** Reducing or eliminating karma matter and using the

three pillars of (1) asceticism or self-denial, (2) absolute respect for all life forms, and (3) meditation to gain enlightenment.

- **Buddhism.** The four noble truths leading to the eight-fold path.
- **Sikhism.** Following the three S's: Simran or meditation; Seva or service; and Sangat or following the guidance of advanced teachers.

Religions of East Asia

- **Taoism.** Living in harmony with the Tao by bringing into harmony the yin and the yang. This is achieved by allowing the natural course of events to take place. Assistance is gained through the use of rituals, pills, magical potions, physical exercises, and dietary practices.
- **Confucianism.** Following the Chung Yung path of the moral man.
- **Shintoism.** Following the four basic elements of "Shinto" worship leading to the way of the Gods. The shinto way involves purification, offerings, prayers, and the sacred meal around popular festivals.

Religions of Southwest Asia

- **Zoroastrianism.** Follow the teachings of Ahura Mazda.
- **Judaism.** Jewish ritual life is the way that Jews remember and re-participate in their history with God.
- **Islam.** Complete submission to the Five Pillars of Faith: witness of faith, prayer, almsgiving, fasting, and pilgrimage to Mecca.
- **Moral Relativism (Humanism).** Moral or ethical propositions do not reflect absolute and universal moral truths. Instead, these propositions are relative to social, cultural, historic, or personal preferences and there is no single standard by which to assess truth. What is true for me may not be true for you.

The Concept of Sin

Within each of these belief systems, there is no "sin" in the traditional Christian definition. Each individual is his own savior, and as he stays on the prescribed "path," his own discipleship will lead him to his heavenly attainment, nirvana, eternal bliss, or whatever comes next. The concept of "sin" and a personal "redeemer" as believed within the Christian orientation is foreign to these religions and philosophies. The monotheistic religions of southwest Asia (Zoroastrianism, Judaism, Christianity, and Islam) are the only major religions that even incorporate a doctrine of "final judgment." One of the most formidable obstacles that Christian missionaries of the first century encountered in teaching Christian precepts to the "heathen" was the absence in their languages of a spiritual and ethical nomenclature. The Greeks and Romans, for example, had a clear conception of a moral ideal, but the Christian idea of sin was utterly unknown to the pagan mind. Vice they regarded as simply a relaxed energy of the will by which it yielded to the allurements of sensual pleasure. And virtue, literally manliness, was the determined spirit, the courage and vigor with which it resisted such temptations. But the idea of holiness and the antithetic* idea of sin were such utter strangers to the pagan mind that it would have been impossible to express them in any of the classical tongues of antiquity.

Jesus Christ, Savior

True Christianity stands alone to raise the word savior from being a common noun to its proper noun status. Let's discuss these ramifications. The unique message of "true" Christianity (as restored in the Restoration through Joseph Smith) focuses upon the true identity and mission of Jesus Christ. Let us examine four domains that elevate Jesus to a standard unequaled by any in mortality.

Jesus Christ represents the perfect model of character, morality, and spiritual attainment. He, without conceit, proclaimed himself to be "the way, the truth and the light" (John 14:6). To the Nephites, he said: "What manner of men ought ye to be? Verily I say unto you, even as I am" (3 Nephi 27:27). To all of the human family, he admonished, "Therefore I would that ye should be perfect even as I, or your Father who is in heaven is perfect" (3 Nephi 12:48). Jesus had a perfect understanding of his premortal, mortal, and future identity. As he labored to manifest or reveal himself in each dispensation of earth's existence, he continually expressed this identity with self-describing titles. Appendix H contains a list of these self-expressions found throughout the four standard works. No other leader or founder has ever proclaimed such a self-identity. Their messages were to follow the "path" they had discovered but not to follow them specifically as the ideal model. A more complete discussion of Christ's credentials as a perfect model is found in Chapter Ten.

Jesus was a God who became man. Jesus' physical birth was brought about through a union between his immortal Father in Heaven and Mary, his mortal virgin mother. Because of his physical birth, he was able to experience the full range of the mortal experience. Alma provides this description:

> And he shall go forth, suffering pains and afflictions and temptations of every kind: and this that the word might be fulfilled which saith he will take upon him the pains and the sicknesses of his people.
>
> And he will take upon him death, that he may loose the bands of death which bind his people; and he will take upon him their infirmities, that his bowels may be filled with mercy, according to the flesh, that he may know according to the flesh how to succor his people according to their infirmities (Alma 7:11–12).

Through his divine Father, he received power over death to initiate the resurrection of himself and of all mankind. No other human being (of a sane mind) has ever claimed such a power, not only for himself, but to extend that promise to all of the human family. Christ also received from his paternal genetic inheritance an endowment of power to perform an act of supreme reconciliation for the payment of the sins of humanity held due by the Law of Justice.

Christ's Atonement and the Law of Justice. God has blessed us with a set of commandments. The intent of these commandments is to bless our lives with joy and happiness. Obedience to each commandment produces some beneficial outcome that brings us closer to our divine potential. Some commandments serve prerequisite purposes. Baptism, for example, is requisite in order to enter into the kingdom of heaven. It also serves as an initial ordinance for entrance in the kingdom of God on earth, the Church. The violation of these commandments retards our spiritual development and offends our divine nature. These acts of disobedience are sin. The Law of Justice lays hold upon these acts that violate our divine nature and retards our course not only back to God but to eventual deification. The Law of Mercy allows the demands of the Law of Justice to be satisfied through Christ's Atonement. In relationship to our sins, our access to the power of the Atonement is through the process of individual repentance. Without repentance, each individual is subject to the full requirements associated with the Law of Justice.

The grace of Christ. The grace of Christ is an enabling power. It is not a mystical force or an influence coming from a correct alignment of the stars. The LDS Bible Dictionary provides this insight: "Through the grace of the Lord, each individual through faith in the atonement and repentance of their sins can receive strength and assistance to do good works that they otherwise would not be able to maintain if left to their own means. This grace is an enabling power that allows men and women to lay hold on eternal life and exaltation after they have expended their own best efforts" (LDS Bible Dictionary, "Grace").

The condition of weakness we experience within the mortal realm can be used to facilitate our desire to humble ourselves in order to call upon our Lord and Savior for his divine help. Enabled by his grace and through our own faith and diligence, "weak things become strong" (Ether 12:27).

Can any other human being compare with this lowly man born in an insignificant province, in an insignificant stable, with mortal parents of the humblest circumstance. He hardly traveled a few hundred miles from his hometown. He received no degrees, no honorary earthly titles, no international acclaim during his lifetime. He left no endowments of monetary wealth. He died on a cross—what seemed an ignominious* death to his crucifiers. His only material possession, his robe, was gambled away. But now, two thousand years later, more than half the world's population indirectly recognizes his person when they acknowledge the Gregorian method of calendaring. Christ's life, acknowledged or not, was the pivotal point in the history of man. President Harold B. Lee gave us this challenge:

> Our greatest responsibility and anxiety is to defend the divine mission of our Lord and Master, Jesus Christ, for all about us, even among those who claim to be professors of the Christian faith, are those not willing to stand squarely in defense of the great truth that our Lord and Master, Jesus Christ, was indeed the Son of God . . . so it would seem to me that the most important thing I could say to you is to try to strengthen your faith and increase you courage and your understanding of the place of the Master in the great Plan of Salvation.[3]

President Spencer W. Kimball, in speaking to a group of civic leaders, gave them this challenge:

> Perhaps the most important thing I can say about Jesus Christ, more important that all else I have said, is that He lives. He really does embody all those virtues and attributes the scriptures tell us of. If we can come to know that, we then know the central reality about man and the universe. If we don't accept that truth and that reality, then we will not have the fixed principles or the transcendent truths by which to live out our lives in happiness and service. In other words, we will find it very difficult to be significant leaders unless we recognize the reality of the perfect leader, Jesus Christ, and let him be the light by which we see the way![4]

One of the great apologists for Christianity and a favorite author of mine is C.S. Lewis. Some of my colleagues jokingly call him our mission president over the Anglicans in the spirit world. He wrote a beautiful treatise entitled *Mere Christianity* as a defense of the Christian religion. He was raised Christian but later gave up his allegiance. The story of his "rediscovery" of Christianity and his newfound understanding is fascinating and involves other significant authors. "Brother" Lewis cuts through traditional Christian chaff which attempts to humanize Jesus.

> There was a time when I believed that the universe was just an accident, that God was just a fantasy, and that Christ was just a good moral teacher. Not so now. You see, I discovered that Christ denied that there was any truth in my arguments. What's more, He said He was the Son of God. Here I was troubled. The man who was merely a man and said the sort of things that Jesus said wouldn't be a great moral teacher at all. He would either be a lunatic on the level with the man that says he's a poached egg, or else he would be the devil of hell. You must make your choice. Either this man was and is the son of God, or else a madman or something worse. You can shut him up for a fool, you can spit at him and kill him as a demon, or you can fall at His feet and call Him Lord and God. But don't let's come up with any patronizing nonsense about his being a great human teacher. He hasn't left that open to us. He didn't intend to.[5]

It is this claim of Christ that has, across the ages, been both Christianity's biggest offense and its greatest attraction. Christ is Christianity. Christianity is based on the bedrock premise of a Savior; not a social revolutionist, not a moral teacher, not a miracle-worker. Jean Danielou, a ranking scholar in modern Catholicism on the religious cultures of the East, posed this choice:

> The danger for Christianity at present is that it should become secularized, worldly, reduced to a kind of socialist humanism. This is not what the world needs; and, if Christians were reduced to offering the world only this humanism, they would soon be set aside and rightly so, since there have always been socialists, teachers of morality, and organizers of society: they have rendered service, but they have never saved anyone. The world today does not need greater social organization but a Savior; man today needs someone who will answer the fundamental problems of his existence, which no social structure has ever been able to answer.[6]

The world not only needs a Savior in the person of Jesus of Nazareth, but each individual needs to come to know the Savior, Jesus Christ. To know him is not to have an academic or scholarly understanding; to know him is not to attend church and learn of his life, miracles, and death experiences; to know him is to have a personal experience, your own sacred grove. The promise is sure. It requires humility. It requires building a hope based on a true understanding of his life, his mission, and his promises. It requires one to "draw near unto me and I will draw near unto you; seek me diligently and ye shall find me; ask, and ye shall receive; knock, and it shall be opened unto you. . . . Therefore, sanctify yourselves that your minds become single to God, and the days will come that you shall see him; for he will unveil his face unto you, and it shall be in his own time, and in his own way, and according to his own will" (D&C 88:63, 68).

1. The only exceptions are Hinduism and Shintoism. These religions rose up out of the religious heritage unique within their culture.
2. Dunn, *American Political Theology*, 114–117.
3. Williams, *Teachings of Harold B. Lee*, 11.
4. Spencer W. Kimball, "Jesus, the Perfect Leader," *Ensign*, Aug. 1979, 7.
5. Lewis, *Mere Christianity*, 41.
6. Shelley, *Church History in Plain Language*, 466.

CHAPTER TEN

"Be Ye Therefore Perfect"

Most people are willing to take the Sermon on the Mount as a flag to sail under, but few will use it as a rudder by which to steer. – Oliver Wendell Holmes

Christianity is not a theory or speculation, but a life; not a philosophy of life, but a life and a living process. – Samuel Taylor Coleridge

What a grand and unique religion—Christianity. Unfortunately, many of its pages of history are marred by war, bloodshed, and persecution. Those events were a dishonor to its true message and brought about by individuals blinded by self-serving interests. "Peace on earth and goodwill toward all men" was the message of the angels to announce the coming birth of the Messiah, the Christ, the Savior of all mankind, Jesus of Nazareth. On a lovely hill on the north shore of the Sea of Galilee, overlooking the beautiful valley setting in which the sea is nestled, Jesus gave the greatest sermon uttered by man. He taught truths that could raise humanity to its grandest heights. A few historic societies have actually realized such an achievement (for example, Enoch's city, Noah's converts, Melchizedek's city, 4 Nephi society, and so forth). The prime premise of this "sermon on the mount" was stated within this injunction: "Be ye therefore perfect." C. S. Lewis said of this pronouncement:

> The command Be Ye Perfect is not idealistic gas. Nor is it a command to do the impossible. He is going to make us into creatures that can obey that command. He said [in the Bible] that we were "gods" and He is going to make good His words. If we let Him—for we can prevent Him, if we choose—He will make . . . us into a god or goddess,

> dazzling, radiant, immortal creatures, pulsating all through with such energy and joy and wisdom and love as we cannot now imagine, a bright stainless mirror which reflects back to God perfectly . . . . His own boundless power and delight and goodness. The process will be long and in part very painful; but that is what we are in for. Nothing less. He meant what He said.
>
> Those who put themselves in His hands will become perfect, as He is perfect—perfect in love, wisdom, joy, beauty, and immortality. The change will not be completed in this life, for death is an important part of the treatment. How far the change will have gone before death in any particular is uncertain.[1]

No one else in Christianity takes this command so literally as do we in Mormonism. The reason for this reverberates back to the very heart and soul of our religion: our knowledge of the nature and character of God. Since traditional Christianity states that God is an essence without body, parts, and human passion, their perfection must be viewed within a metaphoric interpretation. Latter-day Saints define perfection within the doctrine of literal theosis. Peter taught the early Saints of the Church: "According as his divine power hath given unto us all things that pertain unto life and godliness, through the knowledge of him that hath called us to glory and virtue; Whereby are given unto us exceeding great and precious promises: that by these ye might *be partakers of the divine nature*, having escaped the corruption that is in the world" (2 Peter 1:3–4; emphasis added).

The apostle John taught the Saints that if they continued to exemplify the love of the Father they could become like Christ: "Beloved, now are we the sons of God, and it doth not yet appear what we shall be: but we know that when he shall appear, we shall be like him; for we shall see him as he is" (1 John 3:2). The doctrine of theosis provides a paradigm of growth and development toward full, complete, and absolute perfection. There are two scriptural references for this particular command. The first is found in Matthew 5:48: "Be ye therefore perfect, even as your Father which is in heaven is perfect." This was given to the Jews during Christ's mortal ministry. Notice that Christ did not include himself as an example of perfection. Though he was without sin, he still did not qualify as an ultimate example. The next reference is found in 3 Nephi 12:48: "Therefore I would that ye should be perfect even as I, or your Father who is in heaven is perfect." This text was given after his Resurrection to those Nephites who had survived the destruction which had been foretold by

Nephite prophets. Notice that Christ includes himself with his Father as examples of ultimate perfection.[7] Let's investigate this a little further. Joseph Smith was given revealed insight into the gospel writings of John the Baptist. John says of Christ: "And I, John, saw that he received not of the fulness at the first, but received grace for grace; And he received not of the fulness at first, but continued from grace to grace, until he received a fulness" (D&C 93:12–13).

Christ, as well as all of our heavenly family, are on a path of spiritual evolutionary development. Christ led out and is first to accomplish this ultimate triumph. But we are not left in mortality to wallow in our own humanness. We need something to help raise us up above the shackles standing in the way of our perfection. The doctrine of which I speak is simply the "grace of Christ." But to more fully understand this grand concept within the parameters of the doctrine of perfection, we must understand the scriptures that tie this truth together into one grand whole. Paul taught that "by the offence of one, judgment came upon all men to condemnation; even so by the righteousness of one, the free gift came upon all men unto justification of life" (Romans 5:18).

One of the hallmarks of the Christmas season is the giving and receiving of gifts. Not only did Christ and his parents receive gifts from the magi, but Christ returns back to us gifts that aid our quest for perfection. But before we identify these gifts, we need to understand the parameters of perfection—and Christ is our model. Luke records one of the few references relating to Jesus' youth. He states that "Jesus increased in wisdom and stature, and in favour with God and man" (Luke 2:52). There it is—there's the paradigm of perfection. Let me explain. Luke states that Jesus increased, meaning, he grew and developed, and then he lists four domains of life. The domain of wisdom I will call mental. The second domain was stature, that relates to the physical. The third domain indicates that Jesus increased in favor with God. This is the spiritual domain of life—man's relationship with God. Sin estranges us from God. Christ lived a sinless life, thus developing and maintaining a perfect relationship with God. Luke concludes with a reference that Christ increased in favor with man. This fourth domain I will call social or man's relationship to man (speaking generically). This is not to mean that Jesus was the perfect host or the most popular public figure (and I am not saying that he wasn't). This is the domain of social skills or how we interact with and treat one another. Perfection within this domain requires perfect character and virtue. Let me now organize the rest of this development into the following model.

Gifts of Christ unto Perfection

Scripture Chain: Romans 5:18; Matthew 5:48; 3 Nephi 12:48; D&C 93:12–13.

Area of Christ's Perfection	Category of Perfection	Gifts of Christ
Jesus increased in wisdom Moroni 7:16 1 Nephi 13:37; Alma 9:21 D&C 46:11ff; Moroni 10:8ff; 1 Corinthians 12:4ff D&C 130: 9 D&C 130:10–11	Mental: Possessing a knowledge of all eternal truths, doctrines, and principles associated with the reality of God; the earth, its creation and operation; and all knowledge necessary to function as a God Creator and Parent Omniscient.	• Light of Christ • Gift of the Holy Ghost • Gifts of the Holy Ghost • Living on the celestial earth • White Stone = Our personal Urim and Thummim
Jesus increased in stature Alma 40:23 D&C 89:3ff	Physical: Caring for our bodies as appropriate receptacles of our spirit. Receiving perfected bodies in the resurrection and a glory based upon the kingdom of God we are assigned in the final judgment.	• Gift of the resurrection • Gift of the Word of Wisdom
Jesus gained favor with God Matthew 11:28 "Come Unto Me" 3 Nephi 18:32 "Come Unto Me" 2 Corinthians 5:17–18 "God hath reconciled us"	Spiritual: Sin separates us from God. Repentance or the process of reconciling sin allows us to reunite with God and brings us into a state of "at-one-ment" with him.	• Gift of the Atonement

Area of Christ's Perfection	Category of Perfection	Gifts of Christ
Jesus gained favor with man Bible Dictionary: "Grace" Colossians 3:14 Ether 12:27; Jacob 4:7 2 Nephi 25:23 Ether 12:27 Jacob 4:7	Social: Christ's teachings from the Sermon on the Mount direct us to achieve mastery over our emotions and passions and strive for perfection in all of the godly virtues, with assistance from the grace of Jesus Christ.	• Gift of Grace • Gift of weakness

A study of the information in this chart develops the idea that Christ provides us with the gifts sufficient to enable us to achieve full and complete perfection.[2] It is by accessing these gifts of Christ that we ourselves can become perfect as He and our Father are perfect. It is through his loving grace that he enables us ultimately to achieve perfection in every domain, not just overcoming sin. Peter talks about partaking of this divine nature:

> Whereby are given unto us exceeding great and precious promises: that by these ye might be partakers of the divine nature, having escaped the corruption that is in the world through lust.
>
> And beside this, giving all diligence, add to your faith virtue; and to virtue knowledge;
>
> And to knowledge temperance; and to temperance patience; and to patience godliness;
>
> And to godliness brotherly kindness; and to brotherly kindness charity.
>
> For if these things be in you, and abound, they make you that ye shall neither be barren nor unfruitful in the knowledge of our Lord Jesus Christ (2 Peter 1:4–8).

Moroni, just before he closed the last leaf to seal up the gold plates, reminded all who were to read this sacred record:

> Yea, come unto Christ, and be perfected in him, and deny yourselves of all ungodliness; and if ye shall deny yourselves of all ungodliness and love God with all your might, mind and strength, then is his grace sufficient for you, that by his grace ye may be perfect in Christ;

> and if by the grace of God ye are perfect in Christ, ye can in nowise deny the power of God.
>
> And again, if ye by the grace of God are perfect in Christ, and deny not his power, then are ye sanctified in Christ by the grace of God, through the shedding of the blood of Christ, which is in the covenant of the Father unto the remission of your sins, that ye become holy, without spot (Moroni 10:32–33).

That is the message of the Book of Mormon. That is the message of Mormonism. That is the message of Christianity. For that, there is no apologizing.

Faith in the Lord Jesus Christ

The key to our perfection and spiritual progress, then, lies in and through Jesus Christ. Our faith cannot be centered in anyone or anything else. In addition, our faith cannot be centered on the power of our own ability alone. The principle of faith in Jesus Christ was always a principle I felt I had not fully understood. While growing up in the Church, many of the talks and lessons I heard associated faith with events of a miraculous nature: "Faith can move mountains," and, "By faith, miracles are performed." Scriptural accounts document the faith of prophets producing superhuman feats and accomplishments. We are continually reminded of the rich faith of the pioneers who crossed the plains or the exodus of ancient Israel, and the miracles associated with those great dramas. Through my own study and pondering of this first principle of the gospel, I have come to appreciate more of the breadth and depth of this simple principle. Such a principle, however, can be objectively studied. Faith is more of a verb connoting action than a noun naming or denoting a thing. To me, faith in Jesus Christ means that:

1. I accept His divine foreordained role as the Savior of all mankind and the Only Begotten Son of Heavenly Father.
2. I believe in the circumstances of His miraculous birth that brought him the experiences of mortality and endowed him with power to overcome death.
3. I look to him as the only perfect human being who modeled the highest level of the human condition.

4. I accept my dependence on Jesus Christ who, through his infinite Atonement, makes possible for me an escape from death as well as a power that can lift me to an exalted Godlike status.

5. I trust that his example as well as his grace will infuse an uplifting and sanctifying change in my mortal being. This change will affect my perceptions, my assumptions, my attitudes, and my behavior. I trust that it is only as I apply my own concerted efforts and receive of His divine grace that I can have any hope to fulfill the command of "be ye therefore perfect."

6. I believe that Joseph Smith did receive a visitation from the Father and the Son, which resulted in the Restoration of the gospel of Jesus Christ, with it principles, doctrines, commandments, ordinances, covenants, and church organization and structure, possessing the most excellent philosophy and way of life that exists in human society. The gospel is based on absolute truths obtained over time and through divine revelations that have been received from former as well as contemporary prophets.

7. My faith in Jesus Christ translates into clean thoughts, noble words, and Christian actions consistent with the covenants I have made to obey, honor, and keep his commandments. All this is requisite in order to receive the promised blessings in store for the faithful.

8. My questions concerning life's existence in the past, present, and future as well as who I was, who I am, and who I may become are best answered within the "great plan of happiness."

9. As I continue to progress through the great plan of happiness and apply the gospel of Jesus Christ, I can develop to the greatest extent the full potentiality of my gender. I can also establish a paradigm of self-esteem that will assist me to reach out without defensive positioning, fear of reprisal, or self-aggrandizement and extend myself in the charitable service of others.

10. My faith in Jesus Christ allows me to perform and participate in acts and events that transcend the normal mortal experience in a miraculous way.

The Many Voices Calling Out to Us

Paul cautioned the Corinthian Saints with this counsel: "There are, it may be, so many kinds of voices in the world, and none of them is without signification" (1 Corinthians 14:10). Our sense organs are constantly bombarded with stimulation. Our ears and our eyes are flooded continually with a vast array of stimuli. All of this input is fed to our brain for processing. The human mind is a fascinating organ with an amazing power to categorize and organize this input. Within both our conscious as well as our unconscious states, this processing takes place to guide our lives in a safe and productive course. As it is in the physical world, so it is in the spiritual domain. There are many "voices" that sound upon the tablet of our spiritual identity. We are, however, not born into mortality in a "*tabula rasa*" condition (idea of the blank slate made popular by John Locke). We bring from our former existence in the spirit world those proclivities and the personality we developed to a lesser or greater extent. During our infancy years in mortality, we filter through all of our environmental stimuli to "add upon" our evolutionary self-concept. Unfortunately, the source of some of the voices in the world are intent on redefining and modifying our true identity. True and productive self-esteem is the product of the recognition of our divine self and our relationship with our Heavenly Parents. Unfortunately, forces of the natural man use high tech amplifiers to blast its antithetical message: "You are not a person of divine worth. You are a product of nature whose survival is based upon personal power." Worldly self-esteem comes from self-perception of physical abilities like comeliness, athleticism, intellectual prowess, costly attire, talents, and so on. Though these stimuli may be reinforcing, they are *prima facie** only and do not qualify as "prime elements."

Jesus said, "I came into the world to do the will of my Father" (3 Nephi 27:13). Though he was perfect in virtue (manliness), exceptionally gifted, and seemed to display great personal power and accomplished miraculous feats, his concept of self was anchored to his divine origins and his relationship with his Father. He never forgot that central core upon which his self-esteem was centered. From that basis, he withstood all of the evil that the forces of the natural man and the forces of the world of evil spirits could inflict upon him. A conniving lawyer questioned Jesus with this Jewish conundrum, "Master, which is the great commandment in the law?" Jesus' answer not only satisfied the conundrum but provided a paradigm of developmental self-concept: "Jesus said unto him, Thou shalt love the Lord thy God with all thy heart, and with all thy soul, and with all thy mind. This is the first and great commandment. And the second is like unto it, Thou shalt love thy neighbor as thyself" (Matthew 22:37–39).

The development of our mortal self-concept begins at first breath. Our nurturing environment promotes a sense of worth and of being loved. As our cognitive abilities develop, the spirit of Christ confirms truths taught to us of our divine nature. If we hold fast in our youth to remember that "I am a child of God who loves me" and "I am a person of divine worth," then we will be able to withstand the "fiery darts of the adversary" that attempt to dethrone us. God will empower us with a sense of His love and divine acceptance, a message that can distill upon our minds and bury deep within our hearts. As we develop through our infancy and mature into adulthood, this knowledge, this "armor of God" becomes a "defense and a refuge" from the philosophic, agnostic, and humanistic storms of life. With a secure concept of self and divine self-esteem, we can reach out without defensive positioning, fear of reprisal, or self-aggrandizement and extend ourselves in the charitable service of others. As we participate in these acts of charity, our love for others as well as our love for self is enhanced and perpetuated. A full and complete self-concept is a harmonious balance between loving God and loving our neighbor, which promotes and enhances a love and appreciation of self.

How can a person who has lost his way on that broad and winding road find their way back? What is the prime mover that moves people off their divine course and into the back alleys of "worldly wisdom?" What alienates mankind from their "God who gave them life?" The answer is simple. It is pride. Pride is the fuel that fires the rage within the natural man. Pride entertains doubt. Pride encourages independence and selfishness. Pride disallows a dependent relationship upon a Savior. Pride seeks its own. Pride attempts to rewrite divine laws of morality. Pride is the fountainhead of situational ethics. A classic example of this condition takes us back to the "father of lies." "And I, the Lord God, spake unto Moses saying: That Satan, whom thou hast commanded in the name of mine Only Begotten, is the same which was from the beginning, and he came before me, saying—Behold, here am *I*, send me, *I* will be thy son, and *I* will redeem all mankind, that one soul shall not be lost, and surely *I* will do it; wherefore give *me* thine honor" (Moses 4:1; emphasis added). Lucifer, unfortunately, suffered from a deadly disease. He struggled with an "I" disease. So it is with many in mortality. Pride is antithetic to humility and thus to faith in Jesus Christ.

Christ's message, which was first delivered to Adam and Eve and will forever be the saving message of humanity, was, is, and always will be: "Come unto me." He is our Advocate. One day I asked my dear wife what would be the main reason for anyone to turn from their prideful, worldly orientation and to return back to God and their Savior. In one fell swoop she cut through all of their arguments with this simple response: "I can't do it on my own!" Christ said further, "Come unto me, all ye that labor and are heavy laden and I will give you rest" (Matthew 11:28).

Paul described our worldly crisis with these words. "For we wrestle not against flesh and blood, but against principalities, against powers, against the rulers of the darkness of this world, against spiritual wickedness in high place" (Ephesians. 6:12). He then provided the solution to our defensive empowerment.

> Wherefore take unto you the whole armour of God, that ye may be able to withstand in the evil day, and having done all, to stand.
>
> Stand therefore, having your loins girt about with truth, and having on the breastplate of righteousness;
>
> And your feet shod with the preparation of the gospel of peace;
>
> Above all, taking the shield of faith, wherewith ye shall be able to quench all the fiery darts of the wicked (Ephesians 6:13–16).

The Lord adds to this formula through the Prophet Joseph Smith. "And take the helmet of salvation, and the sword of my spirit, which I will pour out upon you, and my word which I reveal unto you" (D&C 27:18). The importance of the "word" as part of our spiritual armament is discussed by the apostle Paul. In his letter to Timothy, whom he describes as being his "own son in the faith," he warns of troubling events coming in the last days. He mentions conditions such as people being "lovers of their own selves, covetous, boasters, proud, blasphemers, disobedient to parents, unthankful, unholy, without natural affection, trucebreakers, false accusers, incontinent, fierce, despisers of those that are good, traitors, heady, highminded, lovers of pleasures more than lovers of God; having a form of godliness but denying the power thereof" (2 Timothy 3:2–5).

Though this condition may have occurred several times after this first century, it certainly describes the conditions in the world today, in these last days. But Paul also provided within the context of his letter (epistle) a solution to these troubling times. He counseled Timothy: "And that from a child thou has known the holy scriptures, which are able to make thee wise unto salvation through faith which is in Christ Jesus. And all Scripture given by inspiration of God, is profitable for doctrine, for reproof, for correction, for instruction in righteousness: That the man of God may be perfect, throughly furnished unto all good works" (JST, 2 Timothy 3:15–17).

Lehi and Nephi were taught in symbolic imagery how important the "iron rod" was along the path leading back to the precious fruit which was "most desirable above all other fruit." This iron rod was the "word of God" that will safely "guide us along the way," as sung in our early years in Primary.

Sometimes "lifers," or individuals who have been faithful members of the Church all their life, lose cognition of their blessed state. The enticements or alluring images off the path portrayed by the entertainment media color the "ways of the natural man" with such imagination that what cannot be seems to be. Isaiah predicted this state, which has been a frequent phenomenon throughout history but certainly characterizes modern western civilization: "Woe unto them that call evil good, and good evil; that put darkness for light, and light for darkness; that put bitter for sweet, and sweet for bitter!" (Isaiah 5:20).

The Book of Mormon prophet Samuel, a Lamanite, saw through the evil social customs of the Nephites and gave them this warning: "Ye have sought all the days of your lives for that which ye could not obtain; and ye have sought for happiness in doing iniquity, which thing is contrary to the nature of that righteousness which is in our great and Eternal Head" (Helaman 13:38).

God reminded Malachi around 400 B.C.: "Ye have said, It is vain to serve God: and what profit is it that we have kept his ordinance, and that we have walked mournfully before the Lord of hosts? And now we call the proud happy; yea, they that work wickedness are set up; yea, they that tempt God are even delivered" (Malachi 3:14–15).

Malachi seemed to fall prey to this same self-deception. God reminded Malachi of some of the long-term rewards of faithfulness: "A book of remembrance was written before him for them that feared the Lord, and that thought upon his name. And they shall be mine, said the Lord of hosts, in that day when I make up my jewels . . . . Then shall ye return, and discern between the righteous and the wicked, between him that serveth God and him that serveth him not" (Malachi 3:16–18).

The promise of long-term heavenly rewards is only part of the payoff for faithfulness. The list of blessings in mortality associated with faithfulness is long and valid. For me, there are two that rise above the others: peace and the spirit. The first was part of the Christmas angelic message, but repeated by the Savior while in mortality: "Peace I leave with you, my peace I give unto you: not as the world giveth, give I unto you. Let not your heart be troubled, neither let it be afraid" (John 14:27). The Lord prioritized this spiritual endowment when he reminded Oliver Cowdery: "Did I not speak peace to your mind concerning the matter? What greater witness can you have than from God" (D&C 6:23). Another gift of faithfulness is identified within God's counsel to Joseph Smith's brother, Hyrum: "Verily, verily, I say unto you, I will impart unto you of my Spirit which shall enlighten your mind, which shall fill your soul with joy." (D&C 11:14).

Truly, saving knowledge (or enlightenment) is that which will "set us free." Within our standard works are many references concerning a "strait and narrow path" leading to eternal life (see Matthew 7:14; 2 Nephi 31:18; Helaman 3:29; D&C 132:22). The word strait has a very different meaning from its homophonic* cousin straight. Strait implies "restriction" or "narrowness." The strait path to eternal life certainly is full of do's and do not's. The natural man is naturally inclined toward resistance and rejection of these authority-based rules of conformity outside of one's self. These road-side commandments, however, come from a loving Father who has only our best interest in mind. Instead of limiting our agency, they are actually conduits that open the gateways into realms of enhanced and expanded freedom. People of faith know exactly what this means: freedom from ignorance, freedom from the bondage of entrapment, freedom from the bondage of greed, freedom from the bondage of indulgence, freedom from the bondage of addiction; and freedom from sin. Faithless people seem to criticize religious rules, external authority, and conformity. Yes, people of faith are viewed as "different." Our critics even go to the extreme and suggest we are "mindless automatons* blindly following old men." The prophet Moses said that the faithful would become a "peculiar people" unto the nations of the earth (Deuteronomy 14:2). The apostle Peter reminded the saints in his day of that same characterization (1 Peter 2:9). In Hebrew, the word for peculiar is *segullah*, meaning "a special possession." People of true faith are secure in the knowledge of their relationship with God.

Being a "special possession," however, comes with responsibility. In the closing days of Jesus' post-resurrection "missionary prep" experiences with his apostles, he gave them this altruistic* injunction: "Go ye therefore, and teach all nations, . . . teaching them to observe all things whatsoever I have commanded you (Matthew 28:19- 20).

The message "come unto Christ" is not discriminatory. We are truly brothers and sisters. Once heeded, life is lived "in the world but not of the world." No matter what our station in life may be, no matter what the condition of our heart, the Lord calls us to his side and to his eternal plan.

> For I will take you from among the heathen, and gather you out of all countries, and will bring you into your own land.
>
> Then will I sprinkle clean water upon you, and ye shall be clean: from all your filthiness, and from all your idols, will I cleanse you.
>
> A new heart also will I give you, and a new spirit will I put within you: and I will take away the stony heart out of your flesh, and I will give you an heart of flesh.
>
> And I will put my spirit within you, and cause you to walk in my statutes, and ye shall keep my judgments, and do them (Ezekiel 36:24–27).

Saul of Tarsus was a devout Jew. He was a disciple and a staunch follower of the Pharisaic tradition. On a single day, the focus of his qualities of devotion, leadership, and dedication were realigned by a call to "come unto me." The course of his life was forever altered along the road to Damascus as he gave heed to the voice of the Lord calling him to true discipleship (Acts 9:4–19). This same Saul, whose name was changed to Paul, was the voice who presented a logical defense of true Christianity to a pagan Roman magistrate governing Judea, King Agrippa. The logic of his defense moved the king to say, "*Almost* thou persuadest me to be a Christian" (Acts 26:28; emphasis added). Paul's response to the call of discipleship led him into a life of service through sacrifice with eternal rewards at the end. Agrippa's failure to heed the call allowed him to continue in self-indulgence and die in infamy. The American poet John Greenleaf Whittier ended his poem "Mauld Muller" with these famous words, "For of all sad words of tongue or pen, the saddest are these: 'It might have been!'" In the final analysis, there are really only two voices. But the final destinations are worlds apart.

1. Lewis, *Mere Christianity*, 175.
2. I acknowledge there are scriptural references that describe Noah, Seth, and Job as perfect (see Genesis 6:9, D&C 107:43 and Job 1:1). Since Paul taught that "all have sinned and come short of the glory of God" (Romans 3:23), the connotation* of perfection associated with these scriptural figures must not be the same as with Christ and the Father as our perfect examples.

CHAPTER ELEVEN

The Pearl of Great Price

You have to pay the price. You will find that everything in life exacts a price, and you have to decide whether the price is worth the prize. – Sam Nunn

All truths are easy to understand once they are discovered; the point is to discover them. – Galileo

Jesus gave a parable: "Again, the kingdom of heaven is like unto a merchant man, seeking goodly pearls: Who, when he had found one pearl of great price, went and sold all that he had, and bought it" (Matthew 13:45–46). During another occasion he taught again using a parable: "What woman having ten pieces of silver, if she lose one piece, doth not light a candle, and sweep the house, and seek diligently till she find it? And when she hath found it, she calleth her friends and her neighbors together, saying, Rejoice with me; for I have found the piece which I had lost" (Luke 15:8–9).

I feel like Alma who desired angelic power to declare the truths of the gospel with a voice that would shake the earth. The restored gospel of Jesus Christ is the pearl of great price. It is worth selling "all that we have" to obtain it. After King Lamoni's father was taught the true doctrines of God and of Christ and the plan of redemption, he said, "I will give away all my sins to know thee" (Alma 22:18). That may be the highest price. That cuts to the core of our resistance: our pride, our independence, our vanity. But in return, what is the payoff? "Rejoice with me; for I have found the piece which I had lost."

The Savior has said, "Come unto me." He could also have said, "Come back to me." In this world of loneliness and despair, the Savior extends his arms and invites a loving embrace. Then together, the rhapsody is played. This synergism of cooperation is dramatized in a popular story ascribed to the famed pianist Paderewski. Unfortunately its genuineness has not been verified. Be that as it may, let's think of it as a story that could have been to teach the principle within.

> Wishing to encourage her young son's progress on the piano, a mother took her boy to a piano concert (featuring a grand master). After they were seated, the mother spotted an old friend in the audience and walked down the aisle to greet her. Seizing the opportunity to explore the wonders of the concert hall, the little boy rose and eventually explored his way through a door marked No Admittance.
>
> When the house lights dimmed and the concert was about to begin, the mother returned to her seat and discovered that the child was missing.
>
> Suddenly, the curtains parted and spotlights focused on the impressive Steinway on stage. In horror, the mother saw her little boy sitting at the keyboard, innocently picking out "Twinkle, Twinkle, Little Star." At that moment, the great piano master made his entrance, quickly moved to the piano, and whispered in the boy's ear, "Don't quit, keep playing." Then leaning over, the master reached down with his left hand and began filling in a bass part. Soon his right arm reached around to the other side of the child, and he added a running obligato.
>
> Together, the old master and the young novice transformed what could have been a frightening situation into a wonderfully creative experience.[1]

It doesn't matter how far one has strayed. A lost sheep who has lost sight of the way back to its shepherd is still lost—one foot, one mile, a thousand miles away. When we lose sight of the Master, worldly values and assumptions fill the void. But our Father's love is without bound and is full of patience. "Remember, the worth of souls is great in the sight of God" (D&C 18:10). When the world gives up on us, our Father never will. Through his Son comes this plea, "Come unto me, all ye that labor and are heavy laden, and I will give you rest" (Matthew 11:28). We could also say, "Don't quit, keep playing."

Remember the words and message of this classic poem written in 1921 by Myra Brooks Welch: "The Touch of the Master's Hand."

> It was battered and scarred,

And the auctioneer thought it hardly worth his while
To waste his time on the old violin, but he held it up with a smile.
"What am I bid, good people," he cried,
"Who starts the bidding for me?"
"One dollar, one dollar, Do I hear two?"
"Two dollars, who makes it three?"
"Three dollars once, three dollars twice, going for three,"
But, no, From the room far back a gray haired man
came forward and picked up the bow,
Then wiping the dust from the old violin
and tightening up the strings,
He played a melody, pure and sweet,
as sweet as the angel sings.
The music ceased and the auctioneer
with a voice that was quiet and low, said
"What now am I bid for this old violin?"
as he held it aloft with its bow.
"One thousand, one thousand, do I hear two?"
"Two thousand, who makes it three?"
"Three thousand once, three thousand twice,
going and gone," said he.
The audience cheered, but some of them cried,
"We just don't understand." "What changed its worth?"
Swift came the reply.
"The Touch of the Masters Hand."
And many a man with life out of tune,
all battered and torn with sin,
Is auctioned cheap to a thoughtless crowd
much like that old violin.
A mess of pottage, a glass of wine,
a game and he travels on.
He is going once, he is going twice,
he is going and almost gone.
But the Master comes,
and the foolish crowd never can quite understand,
The worth of a soul and the change that is wrought
by the Touch of the Master's Hand.[2]

No matter how deep into sin we have buried ourselves, our Savior's grace is sufficient to raise us up and restore our self-worth. The way back is personal as well as institutional. It is personal as we reconcile our relationship with our Heavenly Father through prayer and realign our life away from sin. It is personal as we come unto Christ and request of Him his atoning grace to heal our wounded soul. It is personal as the Holy Spirit re-enters our domain and fills our hearts and our minds with the sweet feelings and sounds of the balm of Gilead. It also becomes institutional as we invite the blessings of the Church back into our lives through the doors of our common judge in Israel, our bishop. He holds the keys to the blessings that await a member in good standing. We are only halfway there if we fail to knock on the door. But knock we must. Then when we do, we will find a loving, understanding, and authorized representative of Jesus Christ. Through his direction, the blessings of full fellowship await.

William E. Hinley, a poet, was very proud of his freedom to act—as all men are—but like the majority of us, he failed to understand and couple this gift with the gift of humility, which also comes from God. Hinley's poem, "Invictus," is the heroic or epic position. We all admire courage, fortitude, and the power to patiently endure. These traits are essential to success, both in spiritual and in temporal pursuits. But these heroic qualities, admirable though they may be and desirable withal, cannot lessen one jot or tittle the need for a Savior and the blessings of church membership. In his wonderfully virile and powerful poem, there is no recognition of any need for divine or institutional help. That, to me, is unfortunate.

Invictus

Out of the night that covers me,
Black as the pit from Pole to Pole,
I thank whatever gods may be,
For my unconquerable soul.

In the fell clutch of circumstance
I have not winced nor cried aloud,
Under the bludgeonings of chance
My head is bloody, but unbowed.

Beyond this place of wrath and tears
Looms but the horror of the shade,
And yet the menace of the years
Finds and shall find me unafraid.

It matters not how straight the gate,
How charged with punishments the scroll,
I am the master of my fate,
I am the captain of my soul.[3]

The late Orson F. Whitney of the Council of the Twelve Apostles wrote a poem entitled "The Soul's Captain." In answer to the declaration "I am the captain of my soul!" Elder Whitney wrote:

Art thou in truth?
Then what of him who bought thee with his blood?
Who plunged into devouring seas
And snatched thee from the flood

Who bore for all our fallen race
What none but him could bear--
The God who died that man might live
And endless glory share.

Of what avail thy vaunted strength
Apart from his vast might?
Pray that his light may pierce the gloom
That thou mayest see aright.

Men are as bubbles on the wave,
As leaves upon the tree,
Thou, captain of thy soul! Forsooth,
Who gave that place to thee?

Free will is thine—free agency,
To wield for right or wrong;
But thou must answer unto him
To whom all souls belong.

Bend to the dust that 'head unbowed,'
Small part of life's great whole,
And see in him and him alone,
The captain of thy soul.[4]

1. Author's retelling.
2. Quoted by Boyd K. Packer, "Touch of the Master's Hand," *Ensign,* May 2001, 22.

3. Quoted by Gordon B. Hinckley, Thomas S. Monson, and James E. Faust, "First Presidency Christmas Devotional: 'My Redeemer Lives'," Ensign, Feb 2001, 70–73.
4. Ibid.

CHAPTER TWELVE

Mormonism—A New World Religion

I am in no position to judge Joseph Smith as a revelator, but as a student of the American imagination I observe that his achievement as national prophet and seer is clearly unique in our history . . . . If there is already in place any authentic version of American Religion, then as Tolstoy surmised, it must be Mormonism, whose future as yet may prove decisive for the nation, and for more than this nation alone. – Harold Bloom in *The American Religion*

Social scientists who professionally study religious movements have developed a keen eye toward the rise of Mormonism. There have been many controversial religious movements that have been espoused by a multitude of followers, then faded into obscurity. Many of these scientists are enamored of Mormonism because of its historic steadiness, its rapid rise in membership, its continued growth rate, its influence in modern society, and its charismatic founder. Organizationally, it was the first new original Christian denomination in America having no roots to European Catholic or Protestant origins. Doctrinally, they find it difficult to position us within the traditional camps of Christianity. We are not Catholic, not Protestant, and surely not liberal. We relate well with Judaism by professing to be of the tribe of Joseph and emphasizing Abrahamic covenants, but we are not Judaic. There is more and more of a tendency among these social scientists to admit to the emergence of a new world religion— Mormonism. One of these scientists puts it this way:

> Some doctrines of the Mormons are so original and so far from any traditional Christianity that many orthodox critics deny their

> Christian profession. In doctrine . . . [they] have so many distinctive doctrines and stand so far apart from all other Christian denominations as to constitute a completely new religious tradition. Some scholars, rather than classifying [them] as a Christian denomination, see [them] as a distinct and separate world religion.[1]

Labeling us as such, they are excited to be in a contemporary position to study the phenomenal growth rates of Mormonism and to research the impact of members of the LDS Church upon society in local, national, and international environments. In the United States, the Church is now the fourth largest Christian denomination. In each of the western states, the LDS Church has the largest number of congregations of all denominations. There are more members of the LDS Church living outside the United States than those living within. One study predicted that if growth rates in individual regions remain constant, the membership of the Church would reach 50 million by the year A.D. 2040. Significant converts come from within all levels of social, political, financial, and educational domains. The fields of entertainment, sports, arts, and dramatics produce a plethora of LDS converts.

On the night of Joseph's first visit with the angel Moroni in his bedroom while his other siblings were fast asleep, Moroni told Joseph "that [my] name should be had for good and evil among all nations, kindreds, and tongues, or that it should be both good and evil spoken of among all people" (Joseph Smith—History 1:33). There is now existing an abundance of books, exposés, and literature written about the Prophet Joseph Smith that easily fulfills Moroni's prophecy. Harold Blood, another social scientist, is one that is both enamored and critical of Joseph Smith. A list of statements by Bloom concerning Joseph Smith is included as Appendix J.

Many years ago, a leading Catholic theologian came to Utah. He was a great scholar, knew a dozen languages, and was well versed in theology, law, literature, science, and philosophy. In a conversation between this theologian and Elder Orson. F. Whitney, he made this declaration: "You Mormons are ignoramuses. You don't know the strength of your own position."[2] Hopefully that opinion is not reflective of our membership today and is one of the motivators behind this treatise.

The strength of our position is in our doctrines, which I have attempted to enumerate.* The following chart simplifies the doctrinal differences between the three differing positions within Christianity.

Doctrinal Differences

Doctrine	Traditional Christian	LDS Position	Other
Concept of God	Trinity	Godhead	Jehovah's Witnesses: Jehovah God Christian Scientists: male/female supreme being
Canon	Closed	Open: two forms of scripture (1) canon and (2) modern-day revelation	Liberal: the Bible is great literature providing moral standards
Priesthood	Apostolic Catholic: The Apostolic authority has continuously resided in the Church through the Pope (Roman) or Eastern Bishops (Eastern Orthodox) or lineage of bishops (Anglican)	Priesthood has been restored through divine angelic messengers who originally held priesthood keys	Protestant: "Priesthood of all believers" as stated by Martin Luther Liberal: No special authority needed because no ordinances are required for salvation.
Salvation	Salvation available only through accepting the sacraments of the Church	Universal salvation, along with other definitions of the word	Protestant: Saved by the acceptance of Christ, who offers his redeeming grace. Liberal: Universal salvation
Plan of Salvation	Examples of unique LDS doctrines: Mother in Heaven, theosis of man, ministering angels, Lucifer's familial relationship, universe organized from unorganized matter—not *ex nihilo*, Garden of Eden doctrines, temple work (ordinances), celestial marriage, paradise and spirit prison, three degrees of glory, sons of perdition, and self-atonement.		

Organizational Differences

Another area of difference is the organizational structure of the physical church. Here again, Mormonism reflects a unique polity* or pattern in contrast to the other four organizational paradigms found in historic Christianity. They are as follows:

Monarchal—Governed by a Theocratic Monarchy

- Characterized by a single or sole presiding leader
- Statements and doctrines taught by this leader are viewed as *ex cathedra* or "inspired," "infallible," and "scripture."
- Religions based upon this polity claim to be of divine origin and solely and singularly representative of Christ's true church.

Example: Roman Catholic Church

Episcopal—Governed by Bishops (Grk. *episkopas*)

- Characterized by leaders claiming authority traced back to Christ's apostles (apostolic succession), which is viewed as an earlier origin than papal leadership.
- The highest level of leadership exists in a council of bishops.
- One bishop is viewed as "first among equals."

Examples:

  - Anglican Family with Archbishop of Canterbury viewed as "first" among their bishops.
  - Eastern Orthodox: Patriarch of Constantinople viewed as "first" among their bishops.
  - Lutheran churches in Europe are presided over by an executive council of bishops.

Presbyterian—Governed by Elders (Greek. *presbyteros*)

- Characterized by leaders coming from the lay or clerical levels.
- A local church is governed by a body composed of the minister and a small group of ruling elders (elected by members, then ordained).

- This form of church polity claims to be the oldest form of government.

Examples:

- Presbyterian
- American Lutheran
- Methodist (has some similarity with different nomenclature)

Congregational—Governed by members united by covenant

- Characterized by each congregation having sole control and authority over church practices and leadership.
- The national organization has no power over the internal life of each congregation.
- Lays claim that the churches of the apostolic age were congregational in nature.

Examples:

- Baptist
- Disciples of Christ
- Pentecostal

If Joseph Smith was just another reformer, he might have investigated the current patterns within Christianity and utilized one in which he felt comfortable. But Joseph Smith was called of God to be the instrument through which the true Church would be organized. He didn't investigate contemporary paradigms but was directed by divine revelation and was invested with heavenly authority through angelic messengers who had previously held priesthood keys. Some of these messengers included Peter, James, John the Beloved, John the Baptist, Moses, Elias, and Elijah. The organization that God revealed to Joseph became, in principle, the "same organization that existed in the Primitive Church" (Articles of Faith 1:6). Ironically, it seems to be an eclectic* blend of those of historic Christianity.

Government of the Church of Jesus Christ of Latter-day Saints

Monarchal

- Revelations and official church doctrine come only through the President of the Church (see D&C 1:38; 21:4–6; 28:2; 43:2–4).
- Inspired statements of the President are viewed as scripture and official church doctrine.
- "The Lord will never permit me or any other man who stands as President of this Church to lead you astray. It is not in the programme. It is not in the mind of God. If I were to attempt that, the Lord would remove me out of my place, and so He will any other man who attempts to lead the children of men astray from the oracles of God and from their duty."[3]

Episcopal

- Leadership based on apostolic succession (refer to any priesthood holder's line of authority).
- The principle of ordination governs calls to priesthood leadership positions.
- The Aaronic Priesthood is governed by an organization of bishops, with the "Presiding Bishop" guiding the administration of temporal affairs.

Presbyterian

- All members of the Melchizedek Priesthood are called "elders," even to the highest leadership level.
- Church leadership originates from the lay membership.

Congregational

- The voice of the people supports the decisions of local leaders (law of common consent).
- Each ward has responsibility to care for the poor and the widowed, maintain their physical facilities, and creatively

sponsor the activities engaged in by ward members.

Naming Differences

It is interesting that by 1830, not one Christian church had legally modeled the name of its church after Christ's name. Christ taught this simple truth to the Nephites during one of his visits to the American continent after his Resurrection. He said: "And how be it my church save it be called in my name?" (3 Nephi 27:8). A research of nomenclature in historic Christianity produces an interesting catalogue of the origins of church names. A representative list follows:

Named after Their Place of Origin

- **Church of England.** Began in England by King Henry VIII.
- **Dutch Reformed.** Dutch followers of John Calvin's teachings.
- **Greek/Eastern Orthodox.** Represents Eastern theology and ties to Greek culture and tradition.
- **Roman Catholic.** Became the legal religion under the reign of the Roman emperor Constantine and the state religion during Theodosius' reign.
- **Moravians.** Followers of John Huss's teachings, beginning in the town of Moravia of Bohemia, former province of Czechoslovakia.

Named after Their Leader or Founder

- **Lutherans.** Named after their spiritual leader, Martin Luther.
- **Mennonites.** Named after their founder, Menno Simons, a Dutch priest.
- **Hutterites.** Named after Jacob Hutter of Austria.
- **Amish.** Named after Jacob Ammann of Switzerland.
- **Campbellites.** Followers of Alexander Campbell; later becoming the Church/Disciples of Christ.
- **Wesleyans.** Followers of John Wesley, founder of the Methodist Church.

Named after the Form of Organization, Doctrines, or Practices

- **Presbyterians.** Governed by elders or *Presbytos.*
- **Episcopalians.** Governed by bishops or *Episkopos.*
- **Congregationalists.** Governed by the voice of lay members, independent congregations.
- **Salvation Army.** As a Wesleyan, William Booth began a "war against sin and poverty."
- **Methodists.** From a nickname given to John and Charles Wesley's "methodical habits" and "strict religious code of behavior" while at Oxford.
- **Shakers.** Their official name is the United Society of Believers in Christ's Second Coming; known for their vigorous shaking behavior during worship services. They also believe that Christ has already appeared in the person of a woman, Ann Lee (see D&C 49).
- **Quakers.** The Society of Friends, started by George Fox, who taught that we should "tremble at the word of the Lord."
- **Jehovah's Witnesses.** An Adventist group whose members are part of a long line of witnesses to Jehovah-God.
- **Seventh-day Adventists.** An Adventist group who looks for the imminent Second Coming of Christ and worships the Sabbath on Saturday.
- **Pentecostals.** Known for their emphasis upon the Pentecostal gifts of the Spirit as evidence of being born again; especially glossolalia (speaking in tongues) and the gift of healing.
- **Christian Scientists.** Emphasize a systematic application of rules based on fixed principles, the science of Christianity that Jesus lived and taught.
- **Baptists.** Emphasize "baptism of believers" by immersion.
- **Church of Christ.** Sought to return to primitive Christianity as true disciples.

The Church of Jesus Christ of Latter-day Saints

On April 6, 1830, in Fayette, New York, and in the home of Newel K. Whitney, Joseph Smith convened a conference of followers to officially and legally (according to the laws of the State of New York) organize the true Church of Jesus Christ. This organization was called by various names until its name was officially designated by revelation. Initially it was referred to as the Church of Christ (see title page of the Book of Commandments). In 1835, when the Book of Commandments was enlarged in its second edition, its title was change to The Doctrine and Covenants of the Church of the Latter-day Saints. Finally, at Far West, Missouri, on April 26, 1838, it was revealed to Joseph Smith what the Lord desired the name of his restored church to be: "For thus shall my church be called in the last days, even The Church of Jesus Christ of Latter-day Saints." In this same revelation, the Lord encouraged all members of this church to "arise and shine forth, that thy light may be a standard for the nations; and that the gathering together upon the land of Zion, and upon her stakes, may be for a defense, and for a refuge from the storm" (D&C 115:4–6).

Members of this church are empowered with truth, with conviction, with testimony, and with a unity of the faithful. We have been, are currently, and will be led by prophets of the living God. We have a stewardship to share the fulness of the gospel of Jesus Christ with all nations, kindreds, tongues, and with those of all religious beliefs. President John Taylor said of this gospel:

> The everlasting gospel . . . is adapted to the wants of the human family, to the world morally, socially, religiously and politically. It is not a sickly, sentimental, effeminate plaything; not a ghostly, spiritual, sing-song, ethereal dream, but a living, sober, matter-of-fact reality adapted to body and spirit, to earth and heaven, to time and eternity. It enters into all the ramifications of life. It does not adapt itself to the philosophy, politics, creeds, and opinions of men, but fashions them in its divine mold. It cannot be twisted into the multitudinous latitudinarian principles of a degenerate world; but lifts all that are in the world, who will be subject to its precepts, to its own ennobling, exalted and dignified standard. It searches all truth, and grasps at all intelligence. It is the revealed living and abiding will of God to man; a connection between the heavens and the earth. It is nature, philosophy, heavens and earth, time and eternity united. It is the philosophy of the heavens and the earth, of God, and angels, and saints.[4]

Empowered by this gospel and with restored priesthood authority, this church will surely be as "the stone cut out of the mountain without hands" and it will role forward to "become a great mountain, and fill the whole earth . . . and it shall stand forever" (Daniel 2:34–35, 44). Joseph confirmed this destiny with this prophetic utterance:

> The Standard of Truth has been erected; no unhallowed hand can stop the work from progressing; persecutions may rage, mobs may combine, armies may assemble, calumny may defame, but the truth of God will go forth boldly, nobly, and independent till it has penetrated every continent, visited every clime, swept every country, and sounded in every ear, till the purposes of God shall be accomplished and the great Jehovah shall say the work is done.[5]

Built to Last: From a Corporate Perspective

In the early infancy of the Church, the Lord continually revealed to the Prophet Joseph Smith visions of the destiny of the Church. Joseph was assured that if he were to remain faithful, the Lord would perform a "marvelous work and a wonder" through him. A year after Joseph complied with the legal requirements in the state of New York to organize the Church with six initial members, the Lord expanded Joseph's understanding of the Church's destiny with a revelation given at Hiram, Ohio, in October 1831: "The keys of the kingdom of God are committed unto man on the earth, and from thence, shall the gospel roll forth unto the ends of the earth, as the stone which is cut out of the mountain without hands shall roll forth, until it has filled the whole earth" (D&C 65:2).

There was to be no apostasy of this Church in these last days. One of the manifest destinies of the Church is to be the "kingdom of God on earth." During this same revelation, Joseph was told to: "Call upon the Lord, that his kingdom may go forth upon the earth, that the inhabitants thereof may receive it, and be prepared for the days to come, in the which the Son of Man shall come down in heaven, clothed in the brightness of his glory, to meet the kingdom of God which is set up on the earth. Wherefore, may the kingdom of God go forth, that the kingdom of heaven may come" (D&C 65:5–6).

As it accomplishes this grand mission, the physical organization of the Church should be something of interest to examine. If it truly is to exist into the millennium, then it must be built to last. In the corporate world, there are visionary companies modeled after principles that they believe will enable them to also last. Many companies and corporations have been successful—for a time, then faded away. During part of my career I was located in the Church Educational System central office in Salt Lake City. In my capacity as Director of Information Services, I became interested in the elements that separated visionary and enduring companies from successful but short-lived companies. The authors of *Built to Last* suggested:

> "Visionary companies are premier institutions—the crown jewels—in their industries, widely admired by their peers and having a long track record of making a significant impact on the world around them. The key point is that a visionary company is an organization—an institution . . . . [These companies] have woven themselves into the fabric of society . . . . The critical question is not "What's common across a group of companies? Rather, the critical issues are : 'What's essentially different about these companies?' How do they overcome and become resilient to setbacks?[6]

Collins and Porras identified the following elements, which uniquely characterize visionary companies:

1. **Become clock builders rather than time-tellers.** Visionary companies are clock builders, not time-tellers. They emphasize building the company rather than employing charismatic leaders, hitting the market just right with an attractive product, or riding a certain market trend.

2. **Avoid the tyranny of the "Or." Embrace the genius of the "And."** Visionary companies acquire the ability to embrace the extremes of A and B; extremes of a number of dimensions at the same time. F. Scott Fitzgerald pointed out, "The test of a first-rate intelligence is the ability to hold two opposed ideas in mind at the same time, and still retain the ability to function."

3. **Core ideology more than profits.** Companies benefit from articulating both core values and purpose in their core ideology. Core values don't change but practices might.

4. **Preserve the core and stimulate progress.** A visionary company carefully preserves and protects its core ideology, yet all the specific manifestations of its core ideology must be open for

change and evolution. This is achieved through the following:

a. **BHAG—Big Hairy Audacious Goals.** Commitment to challenging, audacious—and often risky—goals and projects toward which a visionary company channels its efforts.

b. **Cultlike cultures.** Great places to work only for those who buy in to the core ideology; those who don't fit with the ideology are ejected like a virus (preserve the core).

c. **Try a lot of stuff and keep what works.** High levels of action and experimentation—often unplanned and undirected—that produce new and unexpected paths of progress (which stimulates progress).

d. **Home-grown management.** Promotion from within, bringing to senior levels only those who've spent significant time steeped in the core ideology of the company (preserve the core).

e. **Good enough never is.** A continual process of relentless self-improvement with the aim of doing better and better, forever into the future (stimulates progress).

The Church of Jesus Christ of Latter-day Saints has been built through divine direction and will endure until its mortal mission is absorbed into the millennial reign of the kingdom of heaven. Joseph prophesied that the growth the Church would be described in the latter-days with words like "no unhallowed hand can stop the work from progressing" and that it "will go forth boldly, nobly, and independent till it has penetrated every continent." Utilizing the previous corporate leadership paradigm from Collins and Porras, let's test the organization of the Church to determine its "firm rooted bulwarks [to] outstand the rude blast."[7]

Mormonism's Corporate Strength

1. **Becoming Clock Builders Rather than Time-Tellers.** Although the Church was restored through a charismatic human agent and in a time of heated religious fervor, it was built upon absolute truth through heavenly association and empowered with the divine authority from God. It was not built upon an unused idea as a leftover from the Reformation, the expression of a charismatic personality, the gratification of the originator's ego, or the pursuit of wealth.

2. **Avoid the Tyranny of the "Or"—Embrace the Genius of the "And."** The restored Church is able to maintain a fixed hold on core ideology, yet experiences vigorous change and organizational movement. It embraces conservatism, yet initiates bold, organizational moves. It maintains clear vision and a sense of direction, yet is opportunistic and experimental with new technology. It identifies Big Hairy Audacious Goals, yet experiences incremental evolutionary progress. It espouses ideological control, yet manages operational autonomy. It embraces cultural values, yet promotes holistic behavioral norms. It invests in long-term stability, yet demands short-term performance. It is philosophic, visionary, and futuristic, yet performs with almost flawless "nuts and bolts" execution. It has purpose beyond profit, yet maintains an enviable financial integrity. It maintains an organization aligned with its core ideology, yet shows adaptation to its environmental constrictions.

3. **Core Ideology More than Profits.** The *summum bonum* of the Church's ideology rests within the walls of the family unit and its exaltation, not the perpetuation of the organization. The organization serves the needs of its members and the family rather than individuals and families serving the needs of the organization.

4. **Preserve the Core and Stimulate Progress.** The Church preserves its core and stimulates progress using:

    a. **BHAGs (Big Hairy Audacious Goals):**

        i. Take the gospel to every nation, kindred, tongue, people and religious persuasion.

        ii. Place the good fortune of the missionary efforts largely in the hands of nineteen-year-old boys.

        iii. Expect each member to receive an individual spiritual confirmation as to the divine origin of the restored gospel, the Church, and its ordained leadership.

        iv. Finance the operations of the Church based on the payment of 10 percent tithing; not upon donations, ward and building budgets, or fund-raising projects.

v. Provide primary operations and labor of the Church through the efforts of laymembers, a lay clergy, and voluntary services.

vi. Establish a high-level work ethic and avoid the degrading effects of the welfare dole.

vii. Provide worldwide disaster relief for not only Church members but also brothers and sisters not of our faith.

viii. Build and maintain temples within the reach of every member throughout the world.

ix. Search for and identify family genealogies and histories back to antiquity.

x. Perform saving ordinances for all who have died without gospel covenants.

b. **Cultlike Cultures.** Those members whose behavior reflects gross transgression or capital crime have their membership rescinded or limited. The disciplinary councils of the Church have two basic purposes: (1) to promote the eternal, spiritual welfare of the individual members, and (2) to maintain a high level of purity in the Church (protect the good name of the Church) so that we may indeed be a light unto the world.

c. **Try a Lot of Stuff and Keep What Works.** Throughout its brief 175-plus year history, the Church has "experimented" (through divine mandate or organizational initiative), successfully and unsuccessfully with projects like the United Order and cooperatives, a Deseret alphabet, plural marriage, missionaries without purse or script, adult-only missionaries, handcart migrations, perpetual immigration funding, perpetual educational funding, sugar beet industry, various meeting schedules, leadership roles (such as regional representatives, assistants to the Twelve Apostles), and the list goes on. Failure or dismissal of a project does not denote a failed organization.

d. **Home-Grown Management.** The organizational structure

of the restored Church imitates no Orthodox, Anglican, or Roman Catholic style. Neither does it imitate any Presbyterian, Episcopal, or Congregational Protestant style. Its leadership structure comes from divine origin and utilizes the participation of lay clergy in addition to volunteer and stipend officers who function in hierarchal positions in the worldwide organization. However, there is no tenure of office except within the quorums of highest responsibility. Leaders at mid-level and ground-level positions can be released and later called to serve in the quorums of highest responsibility or receive assignments serving in the (as may be perceived) lowest levels of servitude. Thus the quorums of highest leadership responsibilities are populated with seasoned, tried, and experienced lay members wholly dedicated to service with "an eye single to the glory of God." Contrast this usage of mature and seasoned LDS leadership with a statement describing the Roman Catholic College of Cardinals:

> Since cardinals are rarely chosen until they have had a long career, the College becomes a gerontocracy. Most of the cardinals are still bishops of heads of Roman congregations at ages long beyond the ages at which men are retired from business and government. This has come to mean that the Roman Church rarely enjoys the best and most vigorous years of the human span of life in its most important and sensitive posts.[8]

e. **Good Enough Never Is.** Members of the Church are continually encouraged to seek for excellence, both individually and as an institution. This grows out of the Lord's "be ye therefore perfect" injunction. At all levels, there is great emphasis on seeking for greater efficiency and effectiveness within Church operations as well as in our personal lives. President Gordon B. Hinckley epitomized this standard as he led the Church. The same can be said of each president who has held the keys of presidency. At a BYU devotional, President Hinckley encouraged students to:

> Stand a little taller, rise a little higher, be a little

> better. . . . This is a great day of preparation for each of you. It is the time of beginning for something that will go on for as long as you live. I plead with you. Don't be a scrub! Rise to the high ground of excellence. You can do it. You may not be a genius. You may be lacking in some skills. But you can do better than you are now doing.[9]

When the curtains of history are rolled back and each can assess the determinants of things past, it will be made plain that the success of this Church was not the result of man's genius, but because it was the kingdom of God on earth whose destiny it was to prepare for the Second Coming of the Lord Jesus Christ.

Mormonism—America's Religion

The Old Testament prophet Isaiah prophesied that in a future time the Lord would perform a "marvelous work among this people, even a marvellous work and a wonder." He also predicted that "they also that erred in spirit shall come to understanding, and they that murmured shall learn doctrine" (Isaiah 29:14, 24). The story of the development of Mormonism is captivating. Conceptually, organizationally, and doctrinally, Mormonism stands unique within Christianity. Yet we remain an enigma*—a perplexing, baffling, and seemingly inexplicable matter to other Christian denominations. The ignorant among them attempt to scoff and discount our existence. Many in the Christian community fear our intrusion and see us only as a threat. Those who investigate Mormonism with scholarly interest discover a dynamic past and predict a vibrant future. We are a well-studied phenomenon within the discipline of social scientists. Internal scholarship has also significantly advanced as evidenced by LDS scholarly publications, symposia, seminars, and academic degrees offered.

During the visit of the angel Moroni to the boy Joseph Smith, this prophet-to-be was told that his "name should be had for good and evil among all nations, kindreds, and tongues, or that it should be both good and evil spoken of among all people" (Joseph Smith—History 1:33). One social scientist who has taken an interest in Joseph's contribution to the world of religion as well as the Christian position is Harold Bloom. Bloom has analyzed those Christian denominations that have developed anew in America. He devoted considerable attention to Mormonism and admits to being enamored with as well as critical of Joseph Smith. A list of selected excerpts from his book is found in Appendix J.

The Joseph Smith Papers Project will continue to provide invaluable internal resources to scholarly research related to the Prophet Joseph Smith and the early organizational development of The Church of Jesus Christ of Latter-day Saints. This project is funded by Utah Jazz owner Larry H. Miller. The Joseph Smith Papers Project is expected to produce at least twenty-six volumes stuffed with more than 5,000 related documents, including journals, diaries, correspondence, discourses, written histories, and legal cases. William W. Phelps, an early LDS editor and songwriter, penned the words to a favorite LDS hymn, "Praise to the Man." In the last stanza, Phelps predicted that "millions shall know 'Brother Joseph' again."[10] This project will provide important resources in bringing about that expectation.

Elder LeGrand Richards, an apostle, effective missionary, and author, produced the popular book *A Marvelous Work and a Wonder*. Initially intended to be an outline to assist missionaries in their study and presentation of the gospel, it has become essential reading for members as well as full-time missionaries. In his book, Elder Richards identified Count Leo Tolstoi, the great Russian novelist and social theorist, who expressed an oft-cited opinion as to the possible future destiny of the "American religion" founded under the instrumentality of the Prophet Joseph Smith. Elder Richards includes a discussion between Dr. Andrew D. White and Count Tolsoi as related by Thomas J. Yates. Yates had been a student at Cornell University in 1900. He had the privilege of meeting Dr. White, former president of Cornell and, at the time, U.S. Ambassador to Germany. Upon learning that Yates was a Mormon, Dr. White made an appointment to spend an evening with him, at which time he related an experience he had had with Count Tolstoi while serving as U.S. Foreign Minister to Russia in 1892. Dr. White visited often with Count Tolstoi, and upon one occasion they discussed religion:[11]

> "Dr. White," said Count Tolstoi, "I wish you would tell me about your American religion.'
>
> "We have no state church in America," replied Dr. White.
>
> "I know that, but what about your American religion?" Patiently then Dr. White explained to the Count that in America there are many religions, and that each person is free to belong to the particular church in which he is interested.
>
> To this Tolstoi impatiently replied: "I know all of this, but I want to know about the American religion. Catholicism originated in Rome;

> the Episcopal Church originated in England; the Lutheran Church in Germany, but the Church to which I refer originated in America, and is commonly known as the Mormon Church. What can you tell me of the teachings of the Mormons?"
>
> "Well," said Dr. White, "I know very little concerning them. . . ."
>
> Then Count Leo Tolstoi, in his honest and stern, but lovable, manner, rebuked the ambassador. "Dr. White, I am greatly surprised and disappointed that a man of your great learning and position should be so ignorant on this important subject. The Mormon people teach the American religion; their principles teach the people not only of Heaven and its attendant glories, but how to live so that their social and economic relations with each other are placed on a sound basis. If the people follow the teachings of this Church, nothing can stop their progress—it will be limitless. There have been great movements started in the past but they have died or been modified before they reached maturity. If Mormonism is able to endure, unmodified, until it reaches the third and fourth generation, it is destined to become the greatest power the world has ever known."

I am a fourth-generation Mormon. My great-grandfather, Jacob Zollinger, joined the Church in Switzerland. As reported in the April 2009 General Conference, Church membership is now listed at over 13 million members. Elder Marlin K. Jensen, current Church historian, reported that a nonmember sociologist, Dr. Rodney Stark of the University of Washington, shocked the world of religious sociology in 1984 by characterizing Mormonism as "the rise of a new world faith" and by projecting future membership to be 60 million by the year 2080. In 1996, Dr. Stark published a second essay entitled "So Far, So Good: A Brief Assessment of Mormon Membership Projections." He noted with satisfaction that in 1995 Church membership exceeded his 1984 estimates by almost a million members.[12]

One of President Gordon B. Hinckley's constant concerns was the management of the worldwide growth of the Church.[13] Such a concern is the envy of our antagonists. Such a concern is the by-product of the restoration of the kingdom of God in the dispensation of the fulness of times. The phenomenon of Mormonism literally fulfills the prophetic counsel of the Old Testament prophet Amos: "Surely the Lord God will do nothing, but he revealeth his secret unto his servants the prophets" (Amos 3:7). Mormonism is no longer a secret.

1. Conkin, *American Originals,* 163.

2. Richards, *A Marvelous Work and A Wonder*, 8.
3. Excerpt from Wilford Woodruff, October General Conference, 1890.
4. Taylor, *The Gospel Kingdom*, 2–3.
5. Skinner, *History of the Church*, 4:535–41.
6. Collins, *Built to Last*, 1, 4, 15.
7. *Hymns*, no. 272.
8. McKenzie, *The Roman Catholic Church*, 63.
9. Gordon B. Hinckley, "Stand a Little Taller," BYU Devotional, Nov. 1998.
10. *Hymns,* no. 27.
11. Richards, *A Marvelous Work and A Wonder*, 435.
12. See *Out of Obscurity*, 4.
13. Ibid., 249–50.

CHAPTER THIRTEEN

Do We Really Know What We Have?

It is one thing to show a man that he is in error, and another to put him in possession of truth. – John Locke

To conclude this treatise, this apology, this defense of Mormonism, I ask, "Do we really know what we have?" This church is not merely another Christian denomination or religious belief. This treatise, *Mere Mormonism*, has attempted to develop and convey that significance. Mormonism has been discovered by millions. Noted American historian and social scientist Gordon S. Wood acknowledged that there was a special timing to the advent of Mormonism: "It's timing in 1830 was providential. It appeared at precisely the right moment in American history."[1] He projected that an earlier advent would have made it difficult for the Book of Mormon to have been published. If it emerged later in the eighteenth century, "Mormonism might have been too easily stifled and dismissed by the dominant enlightened gentry culture as just another enthusiastic folk superstition."

It is a core belief within our Mormon theology that the advent of Mormonism was actually a product of divine timing. The Old Testament prophet Daniel foresaw with clarity the historic development of the rise and fall of nations who dominated ancient Israel. This historic prophecy is contained within the "great image" seen in King Nebuchadnezzar's dream. Each part of the image's person represented different empires that were to be. The Bible and the Book of Mormon document the conquest of Judea by the Babylonian Empire. This great empire was then defeated by the Persians, who were defeated in turn by the Greeks. Then came the oppression by the Alexandrian generals who ruled Egypt and Syria. After a short reprieve of Jewish independence under the Maccabees, the Romans came on the scene with ruthless dominion.

The dream of the king included a time represented by ten toes that were part of iron and part of clay. These kingdoms were represented by monarchies of later times that were partly strong and partly weak. Daniel specifically prophesied that in the days of these kings, "shall the God of heaven set up a kingdom, which shall never by destroyed" (Daniel 2:44). The first time when ten monarchies existed concurrently happened to be in the year 1830. Daniel foresaw that a "stone was cut out of the mountain without hands" and that "it shall stand for ever." This stone was the kingdom of God newly restored to the earth, which came not from human imagination and ingenuity but as a result of divine restoration. This kingdom was officially established in a common log cabin on April 6, 1830 at Fayette, New York. Joseph Smith and five other brethren were selected as the first members to satisfy the legal requirements of the state of New York. Daniel prophesied that the stone would grow in size large enough to "fill the whole earth."

Size, however, is not its full purpose. The Lord restored his Church in order to fill the whole earth with truth. The work and destiny of this Church is to perform the preparatory act of spreading the true gospel of Christianity with its attending ordinances to all people of this world, living or departed. What a magnificent challenge! A challenge from which we shrink not away nor hide. As mentioned previously, Joseph Smith added this prophetic vision regarding the destiny of Mormonism:

> Our missionaries are going forth to different nations, and in Germany, Palestine, New Holland, Australia, the East Indies, and other places the standard of truth has been erected; no unhallowed hand can stop the work from progressing; persecutions may rage, mobs may combine, armies may assemble, culumny may defame, but the truth of God will go forth boldly, nobly and independent, till it has penetrated every continent, visited every clime, swept every country, and sounded in every ear, till the purposes of God shall be accomplished, and the Great Jehovah shall say the work is done.[2]

Two such missionaries were serving in Germany. Throughout the day they had been knocking on doors with the hope of sharing their message of the Restoration but without success. Finally, a door was opened by a lady who not only received them warmly but invited the two missionaries into her home. She had been observing the activities of these missionaries in her neighborhood and desired to visit with them about religion. She was well versed in the subject. As evidence of her credentials, she pointed to three Ph.D.'s hanging on the wall of her study: one in theology, one in philosophy, and one in European history specializing in Christianity. In addition, she pointed to a row of books that she had authored. "I am a professor at the University of Munich," she said. "I have been doing this for forty- one years. I love to talk about religion. What would you like to discuss?" During the next twenty minutes these young missionaries shared with her the story of the Book of Mormon and their testimony. Before leaving they handed her a copy with their challenge to read it and pray to determine its truthfulness.

Eight and a half weeks later this expert in religion was dressed in white, anticipating her baptism into the Church. Before entering the waters of baptism she shared with those attending the story of her conversion. She did read the Book of Mormon as well as the Doctrine and Covenant, the Pearl of Great Price, all of Talmage's great writings, and many other volumes of Church doctrine. Her prayers were answered, which brought her to this moment of covenant-making. In conclusion she stated this challenge: "I don't think you members know what you have."3

It is my desire that this treatise on Mormonism will help meet that challenge. I conclude as I bear my own humble witness to the veracity of Mormonism, to the truth in true Christianity, and to the glorious message of the Restoration. As Alma queried his own people in the land of Zarahemla, I too ask:

> Do ye not suppose that I know of these things myself? Behold, I testify unto you that I do know that these things whereof I have spoken are true. And how do ye suppose that I know of their surety? Behold, I say unto you they are made known unto me by the Holy Spirit of God. Behold, I have fasted and prayed many days that I might know these things of myself. And now I do know of myself that they are true; for the Lord God hath made them manifest unto me by his Holy Spirit; and this is the spirit of revelation which is in me. (Alma 5:45–46)

1. Wood, *New York History*, 381.
2. Skinner, *History of the Church*, 4:535–41.
3. Details of this experience taken from a written account of a fireside address delivered by Scott Anderson, CES instructor in the Provo area. A copy of this account is in the possession of the author.

Appendices

APPENDIX A:

Points of the True Church

This list of points of the true church is from a book called *The Greatest Quest* by Blaine and Brenton Yorgason, published by Shadow Mountain Press in 1987. This novel describes the search by five college students to find the one true Church of Jesus Christ. At the end of this book, the authors combine their research with the work of Henry Whiffen, who also developed a list. Together they gave a total of forty-two points. In this list each point has been documented with scriptural references.

1. The Godhead consists of three separate and distinct beings–God the Father, his Son Jesus Christ, and the Holy Ghost (Genesis 1:26–27; 3:22 ; Matthew 3:17; 28:19; Luke 3:22; Acts 7:55; 1 John 5:7).

2. God the Father, as well as his Son Jesus Christ, who is a resurrected personage, both have bodies of flesh and bone and spirit (Genesis 32:30; Exodus 33:23; Luke 24:39, 41–43; John 20:17; 21:13–14; Acts 7:55–56; 1 John 3:2).

3. Jesus is the Christ, the literal Son of God, the Messiah, and the only perfect person upon the earth—not simply a great teacher. (Luke 9:35; John 17:4–5; Hebrews 1:6–7).

4. Jesus Christ, as revealed in the New Testament, is Jehovah, God of the Old Testament (Exodus 3:14; John 8:58; Isaiah 43:11; Hosea 13:4).

5. The Holy Ghost is a distinct personage of spirit and is the third member of the Godhead (Matthew 3:15–18; John 14:26; 16:13–14; 20:21–22; Ephesians 1:17).

6. The Holy Bible is the word of the Lord insofar as it is translated correctly. It is the record of the Jews and will be joined with another record in the last days to relate God's word to his people. This second record will come from a descendant of Joseph (Ezekiel 37:15–17; Isaiah 29:18; Revelation 20:12–14).

7. Jesus Christ is recognized as the head of his Church, with other officers named, beginning with a foundation of apostles and prophets, and including teachers, saints, elders, evangelists, bishops, deacons, priests, and high priests (John 15:16; Mark 3:14–15; Ephesians 2:19–20; 4:11–14).

8. Officers in Christ's Church will be "called of God." They will receive their authority through the "laying of hands." One cannot call oneself to the ministry.

    a. College degree or license insufficient.

    b. Royal priesthood will be known as such.

    c. Bishops and leaders are to marry and to have children (Acts 19:25; Hebrews 5:4, 10; Timothy 3:2; 4:2–3; 1 Peter 2:9).

9. Members of Christ's Church will be "workers," and will be called "saints." In addition, women will be included in activities and leadership (Proverbs 12:4; Romans 1:7; Ephesians 4:12; 1 Corinthians 11:7; 2 Thessalonians 1:7–10).

10. There will exist within the Church separate entities for each of the groups of members. Adult and youth organizations will exist. This point stands to reason, if Christ is concerned with helping each individual from that person's own level of understanding (Ephesians 4:11–14).

11. Christ's Church will believe in the "virgin birth" of Jesus Christ, but will not believe in the "immaculate conception" of Mary (Isaiah 7:14; Matthew 1:19–20, 23; Luke 1:26–31, 42).

12. Christ's Church will believe in immortality or eternal life, and in a heaven and hell. After the resurrection, we will be assigned to different places according to the judgment. The first resurrection

will be for the righteous and will commence 1,000 years before the second resurrection (John 3:16–17; 5:28–29; 14:2; 1 Corinthians 15:20–22; 40–42; 1 Thessalonians 4:16–18).

13. The Savior's Church will honor Sunday as the Sabbath, with the understanding that the resurrection transpired Sunday morning, the first day of the week—and thus replaced Saturday as the Sabbath (Hosea 2:11; Matthew 28:1; John 5:18; Acts 20:7; 1 Corinthians 16:2).

14. Officers as well as members of Christ's Church will receive continuous revelation from God (Amos 3:7; Matthew 16:13, 16–19; Ephesians 1:17).

15. Members of the Lord's Church will be payers of tithes and offerings (Malachi 3:8, 11; Luke 11:42; Hebrews 7:4–5).

16. Members of the Church will regularly partake of the Lord's supper. This sacrament represents the flesh and blood of Christ and is partaken in remembrance of him (Matthew 26:26–28; Acts 20:7; 1 Corinthians 16:1–2).

17. Members of the Lord's Church will experience miracles, such as visions, tongues, and prophesies. In addition, the church will practice divine healing. When members of the Church are sick, elders of the Church will anoint them with oil and heal them (Matthew 9:18; Mark 6: 5; 16:17–18; Acts 5:12, 16; James 5:14–15).

18. Church leaders will teach that the resurrected Jesus Christ will come again to the earth in the last days. This "second coming" will be greatly anticipated (Job 19:25–26; Matthew 24:30; Acts 1:11; 3:19–21).

19. Members of the Lord's Church will be persecuted for their beliefs (Matthew 5:10–12; 24:9; Luke 6:22–23; Acts 8:1–3; 28:22; Hebrews 11:36–38).

20. The Church and its members will be recognized for their "fruits"—as well as the prophets who lead them. The Church will esteem honesty, virtue, and wholesome activity (Proverbs 15:4; Luke 6:43–44; 2 Corinthians 9:10; Philippians 4:17; Hebrews 13:18).

21. The Church must provide salvation for all of God's children, not just those who receive the gospel while living on the earth. It will practice baptism for the dead (Mark 16:16; John 3:1–8; 1 Corinthians 15:29).

22. The Church will build temples similar to the one Solomon built, which was destroyed and built again at the time of Christ. These temples will have unique purposes, including baptism and other ordinances. Temples will also be holy places, contain the Holy of Holies, and be used by members as places of worship (Isaiah 2:3; Malachi 3:1; 3:7).

23. Christ's original Church was organized by him and named after him, and his Church today will also be named after him (Acts 4:10–12; Ephesians 1:22; 4:11–14; 5:23–24).

24. Specific authority to function in the administration of the Church is called "priesthood." It is obtained through ordination by one having the power to ordain (1 Samuel 13:9–14; Mark 6:7; John 7:16; 20:21; Acts 19:2–5; Hebrews 5:4–6, 8–20).

25. A higher priesthood authority is required to bestow the Holy Ghost than to baptize (Matthew 16:19; Mark 1:7–8; Acts 8:15–18; 19:2–6).

26. The Church that Christ originally organized did not baptize infants since the prerequisites for baptism were (1) a capacity for repentance of past personal sins and (2) a personal belief in the divinity and teachings of Christ (Mark 10:14–15; 16:16; Acts 2:38; 8:12).

27. The Church is to send out missionaries (in twos) to preach the gospel of Jesus Christ (Mark 6:7; Luke 10:1).

28. The Church will have a welfare system to provide for the poor and the needy within the Church. Members are to provide for themselves and their families first, and then receive help from the Church (Deuteronomy 15:11; Psalm 9:18; Isaiah 14:30; Mark 10:21; Luke 18:22; Romans 15:26).

29. The Church will have a law of health. Alcoholic beverages will not be used by members of the Church (Ephesians 5:18; 1

Corinthians 5:11; 6:9–10).

30. The Church will be one that is restored to the earth. Christ's original Church experienced a great apostasy or falling away, but his Church will be returned or restored again in the last days (Jeremiah 31:31–34; Acts 3:19–21; 2 Thessalonians 2:1–13; Revelation 14:6–7).

31. Christ's Church will believe in being saved by the grace of Christ through exercising faith in him. In other words, it will teach that when we repent of our sins and forsake them, the Atonement of Christ will cleanse us of our sins (Matthew 7:21–29; Mark 16:15–16; Luke 6:46–49; 1 Timothy 4:10; James 1:22–25; 2:14–26).

32. The Church will preach only the true gospel of Christ, with no variations. It will neither add to the meaning of Christ's teachings nor take away from them—even though current revelation will provide insight into them (Matthew 5:19; Galatians 1:6–9; Ephesians 4:5; Hebrews 13:8–9).

33. Christ's Church will espouse a pre-earth life, or a premortal existence, such as that taught by the Orthodox Jews. Included in this teaching will be the doctrine of foreordination and not predestination. God the Father will be recognized as having created the individual spirits of all people (Genesis 1:26–31; Job 38:4–7; Ecclesiastes 12:7; John 17:5; Ephesians 1:4–5; Hebrews 12:9).

34. The Church will believe in the "original sin" of Adam. Nevertheless, it will teach that Christ atoned for Adam's sin and that we will be punished for our own sins, as Adam's sin has already been atoned for (John 1:29; Acts 24:14–15; Romans 5:6–19; 1 Corinthians 15:21–23).

35. Christ's Church will teach that the gathering of Israel in the last days will be literal (Isaiah 5:26–30; 11:12–13; 35; Jeremiah 3:14–18; 31:10).

36. Members of the true Church will respect the beliefs of others (Galatians 5:22–26; 6:1–2; 2 Thessalonians 1:7–10).

37. The Church will be subject to the laws of the land, regardless of the type of government in power in that land—thus rendering unto Caesar that which is his, and to God that which is his (Matthew 22:21; Mark 12:17; Luke 20:25).

38. It should be recognized that while perfection is to be sought by each member of Christ's Church, the members will have human failings and will make mistakes, and that they will need to grow and learn, line upon line, precept upon precept (Isaiah 28:10; Ephesians 4:11–14; 28,32).

39. After repentance, baptism by immersion is essential, as is receiving the gift of the Holy Ghost. A person performing these ordinances of baptism and the laying on of hands for the gift of the Holy Ghost must be duly authorized to perform such ordinances (Matthew 3:13–15; John 3:5; Acts 2:38,41; 22:16; Romans 6:5–6).

40. The Savior's Church will have an unpaid ministry. This unpaid ministry will be called "by revelation," even as the apostles called new members to their quorum following the Resurrection of Christ (Amos 3:7; Micah 3:11; John 10:13; Acts 1:22–26; 1 Corinthians 9:18; 1 Peter 5:2).

41. Satan is a real spirit being and not a figment of people's imagination (Job 1:6; Matthew 4:10; Mark 1:13; 8:33; Luke 13:16; 22:3, 31; John 13:27; Acts 26:18).

42. The Holy Ghost will bear witness to the truthfulness of the Savior's plan when it is presented. This is the one sure way of knowing which, if any, of the churches belong to the Savior (John 16:13–14; 1 Corinthians 12:4–12; Galatians 5:22–26; Ephesians 1:17).

APPENDIX B:

Athanasian Creed

The following is a literal translation of the Greek text of the Constantinopolitan form, with some words altered or added for Western liturgical use. It is generally agreed that St. Athanasius was not its author. Internal evidences seem to justify the conclusion that it grew out of several provincial synods, chiefly that of Alexandria, held about the year 361, and presided over by St. Athanasius. It was never adopted by any official council, and some even date its origin to the seventh or eighth century. Even as an unofficial statement, it demonstrates how much doctrine had changed by that time. It contains more statements of what one cannot comprehend than statements of what one can believe and testify.

THE ATHANASIAN CREED

(FIFTH CENTURY LATIN COMPILATION)

"Whoever will be saved: before all things it is necessary that he hold the Catholic faith. Which Faith except everyone do keep whole and undefiled: without doubt he shall perish everlastingly. And the Catholic Faith is this: that we worship one God in Trinity, and Trinity in Unity. Neither confounding the Persons: nor dividing the Substance. For this is one Person of the Father, another of the Son, and another of the Holy Ghost. But the Godhead of the Father, of the Son, and of the Holy Ghost, is all one: the Glory co-equal, the Majesty co-eternal. Such as the Father is, such is the Son, and such is the Holy Ghost. The Father uncreate, the Son uncreate, and the Holy Ghost uncreate. The Father incomprehensible, the Son incomprehensible, and the Holy Ghost incomprehensible. The Father eternal, the Son eternal, and the Holy Ghost eternal. And yet they are not three eternals: but one Eternal. As also there are not three incomprehensibles, nor three uncreated: But one Uncreated and one Incomprehensible. So likewise the Father is almighty, the Son almighty, the Holy Ghost almighty. And yet they are not three almighties: but one Almighty. So the Father is God, the Son is God and the Holy Ghost is God. And yet they are not three gods; but one God. So likewise the Father is Lord, the Son Lord and the Holy Ghost Lord, And yet not three lords: but one Lord. For like as we are compelled by the Christian verity to acknowledge every Person by Himself to be God and Lord: So are we forbidden by the Catholic religion to say, there be three gods, or three lords. The Father is made of none: neither created, nor begotten. The Son is of the Father alone, not made, nor created, but begotten. The Holy Ghost is the Father and of the Son, neither made, nor created nor begotten, but proceeding. So there is one Father, not three Fathers, one Son, not three Sons, one Holy Ghost, not three Holy Ghosts. And in this trinity none is afore, or after other: none is the greater or less than another. But the whole three Persons are co-eternal together, and co-equal. So that in all things, as is aforesaid, the Unity in Trinity, and the Trinity in Unity is to be worshipped. He therefore that will be saved: must thus think of the Trinity. Furthermore, it is necessary to everlasting salvation: that he also believe rightly the Incarnation of our Lord Jesus Christ. For the right Faith is, that we believe and confess: that our Lord Jesus Christ, the Son of God, is God and Man. God, of the Substance of the Father, begotten before the worlds: and Man, of the substance of His mother, born in the world. Perfect God, and perfect Man: of a reasonable soul and human flesh subsisting: Equal to the Father: as touching His Godhead, and inferior to the Father, as touching His Manhood. Who although He be God and Man, yet He is not two, but one Christ. One: not by conversion of the Godhead into flesh, but by the taking of the Manhood into God. One altogether: not by confusion of Substance, but by unity of Person. For as the reasonable soul and flesh is one man: So God and Man is one Christ. Who suffered for our salvation: descended into hell, rose again the third day from the dead. He ascended into heaven, He sitteth on the right hand of the Father, God Almighty, from whence He shall come to judge the quick and the dead. At whose coming all men shall rise again with their bodies, and shall give account for their own works. And they that have done good shall enter into life everlasting, and they that have done evil into everlasting fire. This is the Catholic Faith: which except a man believe faithfully, he cannot be saved.

APPENDIX C:

Incorrect Doctrines of Christ Taught within Historic Christianity

Compiled by Ronald R. Zollinger

1. **New Age Modernists.** Christ was merely the creative invention of a new first and second century Jewish sect called Christians who attempted to justify their movement with a supernatural figurehead.

2. **Jesus Seminar.** Christ was a real historical individual but His divinity—His divine Sonship, his miracles, His ability to forgive sin and heal and regenerate human souls, His power over life and death—is not real. Most of the words ascribed to Jesus in the four Gospels (especially the Gospel of John) were never really uttered by Jesus, but reflected the ideas that his followers gleaned from his teachings and later gathered into a collection of oral traditions historically named Q (*Quelle*: German for source).

3. **Ebionites.** Christ was born as any normal human, but later received a divine nature at the time of his baptism. Ebionites were a Jewish Christian sect of the second century.

4. **Docetists.** Christ was a pure spirit-being, uncontaminated by the material world, who only appeared to be human. Docetists surfaced during the second century.

5. **Marcionites.** Christ was not born of a woman, but suddenly appeared at the synagogue at Capernaum in A.D. 29 as a fully grown man whose human experience and sufferings were merely apparent, not real. Marcionites surfaced during the second century.

6. **Monarchians.** God existed in different modes, but only in one mode at any one time. Monarchians practiced during the second and third century.

7. **Nestorians.** Christ possessed two distinct natures—human and divine—which were separate but juxtaposed upon each other. Nestorians existed primarily during the fifth century.

8. **Unitarians.** Christ lived a life worthy of emulation but possessed no additional divinity than is already possessed by each human being. There is no need of a divine sacrificial ransom for the sins of mankind. Christ died and is still dead.

9. **Jehovah's Witnesses.** Christ died a human body, but was resurrected as a mighty spirit creature who is now invisibly present in the world and will always remain invisible to humans.

10. **Quakers (Friends).** The virgin birth and the divinity of Jesus are not essential truths in contrast to each individual's quest to receive the divine light of personal illumination.

11. **Church of Christ, Scientist (Christian Scientists).** There is no reality outside of the All-in-All God. Jesus of Nazareth was the manifestation of the divine in God, who was able to reject the existence of disease and death, thus overcoming the entrapment of the tomb.

12. **United Society of Believers in Christ's Second Coming (Shakers).** Jesus of Nazareth was the fulfillment of the First Coming of the Messianic Christ and represented the male gender duality of God. Ann Lee was the representative of the female gender duality of God and the fulfillment of Christ's Second Coming (see introduction of D&C 49, and verse 22).

13. **Christian myth.** Jesus and Mary Magdalene were husband and wife. Their offspring were scattered throughout Europe and

originated the line of Frankish kings known as the Merovingians (for example, Clovis I). This myth was popularized by the "DaVinci Code" phenomenon.

14. **Traditional Christianity.** Jesus of Nazareth is not the Jehovah of the Old Testament.
15. **Trinitarian Christianity.** Jesus was conceived from a union of the Holy Spirit and Mary.
16. **Trinitarian Christianity.** Jesus is the Triune's incarnate representation of the "Son."
17. **Trinitarian Christianity.** The "Son" was "begotten" (the only begotten) but not created and of the same substance as the "Father."
18. **Arian Christianity.** The "Son" was a creation of the Father and was of like substance.
19. **Traditional Christianity.** Lucifer and Jesus have never had any filial relationship.
20. **Traditional Christianity.** There is no doctrine of Jesus as the "Firstborn" spirit child of our Heavenly Parents, as there is no belief in Christianity of our spirit premortal existence or of our previously existing heavenly family.

APPENDIX D:

The Latter-day Saint Plan of Salvation

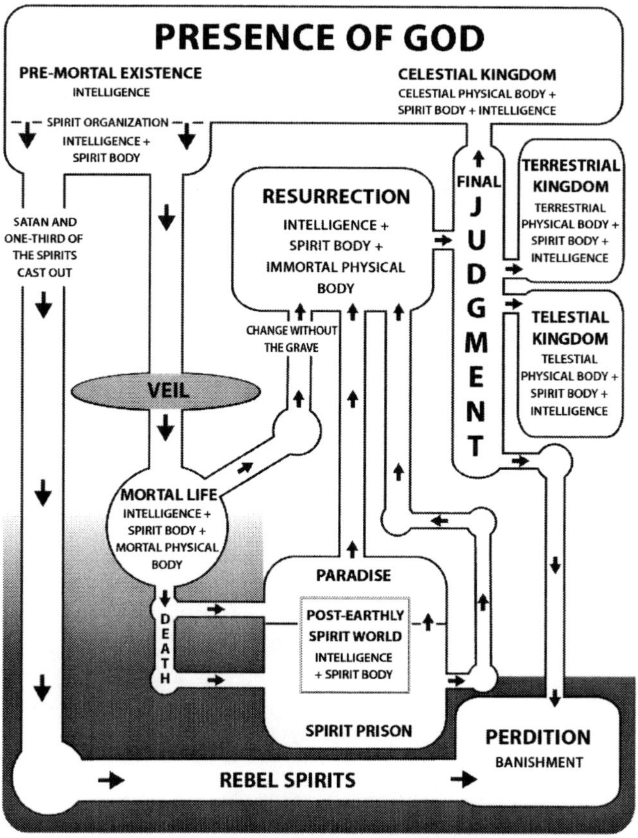

"Modeled after a CES symposium handout which was adapted from a chart published in *The Instructor*, 1961 (inside book cover), and a chart from the 1969 seminary Old Testament Home Study Course, lesson 10, page 33."

GRAPHIC BY R. BRYSEN SPENCER

APPENDIX E:

The Four Types of Sin

FORGIVABLE	PARDONABLE
These are the sins of mankind in which the Atonement of Christ satisfies the demands of the Law of Justice. Forgiveness is possible only through the process of repentance (Alma 11:40).	There are two types of sins that receive pardon. The first are the sins of those who partake not of the Atonement of Christ and suffer self-atonement to satisfy the demands of the Law of Justice (D&C 19:16–17). The second type are the actions of individuals that would otherwise be considered "sin" but which are pardoned through the Atonement of Christ. These actions arise from those who are still within the age of innocence or whose condition of mind or body places them in a state of non-accountability outside the law (Moroni 8:8, 10, 12, 22).
UNFORGIVABLE	**UNPARDONABLE**
The Atonement is unavailable to satisfy the demands of the broken law for these sins. The sinners themselves must pay the penalty in order for the Law of Justice to be satisfied (D&C 19:16–17). Examples include murder by those who are acquainted with the truth (D&C 42:18; 3 Nephi 30:2) and the second offense of adultery after the first offense has been forgiven (D&C 42:24–26).	This sin is also called blasphemy against the Holy Ghost (JST Mark 3:24). This action is of such seriousness that the broken law cannot be paid through the Atonement or pardoned through self-atonement. The law will always lay claim upon the sinner as they will dwell eternally in outer darkness.

APPENDIX F:

What's in a Name?

Compiled by Ronald R. Zollinger

"Thou shalt call his name Jesus: for he shall save his people from their sins" (Matthew 1:21).

Jesus' full Hebrew name was Yehoshua Ben Yoseph. This would translate into an anglicized format as Jesus, son of Joseph.

"Jesus" is the anglicized form of the Latin name, *Iesus,* which comes from the Greek *Iesous.* The Hebrew version of *Iesous* is *Yehoshua* (which means "salvation") of which Yeshua is a contraction. The English version of Yeshua is Joshua (which means "help of Jehovah," and "hoshia" means "to help"). Therefore, the name "Jesus" means "Jehovah is Salvation."

The Hebrew word *Ben* means "son of." The anglicized form of Yoseph is Joseph, the name of Jesus' earthly father in our King James New Testament.

"Christ" is the anglicized form of the Latin *Crist* and the Greek *Chistus* or *Christos,* which means "the anointed one." The Hebrew version of this meaning is *Messhiach,* which in English is "Messiah."

The name Jesus Christ literally means "He who is the Anointed One, our Savior."

Tradition holds that the name of God was first introduced to Moses upon Mount Sinai: I AM THAT I AM. "Thus shalt thou say unto the children of Israel, I AM hath sent you" (Exodus 3:14). This title infers that God is the "self existing one" or "He who has existed through all eternity."[1] In the Hebrew Old Testament, the name of God was written with four consonants: YHWH. Not until 300 A.D. to 900 A.D. were vowels or pronunciation marks included in Hebrew. Therefore, there has been some debate as to the proper pronunciation of this name of God. Modern scholars often write it as *Yahweh*, but the King James translators wrote is as Jehovah, a word popularized by William Tyndale. The Old Testament Jews also used the word *Eloah* or the plural form *Elohim* in reference to *YHWH*. These ancient Jews, however, viewed the name as being so sacred that it should not be pronounced out loud. Whenever they found it written, they would substitute the Hebrew word *adonai*, meaning "my Lord." The translators who produced the King James Version of the Old Testament honored that tradition of the Jews, and where they found the name *YHWH*, they wrote it (with very few exceptions) "the Lord" (*Krios* in Greek). However, *adonai* can also be used as a title of respect for men, as in the phrase "My lord, the king." To distinguish between the two uses, the translators wrote *LORD* in small capital letters if it represented the name of deity and regular upper and lower case letters (Lord) if used normally (see, for example, 2 Samuel 15:21, where both uses are found in the same verse). The declaration of the angels to the shepherds used Lord or *Adonai* in reference to deity; literally it could be translated "Jehovah."

Now we begin to sense the impact of the angel's words upon the shepherds. In essence, here is their pronouncement: "Unto you is born this day in the city prophesied to be the birthplace of the Messiah, Yeshua (or Jesus), the Savior, who is the Anointed One (the Messiah), and who is also Jehovah, the God of your fathers" (Luke 2:11).

1. McConkie, *Mormon Doctrine*, 340.

APPENDIX G:

Evil Thoughts Originating from the Natural Man

Compiled by Ronald R. Zollinger

"Whereas the natural man vents his anger, the men and women of Christ are "not easily provoked" (1 Corinthians 13:5). Whereas the natural man is filled with greed, the men and women of Christ "seeketh not [their] own" (1 Corinthians 13:5). Whereas the natural man seldom denies himself worldly pleasures, the men and women of Christ seek to bridle all their passions (see Alma 38:12). Whereas the natural man covets praise and riches, the men and women of Christ know that such things are but the "drop" (D&C 117:8). Human history's happiest irony will be that the covenant-keeping, unselfish individuals will finally receive "all that [the] Father hath!" (Neal A. Maxwell, *Men and Women of Christ*, 14).

"Among the most common sexual sins our young people commit are necking and petting . . . [which] awaken lust and stir evil thoughts and sex desires" (*The Teachings of Spencer W. Kimball*, 280).

"Just as language can be used to bless or curse, so music is a means of singing praises to the Lord or of planting evil thoughts and desires in the minds of men" (Bruce R. McConkie, *The Promised Messiah*, 553–54).

"Memorize some of the inspiring songs of Zion and then, when the mind is afflicted with temptations, sing aloud, keep before your mind the inspiring words and thus crowd out the evil thoughts. This could also be done to crowd out debilitating, depressive thoughts" (Ezra Taft Benson

"Do Not Despair," *Ensign* Oct. 1986, 5).

"Evil thoughts are sinful (Prov. 15:26; 24:9). They are an abomination in themselves, and they lead to further wickedness. Evils are not committed until they have been thought out in the heart. For from within, out of the heart of men, proceed evil thoughts, adulteries, fornications, murders, thefts, covetousness, wickedness, deceit, lasciviousness, an evil eye, blasphemy, pride, foolishness" (Mark 7:21–22; Matt. 15:19; Luke 6:45). (McConkie, *Mormon Doctrine*, 792.)

"Allowing worldly thoughts to enter your mind," Elder Craven said, "can lead to unrighteous acts." "When evil thoughts arise—Stop! Think! Control your mind! Visualize a large exit sign in your mind's eye. Immediately change your thoughts. Get off that avenue of thinking," he counseled. "To overcome temptation, Church members must control their thoughts," he continued. "Discipline what you allow your eyes to see, your ears to hear, your mouth to speak and your hands to touch" (*The Church News*, Conference Issues, April 13, 1996, 23).

"Lucifer, who fell from heaven . . . set about the opposition of this earth and to wrest the dominion from Adam, and he has been trying it ever since, from the beginning till the present, to wrest the dominion of this earth from Adam and his posterity, and the only means by which he expects or hopes to accomplish it is, in short, to take possession of the tabernacles of Adam . . . He has sought to do this, but he will not accomplish that evil design, for the Father has provided a way of thwarting him. The Savior will displace him. The name of Jesus has power over all these evil spirits, Lucifer and all the hosts of hell who are cast down to the earth, and have set up their abode in the tabernacles of men, and in many instances they have succeeded. They [evil spirits] do not altogether get possession of the tabernacles of men, only in isolated cases. There are cases in which it seems that these spirits so far control the tabernacles of men as to find the natural spirit that owns these tabernacles and suspend the operations of their functions, and usurp the control of the functions of the body, and make these organs of speech speak the language of devils, and make these tabernacles perform the wicked works of the evil one; while the spirit that owns, and should control this tabernacle, is bound, as it were, hand and foot; and where these powers and functions are thus suspended in these isolated cases, we call them maniacs, because their natural powers are suspended, and they are under the dominion of devils" (Erastus Snow, *Journal of Discourses*, 19:275–76, March 3, 1878).

APPENDIX H:

"I Am That I Am"

Compiled by Ronald R. Zollinger

OLD TESTAMENT

I [am] the LORD
I [am] the LORD your God
I [am] the LORD their God
I [am] the LORD thy God
I [am] the LORD that . . . doth sanctify you, hallows, delivers, protect, brought you out, and so forth.
I [am] the LORD which exercise loving kindness
I [am] the Almighty God
I [am] the LORD, your Holy One, the creator of Israel
I [am] the God of Abraham
I [am] the God of Bethel
I [am] the God of thy father, the God of Abraham, the God of Isaac, and the God of Jacob
I [am] the LORD thy God, the Holy One of Israel, thy Saviour
I, [even] I, [am] the LORD; and beside me [there is] no saviour
I [am] the first, and I [am] the last; and beside me [there is] no God
I [am] the LORD that maketh all [things]. . .
Then shall they know that I [am] the LORD their God
For I [am] the LORD, I change not

NEW TESTAMENT

I am the Son of God

I am the bread of life
I am the bread which came down from heaven
I am the living bread which came down from heaven
I am the stone
I am the head of the corner
I am the light of the world
I am the door of the sheepfold
I am the good shepherd
I am the resurrection, and the life
I am the way, the truth, and the life
I am the vine
I am the true vine
I am the root and the offspring of David, [and] the bright and morning star
I am the first and the last
I am the King of the Jews
I am the Christ

BOOK OF MORMON

I am the Lord their God
I am the light
I am the law, and the light
I am the first, and I am also the last
I am the Father and the Son
I am the same yesterday, today, and forever
I am the God of Israel, and the God of the whole earth
I am the light and the life of the world.
I am Alpha and Omega, the beginning and the end
I am the Father, I am the light, and the life, and the truth of the world

DOCTRINE AND COVENANTS

I am the light which shineth in darkness
I am the life and the light of the world
I am the same that spake unto you from the beginning
I am the same who came unto mine own and mine own received me not
I am the same which spake, and the world was made, and all things

came by me

I am the same which have taken the Zion of Enoch into mine own bosom

I am he who was lifted up. I am Jesus that was crucified. I am the Son of God.

I am in your midst, and I am the good shepherd, and the stone of Israel

I am the Lord of Hosts

I am the Son of the living God, that I was, that I am, and that I am to come

I am the true light that is in you

I am the true light that lighteth every man that cometh into the world

I am the Spirit of truth

I am the first and the last; I am he who liveth, I am he who was slain; I am your advocate with the Father

I am the Lord your God, and will save

I am the Lord thy God, and will answer

I am the Lord thy God; and I give

I am the Lord thy God, and will be with thee

I am the Lord thy God, and will destroy

MOSES AND ABRAHAM

I am the Lord God Almighty, and Endless is my name

I am the Only Begotten

I am the Only Begotten of the Father from the beginning

APPENDIX I:

The Christmas Gifts of Jesus Christ

By Ronald R. Zollinger for a Christmas presentation

> I made myself a snowball, as perfect as could be.
> I thought I'd keep it as a pet, and let is sleep with me.
> I made it some pajamas and a pillow for its head,
> Then last night it ran away—
> But first, it wet the bed.

Even though the author of this poem unknown, my guess is that it came from the mind of a clever adult. One of the traits of our humanness is our fanciful imagination. From it we have created cultures full of fairy tales, legends, festivals and celebrations, feasts, and holidays. To the end that they help to identify and deepen healthy and productive social values and traditions, they generally serve a positive function in society.

Now what of the holiday called Christmas. A personal story is told by William F. French of a Christmas party sponsored by American GI's for some Japanese children. It was a party atmosphere with a program that featured a time for Christmas caroling and Santa Claus wearing a big red suit and cotton whiskers, giving out presents. Then little Ito asked his question. "Whose birthday is it?" With all of the focus upon Santa, little Ito was confused when he was told that Christmas was meant to celebrate Jesus's birth.

In the early fall of 1962, Boyd K. Packer performed an experiment with a group of about a thousand teenagers in a fall setting. He asked them to react with the first thought that came into their minds after he gave them a word cue. The word was "Christmas." Ninety-four percent responded with such words as "snow," "lights," "reindeer," "trees," "presents," "shopping," and "Santa Claus." Two percent responded with irrelevancies. One boy responded with "a broken leg." That had been his experience for Christmas the year before. Brother Packer was amazed that no one responded with "broken wallet," but maybe that is reserved for another survey, one including parents. There were just four percent who responded with words such as "Bethlehem," "wise men," "shepherds," "Christmas carols," or "Christ."

Some of our fanciful Christmas traditions have had interesting origins. Even the caricature Santa Claus is based upon a real man named Nicholas who was an eastern Catholic Bishop of Myra in Asia Minor (now Turkey) in the early fourth century. He became sainted in the Catholic tradition and is known as Saint Nicholas. In addition to being a bishop, he was also a man of wealth who used his money to do good deeds, but swore those whom he aided to secrecy. Over time, he became the patron saint of Russia, sailors, bankers, and even thieves and pirates. Many church edifices in Europe were dedicated to him. Originally, he was depicted in a long bright red robe. As his fame and legend spread, he acquired a white horse on which to ride and a black slave boy who carried gifts in a sack that never became empty. In Belgium and Holland, he became the patron saint of children to whom he made an annual visit, leaving gifts for them. The American settlement of New Amsterdam by the Dutch resulted in the importation of Saint Nicholas into the American colonies. Eventually his homeland was changed to the North Pole and his horse was exchanged for a sleigh and eight reindeer. His name went through a transmigration from Saint Nicholas to *Sinter Klaas* and finally, as "r's" are usually dropped by those along the Atlantic seaboard—to Sinta Klaas, or Santa Claus as we know it today. In our day, the remnants of the original Catholic bishop are surrounded with trappings, myth, and fanciful lore.

Quoting T. Edgar Lyon in an old *Improvement Era* article, "Santa Claus may seem to have overshadowed Christ in the popular mind, but to those who listen, penetrating the obscurity of myth and legend, tradition and social custom, the message of the angels sounds above the folk carols; to those who see, the star of Bethlehem shines brighter than tinsel or pagan candle; and to those who feel, the greatest of all gifts is still the gift of the Son whom the Father sent, not to condemn the world, but to redeem it."[1]

In the late 1800s, William Chatterton Dix applied words to the old English tune of "Greensleeves" to give us one of my favorite Christmas carols. This carol begins with the words: "What child is this . . . ?" There have been many children born of which this same question has been asked in retrospect.

In the spirit of the new millennium, several lists of the most influential individuals of the past millennium have been created. Michael Hart has produced a book documenting his choice for the 100 most influential people in history. Among the top of all these lists are included the founders of the world's living religions. Interestingly enough, the founders of five of the world's major living religions were born within sixty years of the date in which the Book of Mormon record begins in 600 B.C.. Out of the nine world religions that credit their beginning to a single individual, four of these founders were born into this world in reported miraculous circumstances. The traditions perpetuated by their followers are full of events suggesting they led an exceptional and exemplary life dominated by a struggle to achieve a mastery over their physical desires and a supernal connection to a higher essence or deity.

How then is Jesus of Nazareth, the central focus of the world's largest religion with over two billion adherents, different from these other founders or any other child that ever has or ever will be born upon this earth? Is the story of Jesus simply to be immersed by our fanciful imagination to become part of the myth and legend associated with the festival known as Christmas?

True followers of Jesus Christ will have none of that. Let us focus upon a few truths concerning this child who is the Son of God, who is the Savior of all mankind without regard to race, creed, gender, or religious affiliation.

First, all prophets from Adam down to John the Baptist prophesied in some way concerning the coming of this child. After the angel instructed Adam as to the purpose of the ordinance of sacrifice, the Holy Ghost fell upon Adam and "he began to prophesy." Isaiah added significant prophetic detail to foretell events in the life of this child destined to be the Savior. For example, in Isaiah 7, "Behold, a virgin shall conceive, and bear a son." In Isaiah 9, "For, unto us a child is born, unto us a son is given and his name shall be called, Wonderful, Counselor, the mighty God, the everlasting Father, the Prince of Peace." In Isaiah 11, it states that "the spirit of the Lord shall rest upon him, the spirit of wisdom and understanding, the spirit of counsel and might, the spirit of knowledge . . . but with righteousness shall he judge." Nephi saw with prophetic clarity how he healed the sick and the diseased and performed many miracles, but that he was also "judged of the world" and was "lifted upon the cross and slain for the sins of the world" (1 Nephi 11:33).

Second, He lived not only an exemplary life, but a perfect life wherein he became the model for all mankind of charity, love, service, leadership, sacrifice, and dedication.

Third, He performed an inhuman act we call the atonement in which he offered himself for a substitutionary sacrifice in our behalf. It is this last truth that, for me, sets Jesus Christ as a human being apart from all others. It means I have a dependent relationship with him in order for me to achieve my full physical and spiritual potential. After all my best efforts and works of moral righteousness, I still fall short to satisfy the demands of the Law of Justice. It is Christ that saves me from the chains of death and offers me a life of eternal happiness and continued familial association. That is the uniqueness of LDS Christianity.

Let me clarify. The founders of all other world religions gave to their followers a legacy of teachings that helped identify truths or a path that each individual needed to follow to obtain his own salvation or heaven. But each individual's success is entirely dependent upon his own efforts, his own achievement. Buddhism comes closest in offering the concept of a "savior." As individuals successfully follow the eight-fold path, they can achieve a release from off the wheel of reincarnation and obtain a Buddha-like state and become a savior. In this capacity, they reach out to inspire and help others discover for themselves the discipline of the eight-fold path, which leads them towards their personal nirvana—a state where the individuality of each saved person is lost and absorbed into a blissful union of the masses.

Matthew records that it was wise men from the East who looked for true signs of the coming of the Messiah, recognized, the star and sought the child who was to be born in Bethlehem. These wise men came from afar bearing gifts that eventually supported Joseph, Mary and the Christ child on their journey and stay in Egypt and their eventual return to their home in Nazareth. Now it is Jesus that reciprocates and offers gifts to those who become wise men and women, who seek for and find their Savior in Jesus of Nazareth. And Jesus will, with his Godly gifts, fully sustain us in our journey through mortality and provide the way for us to return home with a celestial individuality to God, who gave us life.

Paul, in the book of Romans (5:18) refers to the gift of Christ: "Therefore as by the offence of one judgement came upon all men to condemnation; even so by the righteousness of one the free gift came upon all men unto justification of life." A life justified by Christ surpasses a life based upon any other paradigm.

In both the New Testament as well as in the Book of Mormon, the commandment is given to become perfect. After his Resurrection, Christ, as recorded in 3 Nephi, offered himself as well as God our Father as models of perfection. Early in Luke's Gospel, Luke positions Christ's growth and development in four areas or domains of mortal existence. Luke states that "Jesus increased in wisdom and in stature and in favor with God and with man" (Luke 2:52). With all of the glitter and excitement of this coming holy-day season, may we reflect upon the gifts of Christ, which can lead us to a state of perfection that includes eternal life filled with celestial happiness and a fullness of joy.

Christ's gifts may be categorized within each of the four domains of life through which we must grow to perfection. Concerning the first domain: As Jesus himself increased in wisdom and knowledge, he also offers to every individual born into this world gifts of his Holy Spirit. The light of Christ gives light to every man that cometh into the world (D&C 84:46). This light helps establish a base of morality—a knowledge of right and wrong, a conscience.

Second, the workings of the Holy Ghost not only add to the base of man's scientific and philosophic knowledge, but also lead each person to those saving truths that help establish a covenant relationship with Christ. In the second domain, physical perfection is not found in exercise regimes or in dietary controls (although they are helpful to produce a healthy physical state). True physical perfection comes through the gift of Christ's resurrection in that "not a hair of the head shall be lost but all things shall be restored to their proper and perfect frame" (Alma 40:23). The resurrection comes with the added gift of allowing us to overcome the great conundrum that has plagued all of humanity. Job referred to this mystery when he offered these words to his friends, "And if a man dies, shall he live again?" (Job 14:14) Christ's gift of life beyond the grave is extended to all humanity, all that ever was, is, or is yet to come, worlds without end.

The third domain addresses our relationship with God. Since sin leads us to an estranged relationship with God our Father, Christ has provided us with the wonderful reconciliatory gift of the Atonement, which literally refers the process of becoming "at one" with God. Through the events of Gethsemane as well as Calvary, Christ took each of us, as it were, through these temples of sacrifice. In these acts of expiation, Christ offers each of us who use our gift of agency the means to voluntarily, as King Limhi worded it, "give away all my sins to know thee" (Alma 22:18).

The fourth domain, as described by Luke, indicates that Christ increased his favor with man. Christ was one of the most popular social figures in all of Palestine. But it's not social prestige that completes our quest for perfection. The focus of man's relationship with man implies a measure of the quality of that relationship. And the quality of our relationships with each other is centered squarely upon each individual's ability to control his thoughts, his sight, his speech, his emotions, his morality, his judgment, and his full measure of charity and meekness. All of these concepts are contained in Christ's teachings in the Sermon on the Mount, given in both the Old World as well as the New World. The Book of Mormon prophets taught the importance of overcoming the emotions of the natural man (Mosiah 3:19). Paul encouraged us to seek earnestly for the fruits of the Spirit, which are love, joy, peace, longsuffering, gentleness, faith, meekness, temperance, not provoking one another nor envying one another. What gift of Christ addresses all these virtues, which seem to many to be almost impossible to acquire if we are left to our own means? This great gift is known simply as his "grace." We hesitate to talk much of this gift. It seems to be found sacrosanct in Protestantism and Orthodox Christianity, but not discussed much in Mormon theology. Let's end that. The Bible Dictionary teaches a marvelous sermon. "This grace is an enabling power that allows men and women to lay hold on eternal life and exaltation after they have expended their own best efforts. Divine grace is needed by every soul . . . because of man's weaknesses and shortcomings. [Through grace] we receive strength and assistance to do good works that [we] otherwise would not be able to maintain if left to [our] own means (LDS Bible Dictionary, "Grace"). Each of us needs a large measure of Christ's grace to lay hold upon every good virtue necessary for perfection.

May I suggest one more gift in this area. It may be a backhanded offering. Just before Ether concluded his record of the Jaredite nation, he encouraged all men to come unto Christ who will show unto them their weaknesses. You see, by accessing Christ's grace and overcoming each of our weaknesses, Christ will make weak things (us) strong (Ether 12:27). We are taught that each of us is blessed with spiritual gift(s) as described by Paul (1 Corinthians. 12), Moroni (Moroni 10), and Joseph Smith (D&C 46). The corollary to these spiritual gifts as we apply the teaching of Ether is that each of us is blessed with specific weaknesses. Our weaknesses are actually blessings in disguise. Through our dedicated efforts and with the assistance of the grace of Jesus Christ, the process of overcoming these weaknesses and bringing them under control enables us to come closer to acquiring the "countenance of Christ."

Christmas evening, as we all gather together in our family units, or on Christmas morning as we excitedly gaze upon the many gifts we share with each other or that "mysteriously" appear from fanciful caricatures, let us not forget and securely focus upon the man who is true, who is real, who is Christ, our Redeemer, our Savior, the Son of the Highest. God our Father, and may I add, our Mother, gave to us their greatest gift, a gift contained in the life, in the death, and in the Resurrection of their Only Begotten Son. I testify that he lives and loves each of us with a perfect love. In the name of Jesus Christ, Amen.

1. T. Edgar Lyon, "Christ, Christmas, and Santa Claus." *Improvement Era*, December 1943, 756, 791–792)

APPENDIX J:

In Criticism and in Praise of Joseph Smith

Statements written by Harold Bloom in *The American Religion*

Compiled by Ronald R. Zollinger

"Joseph Smith was a religious genius, though only a mixed orator and an indifferent writer."

"All of Mormon scripture is the work of Joseph Smith, and his life, personality, and visions far transcended his talents at the composition of divine texts."

"Whatever his lapses, Smith was an authentic religious genius, unique in our national history."

"It does not matter how retrospective and revised a First Vision this is; all religion necessarily is revisionary in regard to its own sacred origins. What moves me, here and elsewhere in Smith, is the sureness of his instincts, his uncanny knowing precisely what is needful for the inauguration of a new faith."

"The Mormons, like the Jews before them, are a religion that became a people. That . . . always was Joseph Smith's pragmatic goal, for he had the genius to see that only by becoming a people could the Mormons survive."

"Smith's insight could have come only from a remarkably apt reading of the Bible, and there I would locate the secret of his religious genius.

He was anything but a great writer, but he was a great reader, or creative misreader, of the Bible."

"With the Book of Mormon, we arrive at the center of Joseph Smith's prophetic mission, but hardly at any center of Mormonism, because of Smith's extraordinary capacity for speculative development in the fourteen years that remained to him after its publication. The Book of Mormon was not only his first work; it is the portrait of a self-educated, powerful mind at the untried age of twenty-four. It has bravura, but beyond question it is wholly tendentious and frequently tedious. If one compares it closely to Smith's imaginations in the Pearl of Great Price and Doctrine and Covenants, it seems the work of some other writer, and I don't mean Mormon or Moroni."

This book, *The American Religion*, "has only two heroes: the flamboyant Joseph Smith and the quiet twentieth century Southern Baptist religious writer Edgar Young Mullins. . . . I judge Smith to be greater and more interesting than the current faith of the people that he created. Partly this is because he died much too soon, with considerable portion of his innovative prophecy left incomplete."

"I cannot recommend that the [Book of Mormon] be read either fully or closely, because it scarcely sustains such reading. . . . But the genesis of the Book of Mormon is not my concern (though I assume that magical trance-states were involved, so that we can dismiss the literalism both of golden plates and of conscious charlatanry)."

"Whatever account of charisma is accepted, the Mormon prophet possessed that quality to a degree unsurpassed in American history. Other Americans have been religion makers . . . but none of them has the imaginative vitality of Joseph Smith's revelation."

"I am in no position to judge Joseph Smith as a revelator, but as a student of the American imagination I observe that his achievement as national prophet and seer is clearly unique in our history . . . . Joseph Smith did not excel as a writer or as a theologian, let alone as psychologist and philosopher. But he was an authentic religious genius and surpassed all Americans, before or since, in the possession and expression of what could be called the religion-making imagination."

"There have been many other religion-making imaginations in

America before, contemporary with, and since Joseph Smith's, but not one of them came near him in courage, vitality, or comprehensiveness, or in so honest a realization of the consequences of a charismatic endowment. It is clear why Smith . . . and so many other Mormons were murdered, and why the Saints were driven from state to state."

"Joseph's Smith's most remarkable innovation or restoration [was] plural marriage . . . which had to be abandoned by the Latter-day Saints a century ago as Utah's price of admission into the federal union . . . . Smith's genius for restoration exceeded that of Muhammad, and the religious necessity and sincerity of Smith's vision [deification of man, tangible bodies of the Father and Son, celestial marriage, plural marriage, and baptisms for the dead] are beyond doubt."

"One scholar . . . has remarked upon 'the virtually unfathomable complexity of Joseph Smith's early ideas.' "

"Two aspect of the Saints' vision seem starkly central to me; no other American religious movement is so ambitious, and no rival even remotely approaches the spiritual audacity that drives endlessly towards accomplishing a titanic design. The Mormons fully intend to convert the nation and the world; . . . yet the Mormons will not falter. I am optimistic enough to project that hundreds of millions of Mormons will [exist] in the year 3000."

"I do not find it possible to doubt that Joseph Smith was an authentic prophet. Where in all of American history can we find his match? . . . In proportion to his importance and his complexity, he remains the least-studied personage, of an undiminished vitality, in our entire national saga."

"If there is already in place any authentic version of American Religion, then as Tolstoy surmised, it must be Mormonism, whose future as yet may prove decisive for the nation, and for more than this nation alone. But that again returns us to the charismatic personality of Joseph Smith, and to the religion-making genius that was his imagination and that gave his followers the design for their quest."

"The material continuity of Smith's imaginations is assured and will endure at least as long as our nation endures . . . the religion of the Latter-day Saints moves on in ways both seen and unseen, and is certain only to confound all our expectations."

APPENDIX K:

The First Vision

The artist who painted the cover picture is Everett Clarke Thorpe (1904 - 1983). Thorpe was originally from Providence, Utah. He began his figurative art as sports artist for both *The Desert News* and *The Salt Lake Tribune.* His art education commenced at Utah State University in 1934 as a student instructor. He also studied at the University of Utah, Los Angeles Country Art Institute, Syracuse University, and the Hans Hofmann School of Art at Provincetown, Massachusetts. Thorpe's career included a forty year tenure of teaching at USU with extended art experimentation. His work ranged from illustration through portraiture to multiple figurative mural projects. One of Thorpe's murals can be found in the Logan LDS tabernacle.

The First Vision portrait included in this book was painted in 1939. The original oil measures approximately four feet wide by five feet tall. It currently hangs in the home of Ron and Eva Kay Zollinger. This painting is part of a three painting set which was originally painted by Thorpe, then mounted on the front wall of the Thatcher-Penrose LDS Ward chapel. The other two oils, a foot smaller in size, were place on each side of this central picture. The subject of one focused on the miracle of the seagulls during the infestation of crickets. The second scene depicted a wagon train and Mormon pioneers crossing the plains.

All through my years of infancy and adolescence, I attended church at this ward chapel. During my mission, the chapel was remodeled and these pictures were removed. For some years they were forgotten until my brother, Clair Zollinger, the acting bishop, located their presence in the old boiler/coal room during a trouble-shooting inspection of the boiler. They remained in this room for a few years until they were recovered and saved from further deterioration by our mother, Ruth Zollinger. At her expense, they were mounted on oak frames. She then hung them on an entry wall in our home.

When our parents became aged and we could no longer provide for their care and well-being, they established residence at the Bear River Valley Care Center. It then became the duty of their children to collect their earthly possessions and disperse them among the family. We arranged these items into prioritized groups. As I searched among their earthly possessions to determine what value I personally placed upon each item, I paused to reflect on these paintings, especially the First Vision. It was a large, bulky picture which caused me to wonder where I could even place it in my home. As I reminisced, the spirit reminded me of my special connection to this picture which I had not consciously realized.

Every Sunday during my youth as I attended meetings in the Thatcher-Penrose chapel, I would gaze on these pictures, especially the First Vision. Pondering this recollection, I studied this large painting. Suddenly warm feelings of conviction, truth and testimony emerged. This painting represented the seed bed of my testimony. The spirit bore witness as I looked upon it each and every time in my youth that Joseph was a prophet of God; that the Father and the Son did indeed appear to this young lad in answer to his prayer; and that he loves me and will answer my personal prayers. These feelings in my youth were so repetitive that they had become lost to my conscious awareness. Now as I returned to my evaluation of which earthly item of my parents was of most significance to me, the answer was clear.

Glossary of Words

Word	*Part of Speech*	Definition
abrogate	*Verb*	to repeal, to cancel; annul
adamant	*Noun*	not giving in, relentless, unyielding
altruistic	*Adjective*	unselfishly concerned for the welfare of others, the general welfare of others is the goal of an individual's actions
anecdote	*Noun*	a usually short narrative of an interesting or amusing incident
antediluvian	*Noun*	of the time before the Biblical flood
antithetical	*Adjective*	exactly the opposite
apocrypha	*Noun*	Catholic canonical writings dated between Malachi and Matthew
aricular	*Adjective*	from out of the mouth
arrears	*Noun*	unpaid or overdue debt
automaton	*Noun*	a person acting in a mechanical or automatic way
Brahma	*Noun*	the creator God, the ultimate ground of all being in Hinduism
cadre	*Noun*	a nucleus, or core grouping
canon	*Noun*	historical: from the Hebrew word pronounced kaw-nah associated with a measuring reed in Egypt. Christians transliterated the word to associate it with writings that were the standard or rule of the Church. Its Latin equivalent is *kanon*, which became canon in English.
caricatures	*Noun*	comical or exaggerated images with human likeness
caveat	*Noun*	literally "let him beware"; a marker of warning

chiasmus	*Noun*	an inversion of the second of two parallel phrases, clauses
circumvent	*Verb*	to manage to get around by stratagem or ingenuity
cognition	*Noun*	the process of knowing in the broadest sense, including perception, memory, judgment, and so on.
colloquial	*Adjective*	used in or characteristic of familiar and informal conversation
connotation	*Noun*	idea or notion suggested by or associated with a word or phrase in addition to its explicit meaning, or denotation.
conundrum	*Noun*	an intricate and difficult problem having a conjectural answer
deification	*Noun*	the religious doctrine of becoming gods
dharma	*Noun*	cosmic order or law that governs all things
diadem	*Noun*	crown signifying royal power
dichotomy	*Noun*	division into two parts, groups, or classes
dissonance	*Noun*	discord, lack of harmony or agreement; incongruity
divinization	*Noun*	a term unique to Mormonism; the process of man developing into gods
dolorous	*Adjective*	very sorrowful, sad; mournful, painful
eclectic	*Adjective*	selected or composed from various sources, systems
egalitarian	*Noun*	a belief stating that all are equal
empirical	*Adjective*	relying or based solely upon experiment and observation rather than theory
enigma	*Noun*	a perplexing , baffling, or seemingly inexplicable matter or person
enumerate	*Verb*	to list, or determine by number or organization

erudition	*Noun*	learning acquired by reading and study; scholarship
etymology	*Noun*	the origin and development of words
excoriate	*Verb*	to strip off, to denounce harshly
existential	*Adjective*	affirming the self-awareness of one's own person through experience
ex *nihilo*	*Adjective or Verb*	from or out of nothing
exorcize	*Verb*	An exorcism is a rite performed by an exorcist, one of the lower orders within the Roman Catholic Church; its purpose is to drive out demons or evil spirits
familial	*Adjective*	relating to, or characteristic of a family
farcical	*Adjective*	ridiculous, absurd
fiat	*Noun*	something that comes into existence by sanction, order, or decree
filial	*Adjective*	having or assuming the relation of a child or offspring
ff	*abbreviation*	verses following
holistic	*Adjective*	relating to or concerned with wholes or with complete systems, integrated system treating the mind and the body
homophonic	*Adjective*	of the same sound
ignominious	*Adjective*	shameful, dishonorable, disgraceful, humiliating
impetus	*Noun*	a driving force, impulse, incentive, stimulus
incarnate	*Adjective*	endowed with a human body, personified
incognito	*Adverb/Adjective*	with true identity unrevealed or disguised
indefatigable	*Adjective*	cannot be tired out, unyielding
karma	*Noun*	the totality of a person's actions accumulated in successive life states

magnani-mous	*Adjective*	lofty or courageous in spirit or design; having nobility of feeling or design
milieu	*Noun*	social or cultural setting; environment
misnomer	*Noun*	a error in naming or describing
myopia	*Noun*	lack of foresight, narrowmindedness, tunnel vision
neophyte	*Noun*	new member of an organization or newly baptized member
neo-platonism	*Noun*	any of various schools of philosophy based on a modified Platonism; especially a school developed by Plotinus in Alexandria, postulating a single source from which all forms of existence emanate
nirvana	*Noun*	final state that transcends suffering, state of extinction of individual desire and consciousness, state of oblivion or external reality
nomencla-ture	*Noun*	particular word usage or unique conversational language; jargon; the act of naming
paradigm	*Noun*	an example or pattern
paradox	*Noun*	that which seems contradictory to common sense, but which may be true
pecuniary	*Adjective*	of or involving money, penalty or fine
polity	*Noun*	a specific form or system of church government
plethora	*Noun*	to be full or more than full; an excess
pragmatism	*Noun*	a practical approach to problems and affairs; something tested by consequences
prima facie	*Noun*	at first sight, on first view, or before further examination
proclivity	*Noun*	an inclination or disposition toward something
purport	*Verb*	to profess or claim a meaning

replete	*Adjective*	well-filled or plentifully supplied
resonate	*Verb*	to bear a repeated pattern; to produce a harmonious resonance
summum bonum	*Noun*	the supreme good from which all others derive
tenet	*Noun*	a principle, belief, or doctrine generally held to be true
theosis	*Noun*	unique term to Mormonism, the theology of man becoming a god
treatise	*Noun*	a systematic exposition in writing including a methodical discussion of the facts and principles involved and conclusions reached
self-actualization	*Noun*	a full realization of one's own potential
soteriology	*Noun*	spiritual salvation, especially that believed in Christian theology to have been accomplished by Jesus
supernal	*Adjective*	of, from, or through a heavenly or divine source
synergism	*Noun*	the action of separate agencies that when working together have a greater total effect than the action of the agencies working independently
synthesis	*Noun*	the composition or combination of parts or elements so as to form a whole
tangent	*Adjective*	touching or related to
tantamount	*Adjective*	having equal force, value, or effect
Tao	*Noun*	"the way" based upon the doctrines of Lao-tse (sixth century B.C.)
tender	*Noun*	a form of payment to satisfy an obligation
tertiary	*Adjective*	of the third rank in order or type
triune	*Adjective*	being three in one

veracity	*Noun*	devotion to the truth, power of con-veying or perceiving truth
vested	*Adjective*	especially concerned or with a stake in maintaining or influencing a condition or outcome
vouchsafe	*Verb*	to grant as a privilege or special favor; to ensure
vulgar	*Adjective*	original connotation suggested common, popular, or general among the people

List of References

Berrett, William E., *Teachings of the Doctrine and Covenants.* Salt Lake City, Deseret Book, 1956

Besant, Anne Wood, *Four Great Religions.* Whitefish, Mt: Kessinger Publishing, 2008

Best-Loved Poems of the LDS People, ed. Jack M. Lyon and others, 1996. Salt Lake City, Deseret Book, 1996.

Bristol, Frank M., *Providential Epochs,* New York: Hunt and Eaton, 1894.

Brown, Williams Adam, *Christian Theology in Outline.* Whitefish, Mt: Kessinger Publishing, 2007.

Bryant, William Cullen,ed., *Picturesque America; or, the Land We Live In,* 2 vols. (1872–74). New York: D. Appleton and Company, 1872.

Bray, G. L., "Deification," in Sinclair B. Ferguson, David F. Wright, J. I. Packer, ed., *New Dictionary of Theology,* Downers Grove: Zondervan, 1974.

Brotherson, Laura M., *And They Were Not Ashamed, Strengthening Marriage through Sexual Fulfillment,* CFLE, Inspire Books: Boise, Idaho, Sept. 2005.

Burrell, David James, *The Religions of the World; an outline of the great religious systems,* Philadelphia: Presbyterian Board of Publication and Sabbath School Work, 1888.

Burton, Rulon T. ed., *We Believe: Doctrines and Principles of the Church of Jesus Christ of Latter-day Saints,* Salt Lake City: Tabernacle Books, 1994.

Callister, Tad R., *The Infinite Atonement.* Salt Lake City, Deseret Book, 2000.

Cannon, George Q., *Gospel Truth,* Vol. 1. Salt Lake City, Zion's Book Store, 1957.

Catechism of the Catholic Church, 2nd ed. By U.S. Catholic Church, 1995.

Clendenin, Daniel B., *Eastern Orthodox Christianity: A Western Perspective,* Grand Rapids: Baker Academic, 1994.

Collins, James C. and Porras, Jerry I., *Built To Last, Successful Habits of Visionary Companies,* Harper Collins Publishers, Inc.: New York, 1994.

Conkin, Paul K., *American Originals.* The University of North Carolina Press, 1997.

Cowan, Richard O., *Temples to Dot the Earth,* Salt Lake City, 1989. Salt Lake City, Bookcraft, 1989.

Dunn, Charles W. ed., *American Political Theology: Historical Perspective and Theoretical Analysis,* New York: Praeger, 1984.

De mysterio Trinitatis recta confessio est ignoratio scientiae – "Proem ad 1. xviii in Isai.

Durant, Will and Ariel, *The Lessons of History,* New York: Simon and Schuster 1968.

Durant, Will, *The Story of Philosophy, The Lives and Opinions of the Greater Philosophers.* New York: Simon and Schuster, 1926.

Eerdman's Handbook to the History of Christianity, ed. Tim Dowley, Wm B. Eerdmans Publishing Co. Reprint by Lion Publishing Berkhamstead, Herts, England, 1977.

Encyclopedia of Mormonism. Daniel H. Ludlow, ed., New York, Macmillan, 1992.

Fosdick, Henry Emerson, *A Guide to Understanding the Bible,* Harper & Brothers Publishers, New York: 1938.

Fox's Book of Martyrs, ed. Wm. Byron Forbush, New York: Holt, Rinehart and Winston, 1926.

Frankl, Viktor E., *Man's Search for Meaning.* Boston: Beacon and Random House/ Rider: London, 2004.

Gaskill, Alonzo L, *The Savior & The Serpent: Unlocking the Doctrine of the Fall* Salt Lake City: Shadow Mountain, 2005.

George, Timothy, *History of Christianity,* video series. Homewood, Alabama: Beeson Divinity School, 2003.

(Documentary) History of The Church of Jesus Christ of Latter-day Saints, ed. B.H. Roberts, Salt Lake City: Deseret Book, 1902.

Hume, Robert E., *The World's Living Religions,* New York: Charles Scribner's Son, 1959.

Hymns of The Church of Jesus Christ of Latter-day Saints.

Hyrum Smith—Patriarch. Corbett, Pearson H., *Hyrum Smith, Patriarch,* Salt Lake City: Deseret Book Co., 1963.

James, William, *Varieties of Religious Experience: A Study in Human Nature,* Dover Publications, a subsidiary of Courier, North Chelmsford, Mass., 2002.

Journal of Discourses, compiled by George D. Watt and published in

England between 1854 through 1886. The initial printing was then endorsed by the First Presidency.

Kant, Immanuel, *Critique of Practical Reason*, transl. Thomas Kingsmill Abbott, 1788, viewed at http://philosophy.eserver.org/kant/critique-of-practical-reaso.txt

Kimball, Spencer W., Area Conference Report, Munich Germany, 1973.

LDS Church Magazines: *Ensign*, *New Era*, and Improvement Era.

Lee, Harold B., *Teachings of Harold B. Lee,* edited by Clyde W. Williams, Salt Lake City: Bookcraft, 1996.

Lewis, C.S., Mere Christianity. New York: Macmillan Publishing, 1952.

Ludwig, Theodore M., *The Sacred Paths, Understanding the Religions of the World*, 4th ed. Upper Saddle River, New Jersey: Prentice Hall, 2005.

Maitra, Harendranath, *Hinduism, the World Ideal*, New York: Dodd, Mead, 1916.

Maxwell, Neal A., *A More Excellent Way.* Salt Lake City, Deseret Book, 1967.

Maxwell, Neal A., *We Will Prove Them Herewith.* Salt Lake City, Deseret Book, 1982.

Maxwell, Neal A., *That My Family Should Partake.* Salt Lake City, Deseret Book, 1974.

McConkie, Bruce R., *The Promised Messiah.* Salt Lake City, Deseret Book, 1978.

McConkie, Bruce R., *Doctrinal New Testament Commentary*, Vol.1. 3 vols. Salt Lake City, Bookcraft, 1966-73.

McConkie, Bruce R., *Mormon Doctrine.* 2nd ed., Salt Lake City, Bookcraft, 1966.

McKenzie, John L., *Roman Catholic Church*, New York: Holt, Rinehart and Winston, 1969.

McMurrin, Sterling M., *The Philosophical Foundations of Mormon Theology*, The University of Utah Press, 1959.

Müller, Friedrich Max, *Introduction to the Science of Religion*, first published, 1873, Whitefish, Mt: Kessinger Publishing, 2004.

New Catholic Encyclopedia, 17 vols., New York: McGraw-Hill Book Co., 1967.

Nibley, Hugh, *Ancient Documents and the Pearl of Great Price*, ed. Robert Smith and Robert Smythe; from a series of twenty-six lectures given at BYU, 1986, Lecture 3.

Non-Biblical Systems of Religion: A symposium, Cincinnati: Cranston and Curts; New York: Hunt and Eaton, 1893.

Out of Obscurity—The LDS Church in the Twentieth Century, The 29th Annual Sidney B. Sperry Symposium, 2000, Jensen, Marlin K., "May the Kingdom of God Go Forth"; W. Jeffrey Marsh "When the Press Meets the Prophet".

Packer, Boyd K, "The Very Key," *A Brigham Young University Production*, # 28, 29.

Palmer, Spencer J., *The Expanding Church*, Salt Lake City: Deseret Book Co., 1978.

Peters, F.E., "Abraham's Miraculous Journey," *U.S. News and World Report*, a special edition, "Mysteries of Faith: The Prophets," March, 2007.

Peterson, Daniel C. and Ricks, Stephen D., "Baptism for the Dead, Secrecy," *Offenders for a Word.* Salt Lake City, Aspen, 1992.

Providential Epochs, New York: Hunt and Eaton, 1994.

Rause, Vince, "Searching for the Divine," *Reader's Digest*, December 2001.

Reinach, Orpheus, *A General History of Religions*, London: William Heinemann; New York: G. P. Putnam's Sons, 1909.

Ames, Edward Scribner, *Psychology of Religious Experience*, New York: Kessinger Publishing, 2004

Richards, LeGrand, *A Marvelous Work and a Wonder,* rev. ed., 1966.Salt Lake City, Deseret Book.

Roberts, B. H. *The Truth, The Way, The Life*, ed. John W. Welch, Provo, Utah: BYU Studies, 1994.

Ryl, Eden, "You Pack Your Own Chute", video excerpt.

Schaff, Philip and Wace, Henry, eds., *Nicene and Post-Nicene Fathers*, Second Series, vol. XIV, Grand Rapids, Mich.: Eerdmans Publishing Co., 1956.

Schleiermacher, *Discourses on Religion*, chap. 2., 1799 as cited in Robert E. Hume, *The World's Living Religions*, New York: Charles Scribner's Sons, 1959, p. 7.

Shelley, Bruce L., *Church History In Plain Language*, Nashville: Thomas Nelson Publishers, 1995.

Siegel, Alberta, "The Effects of Media Violence on Social Learning," in Violence and the Media: A Staff Report to the National Commission on the Causes of Violence, Washington, D.C.: U.S. Government

Printing Office, 1969.
Smith, Joseph Fielding, *Answers to Gospel Questions*, Vol.2. Comp. Joseph Fielding Smith Jr., 5 vols., Salt Lake City, Deseret Book, 1957-66.
Teachings of the Prophet Joseph Smith, sel, Joseph Fielding Smith, Salt Lake City: Deseret Book, 1938.
Smith, Joseph, *Lectures on Faith*, Salt Lake City, Deseret Book, 1985.
Smith, Joseph Fielding Jr., *Doctrines of Salvation*, Vol.1. Comp. Bruce R. McConkie 3 vols. Salt Lake City, Bookcraft, 1954-56.
Stratton, G.W., *Psychology of the Religious Life*. New York: Macmillan, 1933.
Taylor, John, *The Gospel Kingdom*. Salt Lake City, Deseret Book, 1943.
Teachings of Harold B. Lee, edited by Clyde W. Williams, Salt Lake City: Bookcraft, 1996.
Teachings of Lorenzo Snow. ed. Clyde W. Williams, Salt Lake City: Bookcraft, 1984.
Thavis, John, *Catholic News Service*, Vatican City (CNS).
The Catholic Source Book, 3rd ed. Orlando: Brown-Roa, 2000.
The Church News, Conference Issues 1970-1987.
The Discourses of Wilford Woodruff, ed. G. Homer Durham, Salt Lake City: Bookcraft 1969.
"The Very Key," A Brigham Young University Production, # 28-29.
True To The Faith, A Gospel Reference, published by The Church of Jesus Christ of Latter-day Saints.
Clark, Robert S., Unpublished manuscript: "The gift of tongues in the Church today: Cloven tongues as of fire or smoldering ashes?"
Vajda, Jordon, unpublished master's thesis, University of California-Berkeley: "Partakers of the divine Nature: A Comparative Analysis of Patristic and Mormon doctrines of divinization," August, 1998.
Videotaped panel discussion between Elder Gary Coleman and a Catholic apologist when Elder Coleman was a mission president in California.
Watson, Elden J. ed., *Manuscript History of Brigham Young* 1801-1844, Salt Lake City: Smith Secretarial Service, 1968.
Webster's New World Dictionary of the American Language, 2nd ed., New York: Simon and Schuster, 1982.
Whitney, Orson F., *The Strength of the Mormon Position*, Independence, Mo.: Zion's Printing and Publishing Co., 1917.
Widtsoe, John A., *Evidences and Reconciliations*. 3rd ed. Salt Lake City:

Bookcraft, 1943.
Widtsoe, John A., *Priesthood and Church Government.* rev. ed., Salt Lake City, Deseret Book, 1954.
World Christian Encyclopedia, 2nd edition, New York: Oxford University Press, 2001.
www.wikiquote.org.
Yorgason, Brenton G and Blaine M, *The Greatest Quest.* Salt Lake City, Deseret Book, 1987.
Young, Brigham, *Discourses of Brigham Young*, ed. John A. Widtsoe, Salt Lake City: Deseret Book, 1954

About the Author

Ronald Redford Zollinger graduated from Bear River High School and served an LDS mission to the central states. He earned a BS in 1973 from Utah State University. He majored in psychology and sociology and earned a master's degree in counseling and guidance from Brigham Young University in 1975. He later received a doctorate degree in educational administration from Brigham Young University. He taught in the seminary and institute program of the LDS Church for many years.

Ron is retired and currently resides in Kaysville, Utah, with his wife, Eva Kay. They are the parents of seven children.